REBELS, REFORMERS, AND RACKETEERS

HOW INSURGENTS TRANSFORMED THE LABOR MOVEMENT

BY

HERMAN BENSON

ISBN: 1-4140-5777-6 (e-book)
ISBN: 1-4140-5776-8 (Paperback)

This book is printed on acid free paper.

1stBooks - rev. 02/11/04

(Thanks to the **Furthermore** project of the Kaplan Fund for the grant, which encouraged the writing of this book.)

Table of Contents

Section IV: The Public Impact on the Battle for Union Democracy

Section V: Years of Promise

Preface

Three hundred and fifty unionists and civil libertarians, assembled in 1983 at the conference of the Association for Union Democracy, remained standing for a few moments in silent tribute to five who died in the battle for decency and democracy in unions. Moved by the gesture, Victor Reuther, veteran leader of the United Auto Workers, said that it was the first time in all his experience that union insurgents, killed for battling for union reform, were publicly honored by so many colleagues.

John Harold, once chief counsel for the Association of Catholic Trade Unionists, remembered John Acropolis, his friend and client, president of Teamsters Local 456 who had been murdered for resisting the mob at the Yonkers raceway and in Westchester County, New York.

Joe Rauh, the eminent civil rights and labor lawyer, spoke of his friend and client, Jock Yablonski, the insurgent miners leader, shot to death along with his wife and daughter at the command of a corrupt union president.

John Burton, former Congressman, recalled Dow Wilson and Lloyd Green, the two leaders of Painter locals in the San Francisco Bay Area, assassinated because they fought for union democracy and threatened to expose union officials and employers who were embezzling workers benefit funds.

Attorney Dan Siegel told of Roberto Flotte who had put together a caucus of white, black, and Mexican worker In Longshormen's Local 6. Murdered outside the union hall.

Just two years before the AUD conference, Gene Viernes and Silme Domingo were assassinated right in the hall of Cannery Local 36 in Seattle. As leaders of an insurgent caucus pledged to oust racketeers, they had just won the election, only to be murdered.

Sudden death made these few memorable. But there have been others, many others, unwept, unhonored, and unsung, who fought that same battle in the labor movement. And others who helped them.

In the last 40 years or more, certainly since the adoption of the Labor-Management Reporting and Disclosure Act of 1959, thousands of good, active, loyal unionists have fought within their unions, some to defend basic internal democratic rights; some, to end corruption; some, to eradicate organized crime; some, to fight for equality in job referrals; some, to do it all. For most, it required courage. Some were beaten, lost their jobs. A few were killed. I know about them because I worked with many of them, told their stories, and tried to help them defend their rights in their unions and in the courts.

Only a few were successful, and few of their efforts led to permanently organized oppositions. But in one union then in another, they were there, constituting a broad movement, affecting most major unions in the United States. The seeds were widely scattered and only a few sank hardy roots. But their species remains a hardy perennial. Their persistence up to this very day, is transforming our labor movement. It was the proliferation of these insurgent movements that validated dissent in unions. It was the 1991 Teamster reform victory which tipped the balance in the AFL-CIO. Forty years of broad rank and file reform activity provided both the moral legitimacy and the power that made possible Sweeney's insurgent quest for the AFL-CIO presidency in 1995.

For decades, the International Brotherhood of Teamsters, one of the largest, richest, and most powerful labor unions, had been dominated by organized crime and expelled for corruption from the AFL-CIO. In all this time, no force in the labor movement, no coalition of labor leaders, with all their members and resources, had been able to shake this union — or any other — loose from racket control. This corrupted union remained so powerful that many AFL-CIO and independent unions, from right to left, continued to genuflect before it. And yet, beginning in 1972, a rank and file reform movement, without the material or moral support of a single top labor leader, by its own agitation, leaflets, demonstrations, and conferences built a force strong enough to rally around Ron Carey, then a local union president, and overthrow the racketeer infiltrated administration in 1991.

That year, 1991, recorded the most important single event of our generation in the internal life of the U.S. labor movement. At that point, the racketeers who had been allowed to dominate the powerful Teamsters union were defeated by reformers. Teamster insurgents performed what no other combination of forces had ever been able to accomplish. For the first time in over 50 years, organized crime had suffered a major set back in unions.

The record of these Teamster reformers is the most persistent, the most dramatic, and the most effective but theirs is only one of the insurgent movements that have influenced most major unions in the United States.

The organized labor movement is one of the great forces for democracy and social justice in America. If that was the whole story, it would hardly need repetition, for it has been the frequent theme of talented writers. But the anomaly persists: this great pillar of democracy is itself nibbled away by the mice of bureaucracy. In this, labor organizations resemble all the other great institutions of democracy, even democratic government itself. To paraphrase Emerson: "Bureaucracy is in the saddle and is riding mankind." By battling for democracy inside their unions, union reformers strive to keep the labor movement on course, true to its own ideals. And, precisely because that labor movement is so indispensable a nutrient for the nation's democracy, the quest for democracy in unions is one facet of the broader striving for social justice in the nation.

In one respect, the union reformer stands alone.

In the nation, when the principles of the Declaration of Independence are violated in practice, aroused citizens and organized movements ride to the rescue. If you stand up for human rights, civil rights, women's rights, even animal rights, for the environment, against unbridled global capitalism, for immigrants, for minorities, for religious rights, for civil liberties, for the elderly; and you are in trouble, you can turn to a multitude of dedicated nongovernmental movements and organizations for moral approval and practical support. If you need help against oppressive employers, there are unions.

But if you are a loyal unionist, and you need assistance against arrogant officials to keep your union honest and democratic, you search in vain for an influential ally.

Ironically, the need for union democracy is enunciated in law as a principle but neglected in practice. In the thirties, the Wagner Act recognized the need to protect the right of collective bargaining through unions to offset concentrated corporate power and to assure a measure of industrial democracy. That law has been effective because its enforcement was bolstered by a powerful constituency of organized labor and liberals.

But, as Clyde Summers has written so eloquently, if unions are to serve effectively on behalf of democracy in industry, workers must be assured of democracy in their unions. And so, the Labor-Management Reporting and Disclosure Act of 1959 (Landrum-Griffin) recognized the need for federal protection of the rights of members inside their own unions to keep them democratic and free of corruption. But the LMRDA has been feebly implemented because no organized influential constituency has ever come forward to demand its vigorous enforcement.

The miracle is that despite this lack of enthusiastic public support, but encouraged by the mere existence of the new 1959 law, an insurgent reform wave rippled through the labor movement, in one union then another, and another. By exercising their rights, they freshened up the stale moral atmosphere in the labor movement. It was a demonstration of the power of democracy in action from below. Theirs is an untold story and neglected. What follows here is intended to record the efforts of some of those union reformers and of the tiny band that came forward to help. This account in not complete — none can be so; it is based mainly upon my own experience as a founder of the Association for Union Democracy and earlier as publisher of the newsletter, ***Union Democracy in Action***; but it is a necessary beginning to fill a gap in contemporary labor history. But this is not simply a narrow 'labor' subject; it is an inseparable part of the quest for social justice in America.

AFL-CIO President John Sweeney, understandably alarmed over the decline in union membership, focused the attention of labor leaders on the urgent need to recruit new members. But in their preoccupation with organizing the unorganized, they lose sight of the social power of those who are already organized. Even at this ebb in membership, 16,300,000 people are enrolled in labor unions. With their families, they make up a huge part of the national population and constitute an enormous political potential. The difficulty is that union leaders are unable to summon this army in reserve as an effective force because our labor officialdom, on the whole, is a bureaucracy so obsessed with retaining its own power over their unions that it curbs the rights of its own membership. To release the latent power of that millions-person army as a solid force for social progress requires an infusion of democracy into the life of unions.

Such is the main thrust of this account. I am convinced that such a goal — unleashing union democracy to make labor a powerful force for social justice — is no Utopian fantasy, because I know that for the last 40 years, thousands of active unionists, in most major unions in the United States, — as individuals, in caucuses, in slates for union office, as publishers of independent newsletters — have been striving for integrity, for decency, for democracy in their unions. And I have been associated, in one capacity or another, with many of them. This is their story.

Herman Benson, 2002

Prologue: At the 1995 AFL-CIO convention

On the eve of the 1995 AFL-CIO convention, the leaders of major affiliates set out to depose Lane Kirkland, AFL-CIO president who had held the job since 1979. When he rejected their demand that he step down, they organized a vigorous preconvention campaign to prevent his reelection. Under pressure, he finally resigned and chose Tom Donahue, then AFL-CIO secretary treasurer, to succeed him. But the critics would not relent; Donahue insisted on defending the record of Kirkland's administration; the opponents wanted more than Kirkland's exit; they wanted to make a statement, to repudiate the past, to announce the dawn of a new day. And so they organized their insurgent caucus, won over a majority of the convention delegates, defeated the Donahue slate, and elected John Sweeney as the new AFL-CIO president along with a full slate of new top officers.

It was an astounding development. In the Washington Post, June 29,1995, Frank Swoboda characterized the Sweeney-Donahue contest as "one of the biggest political showdowns within organized labor since Mine Workers President John L. Lewis bolted the AFL in the 1930's to form the rival CIO to organize industrial workers."

The last time any AFL president had suffered such a setback was a hundred years before, in 1894, when John McBride defeated Samuel Gompers. But after that ephemeral mayfly rebellion, McBride was out and Gompers back just one year later.

In publicly repudiating Kirkland, the Sweeney backers had consciously violated those engraved stone commandments which normally govern relations among union officials, a code seldom broken which mandates loyalty, mutual support, live and let live. In smooth transition, the old head of the pack retires or steps down gracefully, always replaced in the celebratory spirit of amiable consensus, honored by accolades for past services to humanity, rewarded with a golden parachute. In its most extreme and debased form, the code prescribes that you may run your union as you see fit, even honestly, so long as I am permitted to run mine as I see fit, without public criticism.

Albert Shanker, Teachers union president, was outraged by that transgression of the traditional etiquette. He told the Associated Press on February 22,1995 that union chiefs who criticized Kirkland publicly should consider whether "they would like it in their own union."

How account for that extraordinary split among the highest AFL-CIO leaders, one that runs counter to their every instinct for retaining a public aura of unanimity?

As they were debating, the labor scene was dismal: a right-wing offensive in politics, retreat on social welfare issues, downsizing and globalization, low wage competition at home and abroad, retreat of unionism from private industry. Labor's critical problem was evident in the decline of the organized sector to some 13% of the nation's work force, the lowest in generations, and in the dilution of labor's power in political and industrial life. The trend had to be reversed: that thought hung over all the proceedings.

In highly touted debates on the convention floor, and in the opposing literature, it may have been impossible to define any clear demarcation of policy between the opposing camps. Still, the pro-Sweeney delegates spoke more vociferously and applauded more loudly for action, militancy, marching forward, and reversing labor's decline.

But the notion that something had to be done was nothing new. Way back in 1960, New York Times labor writer, A.H. Raskin, had written, "American labor is suffering from an advanced case of hardening of the arteries. It is standing still in membership and organizational vigor at a time when radical changes in technology are revolutionizing industry." A year later, in "The Decline of the Labor Movement," Solomon Barkin expanded the same theme into a 66-page booklet. Barkin, a prominent labor intellectual, had been research director of the Textile Workers Union since 1937. "The nature of our industrial society and of the people who comprise it have been changing...The old remedies, the old approaches, will not serve the needs of today. The eventual answer must be provided by the trade union movement through a drastic overhaul of spirit and structure."

The Committee on the Evolution of Work, an official AFL-CIO think tank, headed by Tom Donahue himself, had been mulling over these problems since 1983 and published three separate reports. In 1985 it called for "a resurgence of the labor movement." The New York Times editorialized, "Organized labor has set out to reinvent the labor movement for the post-industrial age."

But none of this led anywhere, certainly not to any split in labor leadership, certainly not to any effort to overturn the AFL-CIO regime. By 1995, however, a new factor had added a new dimension to the discussions. In addition to the nagging sense that something should be done came a realization that action was at last possible.

Simplest to understand is the arithmetic of power politics instantaneously recorded in the 1995 AFL-CIO convention election tally that lifted Sweeney over the top. He defeated Donahue by a weighted roll call vote of about 7,300,00 to 5,700,000, a margin that tells the story. About 1,300,000 of Sweeney's majority came from the Teamsters' union which, only four years before, had come under new reform leadership. If those Teamster votes had been switched from one side to the other, Donahue, not Sweeney, would have triumphed with a comfortable majority of 1,000,000: by 7,000,000 to Sweeney's 6,000,000. What put the Teamsters into the Sweeney column was the victory of the reform forces in 1991 which ousted the Teamster old guard from control of the international. If the Teamster old guard had still held power, Donahue would surely have been guaranteed their support; they were heavily indebted to him and to Kirkland, who had both sponsored and welcomed their readmission to the AFL-CIO. With those Teamster votes available to Donahue, the balance of power against the insurgents would have been so formidable that the Sweeney forces, realistic players, would have hardly attempted any doomed gesture of resistance.

The moral atmosphere for change

Teamster votes provided the obviously necessary arithmetical ingredient for effecting change. But more than raw power was needed. Before the generals could be induced to become rebels, there had to be a change in the moral atmosphere; the traditional repugnance against dissent had to be overcome; There had to be, not only a conviction of the need for something new, but an acceptance of a novel principle: that it was legitimate to organize for the overthrow of a union leadership.

That change in mood was a product of forty years of insurgency by reformers in the rank and file and secondary leadership, movements for democracy against corruption which reached a high point in the victory of the Miners for Democracy in 1972 and culminated in the Teamsters revolution of 1991. Those movements and those victories gave a moral boost to the legitimacy of dissent and democracy in the labor movement and created the power base for Sweeney's victorious insurgency in 1995. Insurgent Miners created Sweeney's candidate for secretary treasurer,

Richard Trumka. In 1968, when Jock Yablonski first raised the banner of democracy inside the United Mine Workers, Trumka, still a member Of the United Miners, was changing careers to become a lawyer. After Yablonski's murder, the Miners for Democracy reform victory opened new opportunities for Trumka. Later, in the newly democratized union, he was elected UMW president. Without the Yablonski martyrdom and the successful rank and file insurgency, Trumka today would probably be known in intimate circles as an excellent pro-labor attorney, talented, and effective, but one among many.

In addition to the Miners and Teamsters there were others, many others. By recording their story we acknowledge one of the principal forces that powers the reinvigoration of our labor movement.

It would require the talents of an experienced labor historian to do justice to rise of movements independent of the incumbent power structure in all unions, those who were spurred on by the Labor-Management Reporting and Disclosure Act of 1959 and then those who were inspired by the victory of the Miners for Democracy. This account is not intended as such a history, but mainly as a record of what came to the attention of the Association for Union Democracy and its precursor. Most of our top labor leaders have always been hostile to rebels and reformers. At best, some have been indifferent. Sweeney and his supporters did not inspire the reform wave or create the democratic spirit that had been infused into the labor movement by those movements of rebellion. They rode it into power.

One obvious difference between Sweeney and Kirkland, perhaps the main difference, was their attitude toward what is inadequately called "the left." Faced by the dissenter: the radical, the critic, the reformer, the rank and file democrat, the unconventional idealist, the independent-minded militant, the instinctive reaction from the Kirkland camp, always uneasy before any stirring independent of the official bureaucracy, was: how do we get rid of that troublemaker?

For Sweeney, however, the question is: How do we utilize them? From the radicals, he plagiarized their slogan: Put the movement back into the labor movement. At the 1995 convention, he called for "a reborn movement of American workers, ready to fight for social and economic justice. A new progressive voice in American life...changing the direction of American politics...a vibrant social movement not simply a federation of constituent organizations...redefine America's (and many of our own members') perceptions of us...a democratic movement that speaks for all American workers..."

Sweeney tapped the spirit of insurgency to reach for power inside the AFL-CIO. The question now is whether our labor leaders can tap that same source, that spirit of insurgency and mobilize that power on behalf of social justice in America. Toward that end, the Sweeney camp induced a thousand student interns to spend a summer with union organizers; they brought women, minorities, and young people into staff and leadership positions; they dispatched more full time organizers, many of them young, into the field in stepped-up campaigns to organize the unorganized, especially low wage workers; they put more money into politics.

But between the hope and the reality, falls a shadow.

The need is democracy. Not only democracy in the nation, but internal union democracy, democracy inside the labor movement itself. The key to making the power of labor effective in the nation is to rekindle and unleash the spirit of democracy inside the labor movement itself, to rely upon the independent-minded unionists who are loyal to unions because they cherish the values of decency, democracy, and dignity and who resent injustice. It is they who can be counted on to bring labor's message of social justice to the nation.

But can our dominant labor leaders release that great potential energy of union democracy? The problem is that, in general, they are so obsessed with the need to maintain their own bureaucratic power that the stirring of democracy in their own unions makes them nervous.

To understand how deep is that distrust of rank and file democracy, we turn back to the late 1950's, just before Federal law was placed on the side of union democracy, and labor leaders were unrestrained in dealing with their own members. Uninhibited by law, their "natural' inclinations were more obviously on display.

Section I
Circa 1959: Democracy v. Corruption

Chapter 1: Labor's Uncertain Trumpet. IAM Lodge 113 and the demise of the Ethical Practices Committee

The year 1955, like 1995, seemed to be a moment of great promise for the labor movement. The American Federation of Labor and the Congress of Industrial Organizations had merged into the united AFL-CIO. Provisions in the new constitution authorized action against corruption in the affiliates; an Ethical Practices Code was adopted; and an Ethical Practices Committee was appointed to enforce the new codes. In 1957, the Senate committee headed by John McClellan opened a three-year investigation of racketeering in unions and of repression of members' rights. With the first sordid revelations, George Meany, AFL-CIO president, told a New York Times Reporter on November 2,1957, "We thought we knew a few things about trade union corruption, but we didn't know the half of it, one-tenth of it or the hundredth part of it." The Ethical Practices Committee, which had already begun hearings into corrupt practices, intensified its efforts. A few unions were expelled, including the mighty International Brotherhood of Teamsters. Looking back in 1986, A.H. Raskin, formerly chief Times labor writer, called it labor's "shining hour."

The chairman of the Ethical Practices Committee, presiding over the expulsion hearings, was A.J. Hayes, then also president of the International Association of Machinists. His career, more than any other, illustrates the dilemma of American labor leadership; it explains why their call for members action against corruption proved to be an uncertain trumpet; it demonstrates that their fear of union democracy outweighed their distaste for corruption. In his role as EPC chairman, he was receiving plaudits in the press and plaques at banquets for his great services to decency and democracy in the labor movement. But in his capacity as IAM president, he was expelling reformers who tried to use their democratic rights to oust crooks from their Machinists local. In 1957, no federal law required unions to afford their members even the most basic democratic rights within their unions; in his own union, Hayes was armed with authoritarian powers.

Some time in the middle of 1958, I got an urgent phone call from Carl Shier, who was then an international representative of the United Auto Workers in Chicago. He told me that a group of machinists in Tool and Die Makers Local 113 in Chicago, a 2,600-member affiliate of the International Association of Machinists, were in trouble.

For more than three years, in a running series of handbills, their insurgent caucus had been warning members against their local officers. After an official IAM auditor found the officials guilty of seriously mishandling union money, the insurgents could count on overwhelming support at membership meetings; and, under pressure, the officers resigned. Then, just as local elections were pending and the insurgents were certain of taking over, the international office, without notice, imposed a trusteeship, suspended elections, and foisted repressive bylaws on the lodge. The reformer-insurgents, campaigning to end the trusteeship and restore autonomy, felt threatened with retaliation from the international. Sure enough, within a few months, two of their spokesmen faced disciplinary charges and were expelled from the union by direct personal order of A.J. Hayes, the international president. Could I help somehow, asked Shier, maybe with publicity, maybe find legal help? Was I interested?

I was more than interested. A bell was tolling for me.

Since 1949, I had been labor editor of *Labor Action*, a left-socialist, bi-weekly tabloid. At that juncture, just as Shier called, I had become preoccupied with the subject of union democracy, some would say, obsessed. For me, the fate of union democracy was inseparably intertwined with prospects for democracy in society. To explain that conviction, I must describe where I was in 1958.

In 1930 at the age of 15, I joined the Young Peoples Socialist League, in plenty of time to campaign for Norman Thomas for president in 1932; and later, when I was old enough, I joined the Socialist Party. Those were the days when talk of revolution was in the air. Walk through Union Square and see hundreds of men, out of work, huddled in little standing clusters listening intently as excited partisans argued over the ideas of known and obscure political sects and assorted philosophic mavericks, all in a medley of native and foreign accents. Long bread lines. Old ladies evicted from grubby tenements, sitting hopelessly in armchairs, their furniture piled on the street, not even a tarpaulin to shield their scattered stuff from the rain.

In the spirit of the times, I became a convinced and dedicated Marxist, left the Socialist Party and ended in the semi-Trotskyist Workers Party, later reborn as the Independent Socialist League. By 1958, when Carl Shier called me, we were about to dissolve the ISL, to discontinue the publication **Labor Action**, and join—actually to rejoin—the Socialist Party.

All this will seem like a strange detour from the story of two expelled machinists. But this digression will explain how I got involved in the case and why it seemed so important to me and how the cause of union democracy came to dominate the rest of my life.

The crux of Marxism, freed from its economic, historical, and philosophical trappings, freed from its intricate intellectual "superstructure," is the conviction that the modern working class, the "proletariat", by taking political power, abolishing capitalism, and "socializing" the basic means of production, will usher in a new era, a classless society of democracy and social justice. While I have concluded, and sadly, that this view is a Utopian dream, I remain convinced that, until its debasement at the hands of the Communists, Marxism was a democratizing and liberating idea that inspired mass movements for justice and freedom throughout the world.

And so I, like so many other young socialists of my generation, was determined to be part of that working class. I became a machinist and toolmaker, working in New York and Detroit, joining the Auto Workers, the Rubber Workers, the United Electrical Workers, the InternationaL Union of Electrical Workers, depending on which union represented my workplace. In time I was active in unions, studied the labor movement, became labor secretary of the Independent Socialist League, and wrote and spoke about union affairs.

As the years rolled by, it dawned even on me that there were more things in the labor movement than were dreamed on in my philosophy. Many unions were riddled by racketeers; union officials, determined to hold on to their jobs, expelled dissidents and blacklisted critics; union elections were stolen; referendums were rigged. Yes, on most political issues, the labor movement could be counted on to stand up for democracy in society. On the other hand, union officials could almost universally be counted on to stand for repression and authoritarianism inside the unions. And most often they were victorious over reformers, democratic-minded critics, and insurgents. The balance of power inside unions was so overwhelmingly on the side of the officialdom against any critics that the very soul and spirit of union democracy survived only precariously. Revelations at the McClellan Hearings simply documented my own growing misgivings.

The more I thought about it, the more one big question continued to nag at me. The future of democracy in society, I was convinced, depended upon the working class. But if this working class cannot defend democracy within its own class institutions, within its own unions, how can it be a dependable force to defend democracy in society? For me, union democracy had become no narrow "labor" issue; it was imbedded in my whole social philosophy. Just at that moment, while I was mulling over all this, along came those machinists. Was it possible to rally public support in their defense by pointing up the broad social significance of union democracy? I had to try.

Moreover, at that point, the subject of union democracy was in the air. In other times, the expulsion of two men expelled from the backwater of an obscure local union would have aroused no ripple of interest anywhere, overlooked as one of those minor injustices routinely ignored in a world so jaded that only major outrages command attention. But just then, something in the air transformed these events into a symbol of larger issues. Corruption in unions and a lack of democracy had become a great national issue and remained so for the next two or three years.

The mood of the times was expressed in a front-page headline of the AFL-CIO News on September 13, 1958: "Rank and File Hold Key to Clean-up, Meany says." The story opened, "A challenge to rank and file workers to complete the rout of corruption from the labor movement was laid down by top AFL-CIO officers..." At the convention of the newly founded American Bakery Workers union, then-Senator John F. Kennedy told the delegates that eliminating "the scourge of racketeering" from the labor movement "cannot be done without the courage and the initiative of the rank and file..." And now, two rank and file machinists were being victimized because they had responded to the spirit of those calls.

The Lodge 113 story opened modestly enough late in 1955 when Lodge President Albert Dency, treasurer Ivar Andersen, and a few close friends studied financial reports prepared by the lodge directing business agent and found the figures skimpy and suspect. There hadn't been an audit for years; and the business agents, they found, had awarded themselves pay raises without authorization. Thereupon, when the directing BA demanded that President Dency sign a book of blank checks, he refused. That act hit the fan of controversy.

In the IAM, as in many unions, the local president occupies a mostly ceremonial position while the real power is exercised by the directing business agent (usually called business manager). Dency worked full time in the shop, presided over meetings and signed checks, but that was about it.

The business agents worked full time for the lodge and conducted its business under the authority of the directing BA.

Dency, Andersen, and Irwin Rappaport, an active unionist, took the initiative. In January, 1956, they announced the formation of a Committee to Save Lodge 113. Between February and October 1996, they distributed a series of handbills, entitled Food for Thought calling for "Full democratic rights of members to speak up freely at union meetings and in the shops without intimidation and threats of reprisals." They demanded full financial disclosure; they questioned expenditures by the business agents, they charged that their supporters were intimidated and beaten at meetings, they circulated petitions. Called upon to attend meetings, the members responded. Meetings were packed; the Committee soon could count on huge majorities. When the supporters of the BA brought charges against Dency for impugning the motives of the BA's, a membership meeting overwhelmingly exonerated him. In June, 1956, after an official IAM auditor finally came to inspect the books, his report vindicated the critics. The auditor demanded changes, adding, "If the officers involved with bookkeeping do not follow through with this, I would think it time for the lodge to consider making some changes in officers at your next election."

The Committee to Save Lodge 113 won the necessary two-thirds support for a series of amendments to the local bylaws. Lodge elections were coming, and the reformers seemed certain of winning. But it was not to be. On October 18,1956, all five business agents resigned, and four days later international President A.J. Hayes imposed a trusteeship over the lodge.

If the reformers had grasped fully the implications of Hayes's reply to their appeal back in early 1956 when their campaign had just begun, they would have been forewarned of what was coming:

In April 1956, shortly after the reformers fired the first shot, Irwin Rappaport had asked International President Hayes for help against "hooliganism." In a letter detailing events in Lodge 113, he wrote, "...if you were fully aware of our situation, you would undoubtedly intervene immediately." He asked Hayes to put the lodge under a temporary period of trusteeship, suspend the business agents, and run new elections. Naively, he appended this P.S.: "Enclosed please find three leaflets which were issued by the Committee to Save Lodge 113." In his hope for Hayes's intervention, Rappaport was blinded by the glow that radiated deceptively from Hayes's Ethical Practices reputation.

But Hayes, with an authoritarian's instinctive ability to smell out the looming menace of democracy, quickly decided where the real danger lay: not from suspect local officials but from Rappaport and his friends. Hayes and his colleagues were obsessed by the threat of "unauthorized" literature. Rappaport should have been forewarned by the tenor of Hayes's suggestion of ominous things to come: "While I do not have any evidence at the present time that has convinced me as to the guilt or innocence of any particular individual," he replied to Rappaport, "I am convinced beyond any doubt that the handbills distributed by the so-called 'Committee to Save Lodge 113' certainly are not serving the best interests of this organization...whoever is responsible for the publication and distribution of these handbills certainly is violating one of the basic concepts of trade unionism and one of the fundamental policies of our organization. I requested General Vice President Siemiller to investigate this matter to find out who is responsible..."

When, in a follow-up letter, Rappaport expressed disappointment, Hayes's rejoinder became openly threatening: "I am not changing my position with regards to the handbills being distributed by the so-called 'Committee to Save Lodge 113'...This is in strict violation of our constitution..."

The irony here is that Hayes, as chairman of the AFL-CIO Ethical Practices Committee, was charged with the duty of rooting out corruption in the AFL-CIO. But as president of the International Association of Machinists, he was about to use his power to crush rank and filers who took the initiative in rooting out corruption in the Machinists union.

Trustee P.L. Siemiller took control of Lodge 113. (Later he succeeded Hayes as international president.) He cancelled the scheduled local elections; he ordered that "all unauthorized meetings of the membership, where union business or policy is discussed and all unauthorized distribution of literature be discontinued immediately."

Six months later, when there was no sign that the trustee would go home, Irwin Rappaport, who was a shop steward, forwarded a request to President Hayes, authorized by a meeting of his shop constituents, asking for a restoration of autonomy. The trustee found this action so subversive that he issued a stern warning: He instructed one of his representatives: "call in whoever chaired the meeting...and advise him that this is not a proper method for discussion at a segment of our union, that things of this kind are what caused the necessity for suspension in the first place...take the necessary steps to see that action of this kind is discontinued..." It could hardly be more obvious that the union hierarchy was disturbed not by the auditor's report of the financial manipulations of the business agents but by the democratic activity of the members who sought to correct the sorry state of affairs. Then came the trustee's menacing forewarning, "...this Lodge must be completely straightened out with a set of bylaws that...will eliminate the cause that necessitated the suspension of this local union before we will be in a position to return it to the membership."

By November 1957, the trustee imposed the necessary bylaws on the lodge. In addition to the prohibition on distributing literature, it included this startling provision: "Any member of this lodge found guilty of causing any petition related to union business to be circulated among the membership, except petitions for a special meeting of the lodge, without express approval of the executive board or the lodge in prior session...shall be subject to fine or expulsion or both..." The insurgents, testing their rights, reported that they were forbidden to distribute copies of the U.S. Constitution Bill of Rights.

Between May 1958 and January 1959, the reformers published Tool and Diemakers Appeal, anonymously to avoid retaliation, criticizing the trusteeship and demanding its removal. They called for the establishment of a Public Review Board of impartial citizens modelled upon the Auto Worker's institution. In October 1958, Irwin Rappaport and Marion Ciepley were among the delegates elected by Lodge 113 to the merger convention of the Illinois AFL and CIO. There, they distributed to the 3,000 delegates copies of a resolution which they proposed for adoption. After denouncing "corrupt elements" in the labor movement, it read in part: "Whereas suspension, administratorship, trusteeships, and similar gimmicks are often used by the corrupt officialdom for the purpose of preventing an effective rank and file movement to cleanse its union of corruption and unethical practices...therefore be it resolved...to set up a committee of seven prominent and impartial citizens consisting of clergy and professional people who would be authorized to review grievances dealing with unethical practices and corruption within the labor unions..."

Later, on the convention floor, Rappaport charged that he and Ciepley had been physically assaulted by a representative of the IAM international office. He said to the delegates, "...if we are going to fight against hooliganism and corruption in the trade union movement, we have to do it right here and now..."

The ax fell swiftly. After 1,000 lodge members signed a petition requesting the IAM executive council to lift the trusteeship, Rappaport was removed as shop chairman for circulating it. Charges were preferred against Rappaport and Ciepley for their acts at the state convention, accusing them of circulating "a false and malicious statement which reflected upon the conduct and attacked the character and impugned the motives and questioned the integrity of members and officers of the IAM..." Their trial took an unusual twist.

International President Hayes waived aside any local trial committee and appointed his own special trial committee of international officers. But a funny thing happened on the way to expulsion. Although appointed by him from among his top international officers, the special trial committee was not malleable enough for Hayes. The IAM international leadership still included men with a nostalgic attachment to socialistic memories. They admired Norman Thomas, the respected Socialist leader, and knew of his support for the intended victims. All of which undoubtedly explains why their verdict was not to Hayes's taste. The two machinists would never know, because the trial committee decision was suppressed; never released to the defendants and never made public.

(Research archaeologists could perform a minor service for history by digging the report out of the IAM files. Years later, after Hayes had retired, Rappaport asked then IAM President William Winpisinger for a copy; he refused.)

On February 12, 1959 Hayes took over and rendered his own verdict, "I am rejecting and striking from the record in the cases the Trial Committee's Report and Recommendations..." On his own personal authority, he ordered both Ciepley and Rappaport expelled. On September 14, their appeal was rejected by the IAM convention.

Back in New York, the rejection of the appeal of the two victims triggered the public announcement of the formation of the Ciepley-Rappaport Legal Fund, appealing for money to finance a court suit for their reinstatement. Their complaint was filed in Federal District Court in Illinois early in 1960, the first under the recently adopted Labor Management Reporting and Disclosure Act of 1959. The sponsoring committee was small, only three, but buttressed by eminent names: Norman Thomas, John Lapp, and Clyde Summers.

Thomas, the famous socialist leader, was the conscience of America, everyman's ombudsman. Ten years earlier, he had helped Noah Greenberg, later an eminent musician but then a seaman, to promote a democratic reform group in the National Maritime Union. In 1959, Thomas was 75, alert and effective as a speaker and writer, but already in declining health. His preoccupation, in those days of the looming atom bomb, was peace; and he devoted his dwindling energies to it until his death in 1968. But he **was** Norman Thomas, and he could not resist the appeal from the two machinists. With him in the lead, our committee had to be taken seriously.

Lapp, a Catholic social action leader was renowned as the Norman Thomas of Chicago. Summers, a professor at Buffalo Law School, had written the ACLU statement on democracy in labor unions and was already a leading expert on union democracy law. I served as volunteer, unpaid secretary-factotum. For me, it was a challenging opportunity to devise a practical program for winning public support for union reformers...and the beginning of years of rewarding collaboration with Summers.

In those days, union democracy was a popular subject for legal review and sociological speculation but not for action. It was hard to find pro-labor public leaders who were ready to stand up against respected union leaders. And Hayes was surely one of those. The mood of the times was illustrated a few months later when Norman Thomas expressed support for organizers of the International Ladies Garment Workers Union who sought recognition for their staff union. David Dubinsky, ILGWU president, denouncing Thomas for daring to intervene on his turf, refused to join him on the platform of a rally memorializing Ehrlich and Alter, two Polish Jewish socialist leaders murdered by Stalin.

Once in court, the case quickly died. The judge ruled that the actual expulsion by Hayes had occurred before the adoption of the LMRDA so that the law did not apply. Tough luck, case dismissed. In later years, protected by the LMRDA, union dissidents disciplined for so-called "slanderous" speech in their unions were routinely reinstated by the courts, awarded damages, and reimbursed for legal fees. Ciepley and Rappaport, premature reformers, never got back into the union. But the campaign for their reinstatement had rallied new moral support to the cause of union democracy.

Our campaign had begun about a year before the public announcement of the C-R Committee when I summed up the case in a detailed report, "The Case of Tool and Diemakers Lodge 113" and circulated it to about 200 people: writers, sponsors of the Fund for the Republic union democracy project, reporters, civil libertarians, labor intellectuals, and others. It pointed up the anomaly: Hayes, Ethical Practices Chairman, expelling members who fought for ethical practices in his own union. And it called for submission of the case to an impartial public review board. The text was picked up by Paul Jacobs who wrote "Mr. Hayes Quells a Disturbance" for the Reporter, then a widely circulated, glossy national magazine. Two months later, the Progressive ran my piece "Labor's Uncertain Trumpet."

At the Cornell School of Industrial and Labor Relations in Ithaca, Professor George Brooks, former research director of the Pulp, Sulphite union, made it a key case study in his courses on union administration. At the Michigan State University, Bob Repas, a graduate student in labor affair, after questioning Hayes, wrote "A Tale of Two Expulsions," which we circulated widely.

The *New York Times* noted editorially on December 4, 1960: "This case is important for the future of American labor unions...it illustrates the need for impartial boards of appeal to review disciplinary actions taken by officials against members who attack their policies." On one live TV interview, Hayes was questioned about the case. Hayes testified on labor legislation on the morning of June 2 at hearings before the House Committee on Education. Before it recessed, he was asked to come back after lunch to answer questions about Lodge 113. He never showed up.

"The notorious Communist"

A.J. Hayes was coming to New York City for a luncheon at the New School for Social Research to be honored for his great services to America as chairman of the AFL-CIO Ethical Practices Committee just as he was about to expel the two machinists who fought for ethical practices. It was an excellent opportunity to expose the hundred or so attendant labor staff representatives to the sordid facts of life.

I prepared a short handbill, neatly mimeographed in those pre-computer days, outlining the facts of the Lodge 113 case and suggesting that Hayes had something to explain as he received the plaudits of his fellow labor diners. Members of the Young People Socialist League passed out this unconventional piece of literature as the audience entered the hall.

At a public meeting after the luncheon, I sat together with three friends: Martin Gerber, regional director of the UAW; Ed Gray, his assistant who later succeeded him as director; and Al Nash, about to become a professor at the Cornell labor school. He had been an auto worker at Chrysler in Detroit, a labor educator and organizer, and an old comrade.

After Hayes finished his post-dinner speech, standard homiletics, it was time for questions. Presiding in the chair was Julius Manson, by then a respected professor in some field of social studies. But in the thirties, he knew me; and I knew him in his youthful career as national secretary of the Young Peoples Socialist League. Perhaps that coincidence explains why I was able to grab the floor and immediately pose the first question. Referring to the Lodge 113 case, I asked: Instead of using your authority as IAM president to discipline your own critics, would it not be more fitting to refer the case to a Public Review Board of impartial people outside your union power structure? Hayes seemed annoyed. My companions grinned.

Not necessary, he replied, and went on to add some derogatory remarks about public review. But his comment allowed Marty Gerber to take the floor. Gerber was a vice president of the Auto Workers, a union which is proud of its Public Review Board as a guardian of member rights against arbitrary action by the union's own officers. Hayes's remarks, said Gerber, compelled him to speak out in defense of the UAW Public Review Board which the union finds a valuable protector of democracy. Somewhat embarrassed, Hayes backtracked: he didn't mean to imply that the institution was not proper for the UAW, but it was not for the Machinists union.

All very diplomatic, but Hayes was more upset than appeared, which brings us back to the little handbill distributed out front. At that point, we had not yet decided to make the Ciepley-Rappaport Legal Fund public; we were awaiting final decision by the IAM convention. The problem, then, was how to identify our handbill, which we solved by signing it "Ad Hoc Committee for Ciepley and Rappaport." Some days later, we got news from Chicago:

At a membership meeting of Lodge 113, the deputy trustee expatiated with indignation on the campaign of slanderous criticism against their beloved international president. And you know what happened in New York, he said, when President Hayes spoke at a luncheon, a notorious communist named Ed Hoc passed out vicious leaflets attacking him.

Hayes's career as labor's ethical czar was brief. After a flurry of activity, the AFL-CIO crusade against racketeers simply evaporated. Once Congress adopted the LMRDA, the AFL-CIO lost interest. The Ethical Practices Committee disappeared from the AFL-CIO constitution and became a missing person, unwept, unhonored, and unsung.

In the fall of 1951, Kermit Eby had written in *Labor and Nation*, "It has been my experience with labor unions that no organizations in America, and no men more than their leaders, stress their democratic aspirations. And, I may add, because of the nature of the power structure in which labor's leaders operate, no men more consistently live in contradiction to their protestations."

His view was grounded in experience: he had been CIO Director of Research and Education, executive secretary of the Chicago Teachers Union; and when he wrote those words, he was professor of social science at the University of Chicago.

That contradiction, one of the eternal verities of power in the American labor movement, is rooted in the divided soul of American labor leadership. To thrive, the labor movement needs a nourishing soil of democracy. Unions and union leaders defend democracy on the outside, in the nation; But on the inside, in their own unions, labor leaders distrust democracy as a threat their own power base. This antithesis has always undermined any effort to eradicate corruption in unions. To eliminate corruption over the long haul, it is necessary to stimulate internal union democracy, to protect the right of union members to organize against their leaders, crooked or honest, and, if need be, to oust them.

The battle for democracy in Lodge 113 was lost, but the campaign for the reinstatement of the two expelled machinists, instructive it itself, had lighted the way for future action. It exposed the Achilles heel of labor's putative war on corruption. For the first time since the thirties, a group of "outside" civic leaders, albeit small, had been inspired to act publicly in support of the rights of union dissidents against a repressive officialdom. It showed that, by stressing the broad social significance of internal union democracy, it was possible to arouse public sympathy for union reformers and exert pressure upon authoritarian leaders.

Moreover, it revealed in dramatic fashion, even in a union whose officialdom enjoyed a reputation for enlightened leadership, the arbitrary, dictatorial quality of union government at a time when the powers of that leadership over its membership were unrestrained by federal law. And now, on the eve of the two expulsions, that power was about to be curbed by the Labor-Management Reporting and Disclosure Act of 1959 (LMRDA.)

Chapter 2: Union democracy then and now: the Labor-Management Reporting and Disclosure Act of 1959.

A. The McClellan Hearings:

Nineteen fifty-nine, the watershed of union democracy, was the year Congress adopted the Labor-Management Reporting and Disclosure Act, the law which gave federal protection for the rights of workers inside their unions. Over 20 years earlier, the National Labor Relations Act had established the statutory right of workers to unions of their own choosing. Now, as Clark Kerr put it, the LMRDA aimed to establish their right to union leaders of their own choosing. Before the LMRDA, union leaders could be unrestrained autocrats. After, they had to observe certain minimal norms of democratic decency. Even then, many continued to resist compliance. It has taken years of battling by union reformers, enforcement by government authorities, and private litigation to put teeth in the law.

In 1926, before LMRDA, when John L. Lewis, in control of the administrative apparatus of the Miners union, reported astounding—and unbelievable—lop sided vote tallies in his own favor, the insurgents had no effective recourse and were simply wiped out. As John Brophy, Lewis's opponent, wrote some years later: "There was no Honest Ballot Association or anything of the sort that could have been called in, and it was contrary to union custom to take such a matter into courts, which I could not have afforded to do anyway," And, of course, in 1926 there was no LMRDA.

In 1969, after LMRDA, when Miners president Tony Boyle performed the same kind of juggling act, his opposition had recourse under federal law.

In a court-ordered rerun election, the Miners for Democracy defeated Boyle and wrote a new democratic union constitution.

In 1957, before LMRDA, the constitution imposed on Machinists Lodge 113 forbade the unauthorized circulation of petitions on union business. Petitions seem so innocuous, why suppress them? Because those who stand guard against subversion understand that petitions can serve to mobilize and organize members independent of the ruling officialdom. The rationale for banning petitions was elaborated in tedious detail in the **Black Worker**, April 1954, the publication of the Brotherhood of Sleeping Car Porters.

A massive front page editorial continues inside, column after column, under the headline "Why Trade Unions Have Rejected and Repudiated the Petition." The piece begins, "Petitions as a method of adjusting problems inside and outside trade unions are outmoded, out-dated, and outlawed." It goes on to explain:

"...The petition is not only in conflict with the sound trade union principles, but it is disruptive and destructive of the purposes and aims of the unions. Petitions are disruptive because they create a caucus-organization situation amounting to an organization within an organization, which is an artificial, unreal, and contradictory condition. This situation is bound to make for chaos, confusion, and conflict. It is utterly impossible for a petition to be planned and executed except by some of the members of the union getting together in some organized form such as a committee to discuss and agree upon a petition and ways and means for getting it before the desired official of the union. Naturally, the members planning for such a petition would not do so within the offices or halls of the union and hence they inevitably are compelled to resort to the use of the caucus, which is the best possible method a group of workers can use to weaken a union or any other organization. As a matter of fact, any meeting for the good and welfare of the members of the Brotherhood rightfully is expected and required to be held under the supervision of the Brotherhood and within its offices or halls. Rump caucus meetings of any union are irregular, unconstitutional and against the best interests of the union and its members..." And on and on in the same spirit, cramming the inside pages.

In those days, organizing an independent caucus was, in many unions, a capital offense. In 1952, insurgents in the Masters, Mates, and Pilots union announcing the formation of their opposition caucus asked in a handbill, "Is the two-party system possible in Local 88? In every nation in the free world, there are two or more parties. Only in Russia is there only one party." They promptly got their reply. Five of their leaders were expelled on charges of dual unionism, unauthorized meetings and related offenses.

Few union administrations were comfortable with standard democratic procedures. Members of the International Association of Machinists could be expelled for "circulating or causing in any manner to be circulated any false or malicious statement reflecting upon the private or public conduct or falsely or maliciously attacking the character, impugning the motives or questioning the integrity of any officer or member..."

Machinist Joe Addison experienced the deadly impact of that clause after he brought charges against his District 727 Lodge officers who had been accused, by an official IAM auditor, of misappropriating $90.000, His charges were dismissed. But he was brought to trial before a special committee selected by International President Hayes and expelled on slander charges.

The constitution of the International Ladies Garment Workers made it a disciplinary offense for members to "organize groups or clubs in the Union or outside of the Union," except in a brief period just before elections. In 1958, fifty Jewish ILGWU members met to prepare a protest against the termination of the Yiddish edition of Justice, the union paper. They were threatened with expulsion for violating the no-caucus rule.

In June 1947, the convention of the National Brotherhood of Operative Potters decided that a member could be penalized, up to expulsion, for "making false accusations, misrepresentations, untruths, or using degrading literature."

For cold bureaucratic suppression, few provisions could compare with assorted sections of the 1957 constitution of the International Brotherhood of Electrical Workers, clauses that could serve as a model for composing any serpentine criminal syndicalism statute. The following offense subjected an electrician to expulsion:

"Mailing, handing out, or posting cards, handbills, letters, marked ballots or political literature of any kind or displaying streamers, banners, signs, or anything else of a political nature, or being a party in any way to such being done in an effort to induce members to vote for or against any candidate or candidates for L.U. [local union] office, or candidates to conventions."

Under this clause, you obviously risked expulsion for passing out cards: "Elect me local president. I am a good union man." So much for the printed word. But what about the spoken word? Here was another capital offense:

"Attending or participating in any gathering or meeting whatsoever, held outside meetings of a L.U., at which the affairs of the L.U. are discussed, or at which conclusions are arrived at regarding the business and the affairs of a L.U., or regarding L.U. officers or a candidate or candidates for L.U. office." Obviously, if you wanted to "campaign" for office, you could only collar members one by one to convince each one of your virtues, always carefully avoiding “false” statements.

There were at least eight similarly flavored repressive clauses of varying nastiness. A typical appeal was decided by the IBEW executive council at its meeting on November 19,1971 when it upheld disciplinary charges against La Forest A. Smith a Local 349 member. The official account published in the union paper informs us that “Brother Smith wrote and circulated amongst a number of members of the local union a document which contained critical comment upon alleged actions of the local union president relative to a pension plan negotiated with the [employers.]...The IEC, upon review of the record, believes that, by his conduct, Brother Smith endangered the rights of the local union members and the local union’s legal and contractual obligations.”

The LMRDA made all these restrictive and repressive provisions, and others, void.

B. Impact of the LMRDA:

LMRDA Title I, the Bill of Rights, protects basic civil liberties in unions, free speech, due process in trials, the right to criticize officials, to assemble in caucuses. to publish literature discussing union affairs, to speak at union meetings, to seek recourse in the courts and before administrative agencies without fear of union disciplinary action. Since this section is enforceable only by private suit of union members, the courts and federal judges are responsible for its effective implementation. This section does not regulate the election of union officers, a subject covered by Title IV.

Title IV is intended to assure the right to fair and democratic election of union officers and an honest count of the ballots. Unlike Title I, this section is enforceable only by the U.S. Department of Labor. Except under certain complex conditions, unionists are barred from initiating suits in the courts in officer election cases; they arc at the mercy of the Labor Department, which therefore bears main responsibility for the effective enforcement of this Title.

Title III, the Trusteeship section, is designed to protect union locals and other subordinate bodies against the imposition of unfair, repressive trusteeships by their national and international union offices. It provides for hybrid enforcement. Complaining unionists have a choice; they can file private suit directly in Federal court or they can complain through the U.S. Labor Department. Precisely because there is a choice between alternate avenues of enforcement, we can test the effectiveness of private enforcement as against enforcement by the Labor Department.

Other Titles spell out reporting requirements by unions and fiscal responsibilities of officers, provisions which enable union members to get certain minimal information on union finances and copies of union contracts and constitutions. Section 610 makes it a criminal offense to deprive members, by violence or threats, of their rights under the law.

Section II
Origins of the Association for Union Democracy, 1959-1972

Chapter 3: Intellectuals and the Lonely Union Reformer

What distinguished the Lodge 113 story from other unheralded insurgent union movements, was the machinists' success, even in defeat, in winning public support and recognition by presenting the union reformer in a new light: Theirs was not a simple "union" story, but part of a wider battle for decency and democracy. The massive social and political institutions of society tend to get out of control; representatives who are chosen to serve people break loose and serve themselves. One of those powerful institutions is the labor movement; by strengthening democracy in unions, we strengthen democracy in society; the fight of the union reformer is one aspect of the fight for social justice in America. Such was the message.

Even before union democracy became a matter of public policy in Federal law, it had become a subject for some public interest. The American Civil Liberties Union, for example, had adopted a statement on democracy in labor unions in which it called for legislation to protect members' rights. And now, the enactment of the LMRDA in 1959 was for me an encouraging spur to action.

It seemed clear, from the IAM experience, that the first step was to prod the conscience of those liberal and radical writers and intellectuals and to win their sympathy, even active support. To launch precisely such an appeal, I wrote a piece for the magazine *Liberation* (March 1960) entitled "Intellectuals and the Lonely Reformer."

Why address an appeal to intellectuals? The short answer is that their influence helps mold public opinion. But there is more: the embattled union dissident needs both moral encouragement and practical aid. There is nothing more demoralizing than to fight on against heavy odds, unknown and unheralded. Amnesty International solicits letters to isolated prisoners of conscience so that they may take heart from knowing that someone, somewhere, knows that they are there and why. The writer, the reporter, the critic, the publicist, the commentator have the power to give that kind of moral boost to the union reformer.

Discussing the factors that strengthen union power, the sociologist Seymour Martin Lipset wrote (1986) in Unions in Transition, "Basically, American labor organizations have declined in their ability to recruit or retain members for the same reasons that the American public generally become less sympathetic to them...[T]he ability of unions to maintain or gain members and to win certification elections is closely linked to the public's view of them." If that observation is valid, it applies even more strongly to movements for union reform which are starved for recognition and morale encouragement. In large part, "the public view" of labor is shaped by intellectuals who pass judgment on its affairs, public and private.

Was it possible, then, to change the "public view," not simply of "labor," but of union reformers by appealing to the conscience of intellectuals? I was convinced that now was the right time.

The Center for the Study of Democratic Institutions, a project generously financed by the Ford Foundation had brought together an impressive assemblage of liberal prolabor academics and writers including included Paul Jacobs and Michael Harrington. Jacobs, a radical critic of the labor establishment, had written the **Reporter** piece on IAM Lodge 113 "Mr. Hayes Curbs a Disturbance." Harrington rose to fame as the author of "The Other America" and later the principal American spokesman for socialism.

The Center's Trade Union Program produced a small library of books and pamphlets, varying in quality. Most authors, independent-minded, refrained from genuflecting before the power of the union establishment. However, the series failed to deal forthrightly with issues of internal union democracy or to do justice to the union reformer. One exception was the book by Lloyd Ulman on the Steelworkers whose concluding words offered this parting advice to the union: "...the best solution to the problems generated by a more difficult and challenging environment consists in taking their traditions seriously and their democratic institutions at face value. This is a radical proposal, but it is offered without apology."

Democracy in unions a "radical" proposal...and offered in a tone of defensive defiance! His comment went beyond what the others expressed, but it was surely a sign of what they were thinking, if not writing. In that thought, I hoped to find a point of support for the lonely union reformer.

Despite the mutual distrust and misgivings between intellectuals and labor, there is a powerful magnetic attraction that brings them together. Without a strong social force to transform ideals into reality, intellectuals remain isolated in the ivy tower of imagination. Labor offers that force. Without validation of its claims as a peoples movement for social justice, the labor movement is subject to charges as a selfish special interest group. Intellectuals can provide that moral validation.

Every other popular social movement —for civil liberties, against sex discrimination, for racial equality, for peace, for every acknowledged worthy cause—could count on a measure of public recognition and for the moral and material aid of support groups. But, despite the new federal law on their behalf, the union reformer had no institutional backing, nowhere to turn for guidance, for assistance, for legal representation. Meet the lonely union reformer!

Could the union reformer win the sympathy and support of the intellectual? Was there a solid basis for an intellectual-labor reformer alliance? To pose this question and test out the possibilities, I distributed advance copies of "Intellectuals and the Lonely Union Reformer," to friends among union activists, civil libertarians, and writers, before publication in **Liberation**.

To those who were disillusioned by union lapses in the battle for democracy and social justice, the message was: "...if the Labor Movement (capital L) is a disappointment, there remain nonetheless thousands of men within unions, rank-and-filers, shop-level leaders, who persist in pressing for democracy and decency in their unions...If it is proper for decent unionists to call for change within the labor movement—and it is— it is no less proper to call upon the intellectual to fulfill his own responsibility to those who stand for democracy within that movement." The quest for union reform and democracy was set forth as one front in the larger battle for social justice.

For the researchers and the frustrated staff intellectuals and the attorneys, not Marxism but philanthropy could be the order of the day. The piece suggested a kind of free clinic for union reformers. Just as doctors and lawyers feel morally obliged to offer at least limited pro bono services to poor clients, so the intellectuals, those who serve unions and those who write about them, should — noblesse oblige— provide at least minimal service to the union reformer. Let the labor lawyer represent just a single group of reformers; the writer and researcher, help at least one; the PR expert, one free client.

The response was mildly encouraging. My closest friends in and around the labor movement contributed a few hundred dollars to finance a mailing of reprints to a targeted audience of several hundred: staff and writers of the Fund for the Republic, labor academics and lawyers, socialistical union staffers, arbitrators, reporters, civil libertarians, labor writers.

There was sympathy but no rush of volunteers to join a crusade. One old comrade and friend, Don Slaiman, then high on the national AFL-CIO staff, was convinced that my concern was "irrelevant" to life in the labor movement. Still, there were enough expressions of interest to make an effort seem worthwhile. John Harold expressed his enthusiastic agreement. I remembered his great contribution as Catholic Defense League counsel to the reform victory in the Masters, Mates, and Pilots.

Liberation asked Sid Lens, one of its editors, for advance comment. He wrote to me on February 18,1960: "...There is no doubt that the interest of intellectuals in the labor movement has declined. But isn't it also true that the number of union reformers is much less today than in the 1930's ...Admittedly there are many good elements still fighting the good fight...but hasn't the number declined? Isn't dissidence per se more latent? Wouldn't the article be stronger if you pivoted it around the fact that <u>both</u> reformers and intellectuals interested in reform have declined...? I get the feeling reading the piece that union reformers would be more numerous if they could depend on aid from the outside. I doubt very much if that's the implication you want to leave...".

But that was precisely the impression that I did want to leave! Lens was an intellectual and radical in the labor movement. He was a union organizer, on the staff of the Building Service Employees and author of "Left, Right, and Center," a critique of what he called "business unionism." If even he was dubious, there was work to do.

Looking back, I realize now that despite a basic strain of skeptical realism, I obviously suffered from a hope-induced naivete. Few lawyers who represented unions could defend even a single dissident—especially without fee— without risking the loss of their paying union clients. A young independent idealistic attorney who initiates a union democracy suit soon discovers that his is not just a case but a longtime ordeal, dragging out for years as the official union defendants extend procedures with delays and appeals and piles of papers. Paying legal fees out of the union treasury, they will spend thousands to block complainants from winning a hundred. To take such a case, a cash-poor lawyer risks bankruptcy. A union staff professional abetting reformers in another union risks instant discharge from his own. The educator who actively tolerates dissidents finds his classes boycotted by union clients.

I learned all that later. And so nothing resembling a union democracy clinic emerged until more than ten years later with the founding of the Association for Union Democracy.

It was Vera Rony who gave me something to think about. At the time she was executive director of the Workers Defense League, the civil liberties organization founded by the Norman Thomas socialists in the thirties. "Your piece in Liberation is nice," she said, "but you have it wrong. It's not that there are no intellectuals available to support the union reformers. The real trouble is that there are so few union reformers for intellectuals to support." She always was — and continued to be — an advocate for the underdog; and I respected her views, which is why I was surprised to realize that even she had no inkling of what I already knew to be a fact: In 1935, the adoption of the Wagner Act gave a powerful impulse to union organizing. In 1959, the adoption of the LMRDA spurred on movements for union democracy and reform, not as powerful nor as well publicized, but manifest. The rising expectations of rank and file unionists was brought home to me when I visited Chicago in 1960 to meet the Lodge 113 machinists and spoke at a public meeting. There I met members of two locals of the IBEW, electricians in locals 9 and 134. Earlier, after the **Progressive** published "Labor's Uncertain Trumpet," my piece on the IAM expulsions, I had been contacted by insurgents in Local 88 of the Masters, Mates, and Pilots who had been expelled and blacklisted for forming their opposition Party for Union Democracy. I got to know Arthur Holdeman, who later took over as MMP Local 88 president, and John Harold, then counsel for the Association of Catholic Trade Unionists. From Philadelphia, the Betterment Committee in Teamsters Local 107 and their attorney, Edward Bergman, wrote to me about their battle against corruption; and, later, I met with them at a public meeting. Later they fell just short of wresting control of the local away from James Hoffa Sr. In 1957 in Labor USA, Lester Velie reported on the battles against corruption in the Operating Engineers union. I was myself acquainted with the teacher mavericks who were creating the United Federation of Teachers in New York.

In the months that followed, and then the next few years, it was obvious that I had only scratched the surface. A lot was going on and more was to come, much more.

In "The Enemy Within," Robert Kennedy wrote that during the McClellan hearings, 1957-9, some 112,000 unionists had written to the Senate committee complaining of abuses. It is impossible to know how many were justified. However, what is clearly on the record, but something overlooked by writers, is that those hearings, followed by the adoption of the LMRDA in 1959, touched off a wave of rebellion in labor unions.

In the Steelworkers' union, a dues protest movement fielded an unknown rank and filer, Don Rarick, to run for international president against incumbent David McDonald in 1957. Even according to the suspect official count, Rarick gathered 223,000 votes to McDonald's 404,000. That result revealed deep dissatisfaction in the ranks and triggered a split in the top leadership, leading to McDonald's defeat by Secretary-Treasurer I.W. Abel in 1965.

In the Masters, Mates, and Pilots, the maritime union of licensed deck officers, a successful revolt in New York Local 88, the union's largest, was the prelude to a reform victory in 1960 with the election of Charles Crooks as international president.

In that same period, in the Marine Engineers Beneficial Association, union of licensed ships' engineers, a series of strong local insurgent movements resisted, unsuccessfully, the dissolution of their locals and the union's reorganization into a single, centralized, national union.

In the National Maritime Union, after President Joe Curran had eradicated his Communist opposition, the union became the arena for vigorous opposition movements, arising in part from within the administration itself.

In the Machinists' union, the national administration had to beat down opposition from Ralph Brown, international vice president for the West Coast, and from fifteen West Coast locals. In St. Louis, the IAM administration faced a revolt from the 22,000-member Lodge 837 at the McDonnell-Douglas plant. The IAM narrowly retained collective bargaining rights in the plant after the United Auto Workers and the Teamsters moved to offer alternatives to the IAM.

In the Musicians' union, in the early 1960's, the elite of the profession organized into the International Conference of Symphony and Opera Musicians as an insurgent caucus to demand basic rights within the union, especially the right to a voice in negotiating and policing their own contracts. After facing denunciation as "dual unionists" by the national leadership, ICSOM won increasing support in the union and from the players in all major symphony orchestras. ICSOM won its battle; it was recognized as an official "conference" in the American Federation of Musicians and became a strong force for democracy within it.

In that same period, in New York City's Musicians' Local 802, an opposition caucus, publishing *Musicians' Voice*, campaigned on a platform for vigorous contract enforcement, against kickbacks to employers, and against blacklisting of critics. The opposition won support from the local's active musicians and dominated local meetings; they suffered defeat in local elections, at that time, only because they were outvoted, in mail balloting, by the part-timers, retirees, and non-playing members who constituted a majority of the membership.

In the United Papermakers and Paperworkers, Frank Grasso, general vice president of this 135,000-member union in 1959, led an insurgent caucus, the Better Union Committee, calling for democratizing the union. At the union's convention in 1960, the insurgents won nine spots on the nineteen-member international executive board. Not enough! In a series of bureaucratic moves, the administration used its thin majority to wipe out its opposition.

In the 170,000-member International Brotherhood of Pulp, Sulphite, and Paper Mill Workers, a powerful insurgent movement succeeded in winning a partial victory. In 1961, the leaders of sixteen locals formed an opposition caucus, the Rank and File Movement for Democratic Action; it aimed "to safeguard the democratic character of the labor movement." Its supporters were driven by a fear that the union was in danger of a corrupt takeover. When they failed to win concessions within the union, five Canadian locals seceded to from an independent Canadian union. In the United States, the insurgents on the West Coast formed their own independent union, the Association of Western Pulp and Paperworkers; the new union won collective bargaining rights for 22,000 workers in 50 mills on the West Coast.

In this same period, soon after the adoption of the LMRDA in 1959, rank and file railroad workers organized the cross-union Right to Vote Committee to campaign for a voice in the adoption of collective bargaining contracts. Local leaders in the International Union of Electrical Workers defeated James Carey as international president after thwarting attempts by administration officials to steal an election. In 1964, Jerry Wurf ousted Arnold Zander as president of the American Federation of State, County, and Municipal Employees. In the International Union of Operating Engineers, rank and filers in Ohio, New Jersey, Detroit, and Los Angeles rebelled unsuccessfully against their local union officials.

Beginning in 1959 and in the early years thereafter, I came to know about these rebels and reformers. But it was obvious that, to stimulate support for union reformers, it was necessary to demonstrate that they actually existed! And so, early in 1960, I began publishing **Union Democracy in Action**, a one-man-band newsletter to break the story of the lonely union reformer. I didn't realize it then, but this was the beginning, not of a few months of spare time activity, but the beginning of a new lifetime career.

Chapter 4: "Union Democracy in Action," 1960-1972

In 1961 at the 14th annual meeting of the Industrial Relations Research Association, discussing the defects in contemporary writings on labor history, George Brooks wrote of "the growing body of third-party practitioners who have become attached to the body of industrial relations — the arbitrators, local advisers, actuaries, conciliators, mediators, public relations experts, and consultants of all kinds...this group is important because it includes large sections of the intellectual community in which genuine labor history might be expected to originate." However, Brooks maintained, their obligations to a union officialdom which tolerates only a sanitized, officially acceptable 'history' renders them incapable of fulfilling that role. "...in labor history," he wrote, "the bureaucratization of research and writing is having the most deleterious results." He quoted labor historian Robert Christie: "...as the [Carpenters] union centralized its administration over the years, the journals, proceedings, and reports made public contained less and less of the material out of which history may be wrought. By 1941, this material had dwindled to a trickle."

"What we now need," he concluded, "is some method of tapping new sources of information." Reading those words, I recognized a kindred spirit — and in the years that followed, Brooks became a close collaborator and a cherished friend. I harbored no grandiose ambition to write the kind of history he looked for, a task beyond my capacity in any event. But, by that time, I knew that I did have the ability, perhaps uniquely, to fill part of the gap with "new sources of information" on the union democrat in action.

To tell the machinists' story, there was the reprint of Jacob's **Reporter** piece, mine in the **Progressive,** and Repas's at Michigan State. Other reprints provided an effective weapon for members of the Masters, Mates and Pilots union.

From the experience of those modest reprints, a more ambitious idea germinated: I would try my hand as a free lance labor journalist, plant stories on union reformers in established publications, and, taking advantage of their respected status, reprint and distribute the stories as part of the battle. I would ask for support from co-thinkers to circulate "Reprints on Union Democracy in Action." (The idea quickly turned out to be an experimental dead end, but it was a start!)

A new scholarly magazine, **Labor History**, asked me to review "The Maritime Story" by Joseph P. Goldberg, a bland product. In my review, I wrote about battles for democracy in the National Maritime Union and in the Masters, Mates, and Pilots, citing them as examples of what should be covered in works on seafarers — not the kind of comment the editors expected. It seemed like a great opportunity for a union democracy reprint. The managing editor told me that he had been uneasy: should he accept my review? He asked Phil Taft, one of the editors, for guidance. Taft was not pleased by the review but said that, having solicited the piece, they were stuck with it. I reprinted it as "Unionism and Democracy in the Merchant Marine." Arthur Holdeman, a leader of insurgents in Local 88 of the MMP, donated $500 toward the costs; (big money in those days) and it was distributed widely throughout the union. But obviously, there was no future for this kind of thing in **Labor History**.

Meanwhile, the MMP battle was heating up. The decisive national election, a mail ballot, was scheduled to begin at the end of July 1960. It was a chance for the reformers to take over after the former national president had been convicted of selling jobs. I wrote a piece for the **Progressive** describing the long battle for MMP reform: the expulsion of critics, the intervention of attorney John Harold and the Association of Catholic Trade Unionists, their battles in ports over the nation. Plenty of time, I was assured by the *Progressive* editor, for the piece to appear before the election. Perfect for another "Reprint on Union Democracy in Action." But it was not to be. At the last moment, on the eve of the MMP election, the *Progressive* changed plans. It ran a literary issue, crowding out all other stories. Mine had to wait. It was published, but a month later; the MMP election was over. My story was another piece of interesting news, but late. I realized that I had to free myself from other peoples' standards and deadlines.

Two numbers of "Reprints on Union Democracy in Action" made it into print. The first announced: "Our [editorial 'we' for a one-man band] aim is to emphasize in the events of our day, the democratic potential of unionism. This is a time of great national discussion on the nature of the labor movement and of the possibilities of union democracy...We hope to report the striving of democratic union reformers and to tell the story of democratic unionism...The revitalization of union democracy is not the task of the rank and file reformer alone, It is the common responsibility of union member and leader, of labor intellectuals, of liberals, of professionals. the defense of democracy anywhere requires a bond of moral solidarity among democratic-minded persons everywhere. Unions are no exception. Writing about the Negro youth at Southern lunch counters, Lillian Smith said, 'They need money, yes, but they need even more to know that we are with them.' The union reformer, too, needs to know that we are with him; as a small beginning, we must tell his story." For the next 11 years and 42 issues, that was the note 'we' sounded. Clyde Summers tells of the cellist who was asked, "Why do you insist on playing over and over only that single note on only one string." The musician replied, "Ah, but what a beautiful note."

Reprint No. 2 publicized the attempt of organizers of the International Ladies Garment Workers Union to form their own staff union, the Federation of Union Representatives (FOUR), and win bargaining rights. The ILG declared war against FOUR as fiercely as any anti-union employer — intimidation, discharges, long tirades in the union paper — and finally wore them down.

Apart from its interest as a minor historical footnote, the issue gave an ironical boost to **Union Democracy in Action**. Moved by self-righteous indignation, Louis Stulberg, then ILGWU secretary treasurer, sent copies of the offending UDA reprint to his entire staff as an example of the kind of warped public attack they had to combat. For me it was an early introduction to the kind of union official who is so convinced of his own virtue that he confidently imagines that he refutes criticism merely by revealing that it exists. Unintended result: he helped lift UDA slightly out of obscurity.

By September 1961, **Union Democracy in Action** began publication as a regular newsletter. The reprint disguise was abandoned as too confining; besides, it was now obvious that enough support was available to sustain a modest newsletter, not quite on regular schedule but quarterly and sometimes more frequently. Norman Thomas, the respected Socialist leader and frequent candidate for president, made the project possible. Upon his recommendation, between $1,500 and $3,000 was granted for each of two or three years by the Prynce Hopkins Fund, which did not require its recipients to enjoy tax-exempt status. An additional $2,000 came from small — quite small — individual donations from 200 supporters.

Technical help came from Jim Peck, pacifist, editor of the CORE newsletter, a former seaman unionist, and one of the Freedom Riders who toured the South at the risk of their lives to break down segregation in bus travel. Jim, a determined participant in high-risk social causes, may have established a world record for the most number of arrests in social protest demonstrations. He wrote about **Union Democracy Review** in the **Independent**, a tabloid then circulated by the publisher, Lyle Stuart. Apart from making annual donations of $100, real money then, Peck typed addresses, stuffed envelopes, and insisted on personally hefting sacks of the first class mail directly to the post office. "You can just drop them into the corner post box," I said. "No," he insisted, "Why should the letter carrier have to haul such heavy mail." Many years later I visited him in the nursing home where he was strapped into a wheel chair after suffering a stroke. He was still able to sound off strongly against some recent injustice. When the attendant, a black woman, came for him, I said, "Do you know Mr. Peck here was one of the first Freedom Riders?" "That's nice," she commented as she wheeled him away.

UDA clearly staked out its territory in January 1962 with a 16-page issue headed "Introducing Union Reformers in Action." It aimed to inform the uninformed; Yes, those reformers are really there, and potentially a substantial force. The issue reported on those painters, teachers, union staff organizers, the Better Union Committee in the United Papermakers and Paperworkers; the Rank and File Movement for Democratic Action in the Pulp, Sulphite union; insurgents in the Marine Engineers Beneficial Association; the victory of democracy in the Masters, Mates and Pilots; Machinist opposition movements in California and Chicago. A first printing of 5,000 was quickly distributed. Two thousand were purchased by the Rank and File Movement for Democratic Action, which mailed them to local officers. An additional thousand was ordered by Pulp, Sulphite locals and caucuses. The Paperworkers Better Union Committee ordered 4,000 copies of the four-page section on their union. Over a thousand copies of the full or partial issue were circulated among marine officers. Some small bundles went to teachers in New York. The section on FOUR, the staff union, was reprinted in an Italian-language socialist and labor bi-monthly in Chicago.

A special four-page issue in 1966 reported on the battle at IAM Lodge 837 in St. Louis; ten thousand copies of the issue were reprinted and distributed by the insurgents. An average print-run, however, was about 2,000, supported by donations from those special 200 readers.

Union Democracy in Action kept going, publishing 42 issues until 1972 when it was superseded by **Union Democracy Review**, the periodical established by the Association for Union Democracy. In those 14 years, roughly 1959-1972, it kept alive the story of union insurgency; it monitored the work of the U.S. Labor Department as an LMRDA enforcement agency; it highlighted developments in union democracy law.

Was all this effort "irrelevant," as some had warned? If I still harbored any subconscious misgivings, they were dispelled by my UDA experience: one fact had been firmly established for anyone who would read: Union reformers were not the figment of some radical's dream. They were alive and active in the labor movement. In the years that followed, that proof became overwhelming.

Still, the road to union democracy is never straight and smooth but a roller coaster of steep ups and downs. Which brings us to the early story of *Union Democracy in Action* and the Painters union.

Chapter 5: Interlude: The Painters' Union, 1962-1972

The sixties were years of hopes aroused but the dreams of union democracy deferred. The cumulative impact of the McClellan hearings, the AFL-CIO Ethical Practices Codes, and the enactment of the LMRDA offered the hope of a new era, the promise of a refurbished union democracy sustained by public opinion and protected by law. It was precisely that promise which encouraged me to begin publishing *Union Democracy in Action*. That same spirit inspired new insurgent movements for union reform, some recorded in UDA; but there were others. Let a hundred flowers bloom! And so they did, but, in those early days, most often only to be cut down.

Within a few years, public interest dwindled; it was disillusioning to discover that the new law would not be vigorously enforced, that the AFL-CIO's concern with issues of democracy and corruption was only a momentary blip. Quelled, the early reform upsurge subsided. The potential for reform was impressive but not powerful enough. The resistance and the obstacles were too formidable. This turn of events was most tragically evident in the Painters' union.

A. Frank Schonfeld fights the mob in New York

The first effort on a mass scale to stifle dissent in unions after the adoption of the LMRDA in 1959 came in the Brotherhood of Painters.

One Saturday afternoon early in 1961, Frank Schonfeld, along with a fellow housepainter, dropped into my Seward Park coop apartment in the Lower East Side. I had just begun publishing *Union Democracy in Action*, without an office, working out of my home, using a Post Office Box address. He said that he expected trouble because he intended to run for secretary treasurer of Painters District Council 9 and was looking for advice. Why from me?

He had first gone to the New York Civil Liberties Union where he met Gordon Haskell, assistant director, who was sympathetic but said regretfully that Frank could not count on the ACLU. Gordon was an old friend and comrade, a co-editor of Labor Action — by then, defunct. He gave Frank a copy of "Intellectuals and the Lonely Union Reformer."

"The lonely union reformer — whoever wrote that," said Frank, "sure knows what he's talking about. There really isn't anyone lonelier. I never saw it put better." Haskell gave him my home phone number.

At that time, Painters District Council 9, with jurisdiction over all union painting in the five boroughs, had about 12,000 members; about 8,000 were building trades house painters organized into a dozen or more locals; 4,000 others were members of several loosely affiliated autonomous locals: bridge painters, glaziers, sign painters, paint salesmen.

Frank told a sorry story: the union and the industry a cesspool of corruption; business agents taking payoffs; collusion between top union officials and contractors to keep wages low; cheating insurance funds; violation of the collective bargaining agreement; pressure on workers to evade safety rules; favoritism in hiring; blacklisting of critics; manipulation of elections and referendums. Above all: heavy infiltration by racketeers.

That was 1961. By now, some 40 years and a multitude of investigations later, these facts about construction are common coin. But back then, the details were shocking. Could this man be believed? Or, was he the victim of hysterical hallucinations? The Painters union! In my mind it still retained a nostalgic "progressive" aura. In the old days it was headed by a right-wing socialist; some of the old timers were still social democratic-inclined Jewish "paintners." It had once been headed by Louis Weinstock, a leading and acknowledged Communist; and then by Martin Rarback, a Trotskyist. It soon became clear to me that I had a lot to learn about the building and construction trades.

Schonfeld said he intended to organize a caucus, run for the top job of district secretary treasurer, and try to clean up the whole mess. The top job! I demurred. Couldn't you start out with more modest ambitions, say, for some local post. After all you've hardly begun to convince supporters...No, he replied, it's got to be the top job with the power to make changes. I listened without commitment. Even if he is describing the scene accurately, and who knows?, does he have delusions of grandeur? I was already wary, having met enough self-proclaimed saviors with Napoleonic visions who quickly faded into the night. And in the years ahead I would meet more. And so I left it vague. We'll be in touch. Meanwhile, I had to check it out. But where?

I asked friends in the auto workers union, and the Ladies Garment Workers, and the Amalgamated Clothing Workers, and the Seafarers' union. Nobody knew a thing. Surely the Jewish Labor Committee must know. Painters DC 9 once had a big Jewish membership and had been part of the New York City socialist-labor-progressive "community." Schonfeld's own Local 1011 had originally been set up for Yiddish-speaking painters. But Manny Muravchik, JLC executive director, had no idea, "It's possible that some agents might be taking a few bucks from bosses," he guessed, "but don't take my word." I begin to realize that nobody I knew outside the union could tell me what was brewing inside.

Then I remembered Lou Cyens, whom I recalled as a former member of the Socialist Workers Party, one who had helped "colonize" the painters union for the party more than ten years earlier. His brother-in-law, Erwin Baur, a toolmaker and auto worker in Detroit and then still an SWP member, whom I knew and trusted as a dedicated idealist, Back in 1937 when I was 22, he was president of a Steelworkers local and took me to my first union meeting.

Erwin told me that Lou was still active in the painters union and a partisan of the administration under its secretary treasurer, Martin Rarback, the very same man Schonfeld would oppose. Cyens, I thought, must know the score, and so I called him.

I hear all kinds of nasty rumors about the Painters' union, I tell him, what can you tell me about Rarback and the union? Cyens is generously willing to talk at length, but he is stingy with basic facts. He expatiates with a heavy social-political analysis, the kind of deep stuff which rang so familiarly in the Marxist movement. There are, he lectured, progressives and conservatives in the labor movement: Harry Van Arsdale, head of the Central Labor Council and president of IBEW Local 3, is one of those admirable progressives. Rarback is in the progressive Van Arsdale camp, which is why, he says, I support him. In my impatience with the deep philosophy discourse, I interrupt: yes, yes, yes, but what about crooks taking money from the bosses? Here, he gets vague. Well, maybe a business agent sometimes takes a bribe, but that's not the important thing…and so back to the philosophy lecture.

What do you know about a Frank Schonfeld?, I ask. Reply; Oh a malcontent, used to be with Rarback. I'm beginning to get the picture. Maybe Schonfeld is genuine. Within a few weeks I'm convinced. Everything Frank told me begins to ring true. On May 27,1961, a drizzly

Saturday morning, 250 painters attended a Schonfeld rally in the Bronx to hear him and speakers from six locals explain why they wanted to get rid of Rarback. Later, I meet some of them; they all confirmed Schonfeld's charges.

Even before the election, disciplinary charges were filed against several Rarback opponents. In June, in an atmosphere of intimidation, the election was concluded. When the ballot count was announced, Rarback was credited with 3,700 votes to Schonfeld's 1,900 but that tally was deceptive. Schonfeld had limited use of the union mailing list. Votes were tabulated by Rarback's supporters with little oversight. In the autonomous locals, where Schonfeld was not able to distribute a single piece of election literature, the vote went 10 to 1 for Rarback. But among painters where Schonfeld was able to get out at least one mailing the vote went for Rarback 2,500 to 1,800. But in locals where Schonfeld had succeeded in compiling his own mailing list and members had received repeated exposures to his campaign handbills, he actually carried a majority. For Schonfeld, they went 1,464; for Rarback, 1,281.

When I first met Frank he was 44, a year younger than me, married to his wife Jean for more than 16 years, with an 11-year old daughter and a 15-year old son, all living in the old Amalgamated Coop Houses in the Bronx. For those 16 years he had earned his living as a house painter, his hands scarred and cracked from the cumulative effects of poisonous paint solvents.

Frank was a rare kind of painter, a rare kind of person. His father and grandfather had been prominent rabbis; and Frank, graduating from a Yeshiva on the way to ordination, seemed destined to follow in the same tradition. But he grew up in the depression-scarred thirties when thousands of young people embraced Marxist social radicalism. In a break with family tradition, he abandoned plans to become a rabbi. For the social justice he once sought through the synagogue, he now pursued through the working class and the labor movement. He joined the Socialist Workers Party, the anti-Stalinist, pro-Trotskyist, current which centered its activities in unions.

He had broken with the family's religious ties, but in character, personal demeanor, and morality he continued its heritage. He was gentle, quiet, considerate, civilized. Painters, puzzled to explain how so mild a manner could conceal so firm a leader, called him "a real gentleman." Strengthened by a powerful core of moral determination and guided by a code of personal ethics, he joined the labor movement not as a desk man but as an overalls worker. Later, when he left the SWP and his dream of changing the world faded, and others drifted back belatedly to professional careers, Frank retained a vision of workers democracy, now purged of earlier illusions.

By the time I met him, Frank had left the SWP years before, disillusioned with the party and with Rarback; but he remained an active member of Local 1011. No longer part of the Rarback administration, he was nonetheless elected a local recording secretary in the late fifties. It was his job to take minutes —in English and Yiddish. But one day he missed a meeting to attend a niece's wedding. Upon return he read, in the minutes written by someone else, that the meeting had adopted a motion to impose a 50-cent assessment by a vote of about 700 to 15. He knew such a result to be an unlikely miracle because no more than 50 had ever attended meetings. Disgusted, he resigned the secretary job.

Earlier, during World War II, he had served in the merchant marine. In 1945, together with other comrades in the Socialist Workers Party, he became a painter and a member of Local 1011 in District Council 9. Their SWP cadre formed the core of a new opposition coalition caucus which, in 1947, defeated Louis Weinstock for the top job of DC 9 secretary treasurer and elected Martin Rarback. Then in his late forties, "Marty," like Schonfeld, was still an SWP member; but he had joined the party years before Schonfeld.

When he was younger and still in the SWP, Marty admired Felix Morrow with a trace of that awe which party leaders inspired in their young followers. Morrow, a half-generation older, was an intellectual leader of the party, an effective speaker, the author of a book on the Spanish civil war highly praised among the comrades. In the SWP, Morrow was Rarback's mentor, his model. Time passes. Sometime in late fifties or early sixties, Rarback had been out of the party for a long time, Felix Morrow was commuting to the city on the Long Island Railroad, when a former close acquaintance, whom he had not seen for years, sat down beside him. It was Rarback, a chance meeting. This is Morrow's account to me a few years later:

Marty, eager to talk, seemed determined to prove to Felix that he had made good in the intervening years; he was more than a mere union official; he was a man of affairs owed deference by others, as demonstrated by his recent trip to Florida. Two gangsters had been embroiled in a messy dispute over which was entitled to receive the ample fruits of some successful racket venture. Rarback, asked to arbitrate, went down to Florida to preside over the hearings, along with his aide Frank Grattano. After Marty had listened impartially to both sides and made the award, the lucky winner thanked him by proffering a big bundle of cash. Marty turned up his nose. "I don't handle that," he said condescendingly, "Turn it over to Grattano." Morrow, not impressed, was dumbfounded. (At hearings before one House committee, documentary evidence revealed that Rarback and Grattano had jointly received over $188,000 in one single payment from Jack McCarthy, a labor racketeer.)

When Rarback was first elected secretary treasurer of District Council 9, racketeers were still entrenched in the locals. Louis Weinstock, the Communist leader who had been elected secretary treasurer some ten years before, had to maneuver carefully and make concessions to retain power. In other unions, racketeers had entrenched themselves even while socialists held top office. John Burke president of the Pulp, Sulphite union and Pat Gorman president of the Meat Cutters were both socialist trade union leaders who failed to prevent the infiltration of racketeers. The difference between them and Rarback, however, was this: they failed to ward off racketeers; Rarback joined them.

One day, while Schonfeld was still in the Rarback camp but becoming uneasy with the direction of the union, the two men were arguing mildly over some aspect of union policy. "Painters are whores," said Rarback, "They'd sell out their own grandmothers for a few days work." He had learned contempt for the members who continued to elect him. They were anxious to make a living, sometimes desperate. He despised them for their need.

For eight years, between 1953 and 1961, Rarback faced no challenger and so was automatically declared reelected. The old CP- dominated Rank and File Caucus had reached an informal live and let live arrangement with Rarback. They grumbled now and then but after 1951, they never ran a candidate against him. However, when Schonfeld finally raised the banner of revolt, most of them supported him against Rarback. The union continued to crumble; it ceased to exist on the job sites as a protector of working conditions. The contract was not enforced. Between 1953 and 1967, there was not a single general membership meeting of DC 9 painters. Rarback was busy with more lucrative activities; in collusion with employers and crooked city officials he was running a bid-rigging conspiracy in city housing painting. Shop stewardships, filled by the union, became sources of illicit income. Rarback's brother ran the insurance funds. The son of one of the big employers set up a brokerage firm to handle the fund's investments. Favored employers were allowed to fall behind on their insurance fund payments. In 1964, contemptuous of the members, Rarback negotiated a three-year contract which provided a total wage increase of four cents an hour. One and a third cent per year! (He justified the deal by negotiating an annuity plan which swelled the insurance fund coffers, a common source of manipulation.)

For Schonfeld it was depressing to watch the degeneration of the man he had helped raise to power. He rejected every offer to board the gravy train and severed relations with Rarback. At first it seemed impossible to oppose a solidifying machine based on fear and favors. For a time he dropped out of union activity and earned his living unobtrusively as a painter. But by 1960, after the adoption of the LMRDA and a new public interest in union democracy, Schonfeld and a few others decided to take a stand. They formed a Committee for Democracy; Schonfeld announced his candidacy against Rarback, which is when I met him. His organized caucus never totaled more than a dozen or two, a small band but not unusual in union opposition groups. But, as the election results proved, even in defeat they could count on a big reservoir of membership sympathy.

For the next six years, the Schonfeld opposition persisted in a flurry of activity. They ran candidates in some locals, published the Painters Free Press as an occasional tabloid newspaper, distributed handbills, organized small meetings of supporters. Slowly, they were winning support, but it was impossible to know its full extent, because elections and referendums were routinely stolen. It was impossible to get an honest count.

When the dissidents were brought to trial before a board staffed by their enemies, Schonfeld's public appeal for the establishment of an impartial public review board, as in the auto workers union, was circulated to the list of three or four hundred writers and public leaders which I had compiled during the machinists affair.

Norman Thomas, everyman's ombudsman, who had sponsored the defense of the Chicago machinists, was available to help the painters. On August 24,1961, just as the painters were coming to trial in their union, 300 people came to Judson Memorial Church in Greenwich Village, at a public forum sponsored by *Union Democracy in Action*, to hear Thomas, Schonfeld, and Dan House, head of UAW Local 365, speak on the need for Public Review in the labor movement. Rarback, accompanied by an official from IBEW Local 3, was there in the hall expecting, no doubt, to "expose" the affair. Taking the floor during the discussion period, he denounced his critics as disrupters and shouted scornfully that the audience consisted of nothing but an assemblage of painter malcontents. Whereupon loud calls came from scattered sections of the hall: Teachers here! Seamen! Carpenters! ILGWU members! Building Service! Paperworkers! It was a first preliminary hint of what, over the years, would become an informal national network for union democracy.

Schonfeld and his supporters were being starved out, blacklisted, denied the right to work. Under the terms of the collective bargaining agreement, the union had no hiring hall rights; painters had to solicit their own jobs. Business agents made their own private arrangements with contractors to make sure that their cronies got plenty of lucrative work. But when active

Schonfeld supporters arrived: nothing available today! At one point in 1966, Schonfeld wrote to Mayor Lindsay "A systematic blacklist is operating against us, not only in private industry but even against some who have worked for the city as provisional painters."

Schonfeld himself had worked regularly for many years for a large contractor, the Schatz Painting Company; but after coming out openly against Rarback his work with the company suddenly dried up: "Sorry, nothing today, Frank." Here again, Norman Thomas to the rescue. He wrote a concerned letter to the company president, appealing to his sense of fair play. Who knows what deeply buried sense of guilt the letter prodded in the mind of this Jewish entrepreneur? It worked. Frank went back to work, still able to support his family and to fight another day.

All the expressions of public sympathy contributed little tangible practical aid to the embattled painters; but, modest as it was, it did provide a measure of moral encouragement. But after the adoption of the LMRDA in 1959, union reformers expected more than moral encouragement. They presumably had gained the right to protection under federal law. The painters were the first to test the effectiveness of the law and to test the reliability of the government agencies responsible for enforcing it. In short, they discovered that the U.S. Labor Department was a weak reed and that they were more likely to find recourse and relief in the Federal courts.

As soon as Rarback was installed in 1961, he preferred disciplinary charges against all his major critics, heard before a trial committee of his own supporters. Guilty! Of course. And in the normal course of events, normal that is before the enactment of the LMRDA, they would have been summarily dispatched and would have vanished from the radar screen. But not now. By October 1962, Schonfeld's case was decided in Federal court. Overturning the trial committees verdict and restoring Schonfeld to good standing, District Judge Murphy expressed his contempt for the union proceedings, "If this be due process," he wrote, "the moon is made of green cheese." All the trials were abandoned, the intended victims exonerated.

The new law was being tested. I decided to work with these insurgent painters to help defend their rights under the LMRDA. For Frank and me, it was the beginning of a lasting collaboration and friendship that will surely endure for the rest of his life or mine, whichever comes first.

The case of Solomon Salzhandler, a retired painter in Local 442, made legal history. He got into trouble in 1960 because he took his duties seriously as local financial secretary. After inspecting a group of canceled checks, he concluded that the local business agent had forged endorsements and cashed checks for his own benefit. In a little handbill message to local members he called the BA a "petty robber." Not the BA but Salzhandler was brought up on charges in the union, tried, found guilty of slander, removed from office, and suspended for five years. Earlier, three anti-Rarback oppositionists had also been disciplined on slander charges.

In a ringing defense of union democracy, the Court of Appeals in New York, voided the union decision and ordered Salzhandler reinstated. "We hold that the LMRDA protects the union member in the exercise of his right to make such charges without reprisal by the union; that any provision of the union constitution which makes such a criticism, whether libelous or not, subject to union discipline are unenforceable; and that the Act allows redress for such unlawful treatment." The union, the court held, is simply not to be trusted is such cases. "The Trial Board in the instant case," it wrote, "consisted of union officials not judges. It was a group to which the delicate problems of truth or falsehood, privilege, and 'fair comment' were not familiar. Its procedure is peculiarly unsuited for drawing the fine line between criticism and defamation..."

Union Democracy in Action commented, "If a critic of a ruling administration charges that he has been slandered by the officials, his complaint is contemptuously ignored or dismissed. But if the official charges that he has been slandered by a critic, the result is usually quite different. The oppositionist can expect triaL before a committee chosen by his enemies and prompt punishment. This farce, as a result of the Appeals Court decision, is now illegal."

Salzhandler v. Caputo was a landmark decision in union democracy law. All union trials on slander charges were abandoned in Painters DC 9. There were prompt repercussions in other unions. The conviction on charges of slander of John W. Anderson, by his UAW Local 15, was overturned by the UAW international executive board. The trial of Dow Wilson in the Painters union on the West Coast was abandoned. The MEBA was forced to drop slander charges against dissidents Nick Priscu and John Roman.

For seven years, elections and referendums in DC 9 were stolen. To turn their energies and their mounting support into power, the Painter reformers needed a fair count in democratic elections. At one gathering, I think it was a convention of the Socialist Party, I met Don Slaiman, who was then director of the AFL-CIO organizing department in Washington. I asked him, "How can Schonfeld get an honest election in the Painters union?" He shrugged, "How should I know!" But opportunity knocked in 1967.

A crack in Rarback's protective stockade opened violently one evening in March 1964. In the parking lot of a city housing project, Jack Graham, a contractor, was beaten by two thugs with tire irons so badly that he almost died. Luckily, he survived; and, after agonizing over the event for six months, he went to Manhattan District Attorney Hogan with his story.

Graham was the owner of the Westgate Painting Company, a contractor under agreement with Painters DC 9. He provided evidence of a corrupt bid-rigging conspiracy in the repainting of city housing, a lucrative $7,000,000 annual business. Crooked contractors parceled out work among themselves assigning one, then another, to be low bidder on projects. To make an extra buck on top of their inflated "low" bids, they did substandard work, using inferior paints, stealing coats of paint, pushing workers to do shoddy work under intense speed-up pressures. For overlooking obvious violations, city inspectors and union officials got bribes of 3% of the total contract prices. In six years, $840,000 went to Rarback and $420,000 to crooked inspectors. Legitimate bidders could not compete. Graham, for defying the system, was almost killed.

The plot involved contractors, city paint inspectors, and the union. A ring of employers would agree on the price to be charged the city for repainting of city-owned houses, decide on which of them would be the successful bidder, and submit higher prices to assure that their lucky choice would win out. Any unwary or recalcitrant bidder, not part of the clique, who won a contract by submitting a lower bid would soon find himself in deep trouble. The inspectors would examine his work with microscopic care and find it defective. Do it over! The union would harass him with charges of violating the collective bargaining agreement and stop work on his job.

Soon everyone got the message. According to the indictment, Rarback as the mastermind collected at least $800,000. One city housing official, Nathaniel Wheatman was indicted in June 1965. Suspended from his job, he was hired by the Schatz Painting Company, first as a lowly painter then promoted to a desk job as a dispatcher. By coincidence, Schonfeld worked for that same company, so that the reformer who was urging painters to come forward with evidence against the crooks now depended for job assignments upon a man indicted on the basis of such evidence.

Rarback was indicted in October 1966, which put pressure on Frank Raftery, Painters international president, to impose a trusteeship over DC 9. But his action was a face-saving sham from the start. The status quo remained untouched. All the old officials were retained in their jobs, including the business agents and the council president who had refused to testify at the grand jury investigation into bid-rigging. Rarback was removed as secretary treasurer but then promptly appointed to a newly created full time job of educational director at a salary only $25 a week lower than before. Life in DC 9 remained unchanged. All elections were postponed, effectively insulating the old officials from challenge.

The trusteeship, because it was so obvious a whitewash designed only to solidify the corrupt incumbents, opened up an avenue of recourse unforeseen by the officials. LMRDA Title III, which regulates trusteeships, permits alternative recourse: either by complaint to the Labor Department or by private suit in Federal court. It presented the Schonfeld reformers with the opportunity they had sought in vain for years. They went promptly and directly before Federal Judge Marvin Frankel asking that the trusteeship be lifted and that the court order an election of officers under strict government controls.

The scene was set for a double confrontation, a challenge to the union officialdom, of course, but also a challenge to the U.S. Labor Department which had failed abysmally to act during the reformers six-year ordeal. The case of *Schonfeld v. Raftery* became a kind of scientific experiment, contrasting the responses of the Labor Department and of a Federal judge to the same set of identical facts.

Judge Frankel conducted seven days of evidentiary hearings. Here, at last, the reformers were able to record under oath the stolen elections, the corruption, the intimidation, the whole sordid story which they had presented time and again, but in vain, to the Labor Department.

Here we come to an odd aspect of Title III. The law provides that in any action in federal court, a union-imposed trusteeship shall be presumed valid for the first 18 months. The DC 9 trusteeship had been imposed in October 1966. But when the insurgents filed their suit in April 1967, less than six months had elapsed. Was the evidence amassed by the insurgents shocking enough to overcome any presumption of validity? After hearing all the evidence, Judge Frankel asked the Labor Department for its opinion and received its familiar kneejerk response.

For six years, the department had manipulated law and logic to validate the actions of grafters and dictators in control of the New York Painters union; it was not to waver now. The department urged the judge to dismiss the complaint and uphold the trusteeship. Its attorneys wrote, "...the defendant's action in imposing the trusteeship, and its subsequent ratification, complied with the provisions of section 304(c) and, therefore, the trusteeship is entitled to be presumed valid for a period of 18 months..." But the judge, whose assessment of credibility was based upon actual evidence, waived the department's recommendation aside and in a sweeping decision upheld the reformers on every count.

Frankel concluded that "...the evidence offered at the hearing by the plaintiffs in support of their serious charges against Rarback, his fellow officers, and the Brotherhood was clear, consistent, careful, and highly credible…the Trustee's testimony was false…it begins a train of evasive, misleading, and plainly untrue testimony for the defendants."

In rejecting the Labor Department's position, he wrote, "the weakest area of the Secretary's [of Labor] brief…is in its thin treatment of the facts largely rested upon the testimony of the Trustee." Examining the same background of facts which failed to impress the Labor Department, he held, "the history of D.C. 9 elections extending into the period of the trusteeship, has been marred by fraud and other irregularities." He noted that the international officials, "witnessed, with apparent indifference, the repeated silencing of opposition views at meetings, and blatant improprieties in local balloting."

Unlike the Labor Department which would have validated the trusteeship, Judge Frankel wrote: "The proof is clear and convincing that the Brotherhood has not proceeded in good faith for any of the purposes authorized by law…The primary reason for establishing or maintaining the trusteeship was to maintain the status quo…and thwart the efforts of Rarback's opponents to achieve power by democratic means."

In June 1967, Judge Frankel ordered an election of DC 9 officers under supervision of the American Arbitration Association and, following their installation, an end to the trusteeship. At last the insurgents could achieve what they had strived for: a democratic election under impartial control.

For seven years, Schonfeld and his supporters had maintained a semi-underground existence in this union of some 13,000 members where perhaps a dozen or two dared to speak and act openly. An urgent need was to lift that cloud of fear.

But with Judge Frankel's decision, the atmosphere was transformed. Where once a bakers dozen came to local meetings, now there were hundreds. Freedom was in the air. DC 9 was like a nation suddenly liberated from autocracy. A few days before the final voting, 200 came to hear Schonfeld at a caucus rally. "The streets around the polls," he said with some pardonable exaggeration, "will be federal territory policed by federal marshals. You will be under the protection of the United States!" A burst of resounding applause. No civil rights election workers in Mississippi were happier at this news of impending federal intervention. And this was 34 Street and 8th Avenue in Manhattan.

When the tally was ready at Manhattan Center on September 6, 1967, a thousand DC 9 painters had gathered in the hall. When the final count from 27 locals was announced, a roar of jubilation resounded: 3,230 for Schonfeld; 2,529 for Rarback. Schonfeld, the new secretary treasurer, was hoisted on the shoulders of enthusiastic supporters and paraded around the hall. He needed a police escort to free him from the press of admiring followers as he walked to his car.

But this is no fairy tale with a lived-forever happy ending. It was only the beginning of another ordeal, even more onerous. Corruption and organized crime, stubborn things, were still entrenched in DC 9.

In 1967, Schonfeld took office as secretary treasurer, the only post filled by direct vote of the entire membership. But most business agents, elected in the locals, were unopposed and resumed their jobs automatically. The deadline for BA nominations had expired before Judge Frankel's order and at a time when the fog of fear still was hanging over the union; few dared to stand up. By some strange quirk, the judge failed to order a reopening of BA nominations. Schonfeld had been elected to the top position; but, the union structure left actual power in the hands of the old gang. The painter business agents, about 20 in number, held a strong grip over their locals, a familiar scene in the building trades. Painters had no union hiring hall, no seniority protection, no hiring rights, no security. Business agents, in collusion with employers, constructed effective political machines by distributing the best jobs to small bands of supporters and by starving out critics.

On paper, the highest authority in District Council 9 was the district council composed of delegates from the locals. Formally, they were elected by the local membership; actually they were handpicked by the business agents. When the BA's, the employers, and Rarback constituted one happy consensual family, this constitutional setup was a fiction. Rarback, always assured of the backing of the international office, could disregard the council. He could do as he pleased because it invariably pleased his cronies. But once Schonfeld took over, the moribund council suddenly sprang to life, asserted its authority, and, with the international on their side, Schonfeld's enemies could undercut him at every point. By itself, Schonfeld's election could not change that pattern. But it did present a first threat to the cozy collusive coalition.

While his enemies were still stunned by the early flush of reform enthusiasm, Schonfeld proposed bylaw amendments to establish conditions for democratic elections: supervision by the American Arbitration Association, guarantees for a secret ballot, identification of voters at the polls, the end of restrictions on the right to run for office. The district council, backed by the international office, managed to delay action for eight months, but when the proposals were finally submitted to a membership referendum, they were adopted by a massive 3 to 1 majority.

Meanwhile, in 1968, Schonfeld led the first general strike of New York painters in 23 years. Three years later, in 1971, when the contract expired, negotiations teetered on the edge until a new agreement narrowly averted another strike. The new militant stance of the union under Schonfeld lifted wages on most painters work from $4.20 an hour in 1967 to $7.25. Maximum pensions went up from $90 a month to $130. Benefit funds were taken out of the hands of political hacks and turned over to professional management.

Schonfeld was convinced, however, that painters gains could be sustained only if the union became an effective policing force in the industry and that, he knew, was impossible without rooting out the corrupt system of collusion with unscrupulous employers. But the business agents, backed by the international were relentless in their drive to get rid of this reformer. In the locals, where elections were set on a staggered schedule, Schonfeld carried on the fight in the BA's home territories by supporting local slates pledged to reform and democracy. His supporters made some gains in the council but not enough to shake off control by the BA coalition.

The year 1969 was a turning point. Schonfeld submitted to membership referendum a series of proposals to reorganize the district council to shift power into the hands of painter locals and eliminate the influence of the autonomous locals, non-painter locals that invariably supported the old corrupt coalition. The amendments passed by a 2 to 1 majority. But when the international office vetoed the change, it was a clear signal to Schonfeld's enemies that his powers would be clipped and that the international would protect them from the reformers. Later that year, an international convention rejected Schonfeld's appeal and upheld the international board's decision against him.

With the open support of the international now assured, the corrupt combination unleashed its campaign to defeat Schonfeld when he came up for reelection in 1970. The drive to unseat him took a bizarre turn at a testimonial dinner sponsored by one autonomous local, ostensibly to honor International President S. Frank Raftery. On the stage was an assemblage of Schonfeld enemies, inside and outside the union. There was Jimmy Bishop, selected by organized crime and backed by the international to run against Schonfeld. There was the head of the Carpenters District Council which had just completed a successful raid against DC 9. There was the president of Teamster Local 237 which, at that moment, was actually engaged in raids against DC 9 among civil service painters. There was no seat for Schonfeld on the dais with the dignitaries; he was shunted off to a lowly spot on the floor with the masses.

It was a near miracle: in the 1970 election Schonfeld defeated the combination with a comfortable majority. But power in the council still remained in the hands of the old guard combination. For the next three years, backed by the international, they continued a relentless drive to undermine his authority, using their majority on the council to turn meetings into extended diatribes against him, subjecting him to a multitude of disciplinary charges, and finally voting to remove him from office and barring him from running. But, by court order, he was reinstated and was able to run for reelection in 1973.

In the six years of his administration, because he held office but limited power, many of his key supporters found it hard to get regular work. Demoralized by their inability to break through the local and international power structure, some retired, some gave up, some lapsed into neutrality, some even went over to the enemy out of sheer self-preservation. During the six years of Schonfeld's incumbency, some 1,500 new workers were brought into the trade by the business agents and employers; workers who were unaware that they were benefiting from the improved wages and conditions that arose out of the long reform struggle. They knew only that, for their jobs, they were beholden to Schonfeld's enemies.

When he was reelected in 1970, 5,600 had voted. By 1973, when he was defeated, the number of voters declined to 4,600. By then, the combination could no longer be denied. Schonfeld went down; Jimmy Bishop, the choice of the Lucchese crime family, now occupied the top office. The tide of reform had been swept back.

By that time, I had been associated with Frank for over 12 years, beginning with 1961 when he first visited me on the East Side. From 1967, when Schonfeld was first elected as DC 9 secretary treasurer, until 1973 when he was defeated, I served part time as his consultant. Among other tasks, I edited the DC 9 Newsletter. During the 1968 strike, I got out a daily strike bulletin and wrote ads in the daily press to present the union's case to the public. I helped mount a successful campaign to ward off two raiding attempts by Teamster Local 237 to take civil service painters away from DC 9. For this work, DC 9 paid me $750 a month.

For me they were gratifying years and instructive. I learned what it was like to live and work in the building trades, and how difficult it was to survive in an atmosphere dripping with corruption.

When Frank was still an insurgent battling the crooks, he took up the cause of Carl Blum, a woodfinisher, a member of DC 9. Blum had been discharged from his job and deserted by the union when the Carpenters tried to raid DC 9 in woodfinishing shops. Carl was personable, intelligent, a convincing talker, and in his way, a fighter. He and Frank seemed to work well together; And so, when Frank was elected, he appointed Carl as his assistant. I worked with Carl visited him once or twice at the two-family home he owned in Brooklyn. It was deep into Frank's first term —Carl was still his assistant — when Carl told me that he had visited Harry Davidow. It was a strange visit and even stranger that Carl should tell me about it. Davidow was the head of Teamsters Local 295, a powerful mob-dominated union, at the Kennedy Airport. [Many years later, Davidow was ousted when the Federal government imposed a trusteeship over the local.] I wondered how Carl had gotten to Davidow and why. Carl told me that they had a long talk about Schonfeld. He said that Davidow insisted that Schonfeld would never get anywhere because "We will just get around him." We? Remember Davidow was a Teamster, not a Painter. Obviously he was talking about the mob.

Then, during Schonfeld's second term, while Carl was still his assistant, Frank was in tough negotiations with the employers over the terms of a new contract. At that moment, Frank learned that Carl was engaged in secret dealings for the top job of secretary of the employers' association. Louis Elkin, who had the job, was about to retire. When Frank explained to a meeting of his Local 1011 that he could not tolerate that kind of apostasy and had to fire Carl as his assistant, Carl was not defensive, not in the slightest, when he explained to the assembled painters. "This is America," he said, "Everyone has the right to try to advance himself." As Frank's second term was about to end in 1973 and the racketeer-employer-Carpenters-Teamsters- Painters international combine was out to cut him down, Carl joined the anti-Schonfeld camp and was later rewarded with a job as international representative and, in that capacity, served the old gang.

Burton Hall

When I first met Burton Harrington Hall around 1960 at a Socialist Party weekend social affair, he was in his early thirties, recently admitted to the bar, with his office at 136 Liberty Street in Manhattan. His rent was somewhere around $35 a month for a hole in the wall in this rundown area full of schlock shops selling discontinued job lots, hardware seconds, cloth schmatas, and nondescript electrical parts bristling with indeterminate wires. He fitted in. It was out of this cubicle that he typed his own briefs, as in **Salzhandler**, on an old second-hand manual typewriter equipped with a worn ribbon. (Years later, the World Trade Center transformed the neighborhood into a high-priced luxury center where no mere mortal could afford space.)

He was brash, a confirmed bachelor, and looking for something socially useful to do, I was looking for someone to do something useful about union democracy. And so our interests coincided.

I was scheduled to speak the following week on my favorite subject, union democracy, at two meetings in Philadelphia. Hall owned a little foreign compact car; I owned nothing mobile, couldn't drive, and could use a lift. He agreed to drive me down and attended the meetings where we met a few union insurgents. The ones I remember best were from Teamsters Local 107, then engaged in a bitter battle against a corrupt officialdom. Hall was bitten by the bug; that's what got him linked up with Schonfeld and Salzhandler and turned him into a union democracy attorney, devoting the rest of his life to representing a variety of union insurgents. In 1973 before the Supreme Court in **Hall v. Cole,** representing an insurgent in the Seafarers international Union against its president, Paul Hall,[no relative] he established the right of successful union complainants to collect legal fees in union democracy free speech cases.

In 1961, when Solomon Salzhandler was suspended on charges of slander, he came to Schonfeld for help; and Schonfeld asked me to suggest an attorney who might take the case pro bono. Even today, it is difficult to find pro bono assistance in union democracy cases; in those days it was almost impossible. By then, I knew Burt Hall; without hesitation, he agreed to take on what became the leading case in union democracy law: the landmark *Salzhandler v. Caputo.*

As long as Schonfeld was an insurgent, Hall served him well. He performed admirably in *Schonfeld v. Raftery*, the successful challenge to the DC 9 trusteeship which opened the way to Schonfeld's victory in 1967. But once Schonfeld was elected, Hall made a bizarre turnabout, attacking his recent client in the press, deploying his legal talents to torment and undercut him. It makes a strange story, revealing an eccentric, unpredictable, even malicious streak in Hall's personality. This aberrant series of events in Hall's career was triggered, but not psychologically explained, by a disagreement with Schonfeld over Hall's future role as an attorney in the new DC 9 administration.

There has always been an delicate problem in the labor movement over the proper role of union attorneys. One can sympathize with a brilliant attorney who pilots union leaders through dangerous waters, legal, nonlegal, and illegal. He begins to think that he is far more capable of running the union than its elected officers. (Sometimes, it is true.) Sometimes, lawyers end up in the top power positions, like Arthur Coia in the Laborers and James Hoffa, Jr. in the Teamsters. Often, attorneys, confused about their role, forget that the client is the real boss. This phenomenon is intensified among those crusading attorneys, ready to take on worthy causes, who volunteer to represent clients without fee in civil liberties cases, especially in union democracy cases. After all, they spend huge amounts of time, effort, and even money, ignoring their immediate self-interest, with little pay, usually none. Their true reward becomes their participation in the battle for social justice. Preoccupied with the cause, they tend to forget who serves whom, the client, often a grassroots insurgent, or the brainy lawyer. In the case of DC 9, this kind of confusion, I am convinced, drove Burton Hall over the edge.

Having rid the union of the legal firm that served Rarback's interests, Schonfeld sought a new legal setup for DC with its 13,000 members and 20 locals. He respected Hall as a dedicated attorney effective in court. But life requires more than legal papers. Justifiably or not, he distrusted Hall's judgment outside the courtroom. (That distrust was vindicated soon after precisely by Hall's vituperative public attacks on Schonfeld.) Moreover, knowing that Hall worked normally as a one-man band, with no team backup, Schonfeld had misgivings over depending exclusively on him to take over the whole DC 9 legal burden. As a compromise, he proposed that Hall become the attorney for the DC 9 insurance funds and that a second attorney, Henry Easton, whom he knew as a friend and was a partner in a larger firm, represent the union itself. Hall rejected the proposal, insisting upon all or nothing, and that was the end of the happy Schonfeld-Hall relationship. From that moment on, Hall became Schonfeld's inveterate enemy, attacking his erstwhile client, in private, in public writings, and in court.

Hall publicly denounced Schonfeld for capitulating to the corrupt old guard at a time when I was working hard with Frank in campaigns against them. Hall hailed Carl Blum as a "reformer" who was battling against the Schonfeld sellout when I knew of Blum's overtures to a racketeer. Hall tried to press criminal charges against Schonfeld on a nonsensical technicality but the district attorney's office threw out the complaint. His incredible campaign against Frank reached the heights of absurdity in 1973 when the old guard, in control of the council, preferred fabricated charges against Frank and removed him from office. When Frank appealed to federal court under LMRDA Title I, it was hard to believe but Hall represented the chairman of the DC 9 trial committee, Joe Presser, a relative of the Teamster's Jackie Presser, to defend the removal of Schonfeld. He denounced Frank for "rushing" into court to defend himself, the same Hall who "rushed" into court in scores of union democracy cases! He argued that Schonfeld had no recourse under the LMRDA because it protected the due process rights of members not of officers.

Represented by Hall, the Painters old guard lost that case. Schonfeld was reinstated by court order when the judge ruled that elected officers are entitled to due process under the LMRDA where there has been, as in this case, a pattern of repression in the union. And so here was the only landmark advance in union democracy law achieved because Hall, representing the side of corruption and repression, was defeated. In *Schonfeld v Penza*, Federal Judge Brieant judge wrote:

"...the abuse of process in the District Council as against Schonfeld appears...egregious." He added that the charge was "a smokescreen to give a basis to oust Schonfeld from office and prevent him from running for re-election."

I should make clear that this whole business was a crazy episode in Hall's life, at a moment when something threw him off balance. Apart from this deviant aberration, he spent his whole life, until his death in 1991, representing victimized unionists against autocratic officials, in the course of which he strengthened union democracy law in landmark cases. I have always respected him for that record and appreciated what he accomplished in our common cause.

I write of all this at some length, however, because Hall's irrational assault on Schonfeld was printed in *New Politics*, which later preserved this performance in hard covers as a chapter on union autocracy. It was a vicious, distorted, sick diatribe against a man I knew as an incorruptible straight-arrow unionist who had the courage to stand up against organized crime domination in his union and who was finally defeated because the odds against him at that time were too heavy for anyone to withstand. It was sad to see Hall join the pack tearing at Schonfeld. My intention is not to derogate Hall, whose lifetime record I otherwise admire, but to set the record straight about Schonfeld whose unwavering defense of decency and democracy I admire.

Frank Schonfeld was a premature battler against organized crime, fifteen years ahead of his time, too soon to enjoy the protective shield of a later government crusade against the Mafia. Isolated in this corner of the construction trade, at a time when the nation became preoccupied with the war in Viet Nam, no echo within the labor movement, no support from administrative law enforcement authorities, and little interest in the broad public.

Post script: With the defeat of Schonfeld in 1973, organized crime fastened its hold tightly over the Painters union in New York City. By 1990, the Lucchese Crime family was in total control. Jimmy Bishop, selected by the mob in 1973 to defeat Schonfeld was murdered by the mob in 1990 after he defied orders to step aside for a new reigning family faction. In the interim, the Schonfeld reforms were obliterated. In 1991, in a new state corruption trial, officials of DC 9 were convicted on racketeering charges; the indictment charged that the union was dominated by the Lucchese crime family. However, unlike Teamster and Laborers locals in

New York, Painters District Council 9 was never reorganized by action of Federal authorities under the RICO statute.

B. In California: the murder of Wilson and Green

Now, we turn back the clock ten years to 1963; Schonfeld is still bogged down in frustrated opposition, isolated in New York City. But independent of his efforts, and unknown to him, a vigorous reform movement is shaping up among painters in the Bay Area of San Francisco.

One day in that year of 1963, seated at his desk in the office of Painters Local 4, Secretary Dow Wilson, its leading officer, happened to glance into the wastebasket where the office clerk normally deposited the day's collection of junk mail. His eye caught the headline in an obscure little newsletter: "Our Day in Court." Curious, he picked it out and discovered issue No. 9 of *Union Democracy in Action* with the full text of *Salzhandler v. Caputo,* the New York painters case in which the Court of Appeals, establishing a firm basis in federal law for civil liberties in unions, had voided internal union charges of slander against critics. Facing precisely such charges in his San Francisco District Council 8, he realized how important the decision could be for him. His local reprinted the UDA issue and distributed it to union activists all over the West Coast. He decided to link up with the reformers in New York.

That's how he got to know me and Frank Schonfeld. Within a few months he provided us with a bulging sheaf of documents, and for the next three years kept us informed. Early in 1966, UDA got a $1,500 grant from the Prynce Hopkins Fund which enabled me to write, print, and distribute the story of the California Painters in UDA No.18: "California Painters: Fight for tenants' rights; defend union democracy; win hard strike." When Wilson saw the advance text, he ordered several thousand copies for circulation in California. We did print the issue, but he never got the copies, because while we were awaiting delivery from the printer, his enemies in California were preparing to kill him. On April 5, 1966, he was shotgunned to death. Later, *Union Democracy in Action* told his story:

In 1963, Wilson, then 37, was known only to a small circle of admiring associates and a much smaller circle of bitter enemies; but his leadership qualities were exceptional. He could easily rally a hundred supporters to picket and protest. Flamboyant like John L. Lewis, he spiked his speeches with colorful phrases and literary quotations. No conformist, no suits, no white shirts, and ties. At a time when it was unfashionable, he sported a beard, black and visible, a blazing hunters jacket and cap. He was murdered just as he was about to break out of obscurity into prominence as a national union leader.

Wilson was born in Washington DC in 1926, dropped out of high school to become a seaman. He married Barbara in 1946, became a housepainter, settled in San Francisco where he raised three children. In 1958 he was elected business agent of Painters Local 19, merged it with another to form Local 4 which, with its 2,500 members, became the largest single unit in the international Brotherhood. As the local's recording secretary, he became its de facto leader, turning it into a powerful force in the painting industry and a respected factor in community affairs.

In New York City, while the painters union under Rarback was running a criminal bid-rigging conspiracy in city housing painting, Wilson's local, in San Francisco, exposed and eradicated the cheating of the city, of tenants, and of the federal government in the painting of public housing. Ominously, he was denounced at the union's district council for upsetting "fine relations" between the union and the city's Housing Authority. He silenced his suspect critics by assembling delegations of rank and file members to attend council meetings. Each Bay Area Painter local was assigned to one of three district councils. Some locals were authentic housepainter locals, but others were so-called autonomous locals on the periphery of the trade. Traditionally, the three district councils negotiated jointly with the employers' association.

Representation In District Council 8, which included Wilson's local was gerrymandered by a lopsided system of representation which gave inordinate power to the autonomous locals and reduced the influence of the housepainters. Wilson's Local 4 with its 2,500 members was awarded five delegates to the council; one autonomous local with only 13 members got the same five. Wilson's supporters initiated a campaign for a new council structure based upon a democratic one-man, one-vote, system. They successfully pressured the council to submit the plan to a membership referendum where it passed by a big majority: 1,277 to 379. But, in October 1965, just as it later ruled against a New York DC 9 similar proposal, the international vetoed the change. Those who wanted the democratic reforms would not supinely submit. In November 1965, they published the first issue of their own tabloid, the *Bay Area Painters News*, to campaign for democratization of the council. The publication became the rallying force for reform forces in the Bay Area. Its first issue wrote, "Power doesn't scare us. We want our rights. What country do they think we are living in?...Now or never will we ever permit the G.E.B. [international executive board] to have that power of crass dictatorship."

The festering situation had come to a head earlier that year during a Bay Area five-week housepainters strike, July 1 - Aug 6. Painters walked out when their union contract expired in June 1965. The three district councils had agreed, as usual, that none of their locals would settle without provisions for a uniform Bay Area contract. Wilson was elected to the bargaining committee; and, from that position, he became the effective leader of the strike. Then, without warning, while the strike was still on, District 33 unilaterally signed a separate contract with employers and ordered its locals back to work, undercutting those locals still on strike. One local in Wilson's District 8 and another in District 16 followed suit in abandoning the strike.

Wilson fought back. He mobilized mass picket lines; he brought mass delegations of strikers to meetings of locals in District 16, whose secretary treasurer, Ben Rasnick, was Wilson's bitter enemy. Despite DC 33's attempted defection, the strike lines held, and the stoppage remained solid. Three weeks later, after Wilson had led a two-front battle against the employers and against the sabotaging union officials, the strike was won. The victorious strike leaders boasted that 7,000 painters had achieved one of the finest contracts in the union's history. Later, Wilson announced that he would be a candidate for vice president of the international and initiated a national campaign to round up support.

Convinced that high-ranking union officials had been paid off to try to break the strike, Wilson publicly denounced local officials who had led the back to work movement as "finks and strikebreakers". He reserved choice words of opprobrium for Ben Rasnick, whom he excoriated as a "scabherder."

Wilson had defeated the employers; he had fought off the sabotaging area union officials. Now, he faced an attack from the union's international officialdom. When Wilson's enemies charged him with slander, the international office, bypassing the locals, took over the trial proceedings and dispatched two international representatives to investigate Wilson. As the trial opened in November 1965, a delegation of 300 painters protested; the American Civil Liberties Union asked for the right to monitor the proceedings, and Congressman Phil Burton protested.

The trial soon had to be abandoned; because the central charge against Wilson of "slander" clearly violated the federal court decision in *Salzhandler*.

The union's general counsel, Herbert S. Thatcher, had represented it in an unsuccessful appeal to the U.S. Supreme Court against *Salzhandler*, the very decision which made the slander charge against Wilson illegal. When Thatcher was rebuffed by the Court, he knew that the charge against Wilson could not stand up.

After three days of testimony, the trial committee suspended the effort to suppress Wilson, but only for the time being. Under federal law, it could not find him guilty; but it would not declare him innocent. Leaving an overhanging threat, an ambiguous verdict sounded this ominous warning: "...the present charges against Brother Wilson should be dismissed without prejudice to the renewal of such charges or similar charges should it become necessary to do so and if a repetition of the conduct alleged in the charges should thereafter take place..."

"I firmly believe, "wrote Wilson in the Bay Area Painters News on December 20,1965, "that further attempts will be made to nail my hide." Tragically, his prediction proved accurate. Success in beating off the illegal prosecution actually led to a verdict of death for Wilson. He had become a dangerous threat to a corrupt conspiracy. Only his death could remove that threat.

By early 1966, Wilson's reputation in the union had extended nationally, as a militant unionist, a stand-up guy who could fend off employers and arrogant union officials; other locals looked to him for leadership. Sacramento Local 487, impressed by his achievements, asked him to represent it in negotiations; at this point, he became suspicious of the management of the local's Health and Welfare Fund. Working closely with Wilson, was Lloyd Green, secretary of Local 1178 in Hayward; Green was a leader in opposition to Ben Rasnick, secretary-treasurer of District Council 16, the "scabherder" target of Wilson's barbs.

As April 1966 drew near, copy had been completed for UDA No. 18 with its background story of Wilson's battle; but it had not yet come back from the printer, "The strike is won," it reported, "the trial is over. The campaign for internal democracy in the Brotherhood of Painters continues. A notable success has been recorded in California."

It was late afternoon, New York time on April 5,1966, that I got the horrible news. Morris Evenson, Wilson's second in command, phoned from San Francisco to say that Wilson had been murdered late that night by three shotgun blasts to the head. So far, by parties unknown. He was so terribly upset that he could say no more. I felt a heavy responsibility to do something, something. If we hadn't saved Wilson in his internal union trial, he might still be alive. I knew it was a crazy thought, but I couldn't repress it. But what to do? what do you do when someone you've been working with is murdered? Isolated and without resources in my little Manhattan apartment, what **could** I possibly do? I owned no copying machine. No computers, no faxes, no internet in those days. How to let the world know?

The full total of modern technology at my disposal was a 20-year old manual Royal typewriter with a faded ribbon, a telephone, a stack of ultra-thin (now obsolete) onion skin sheets, and fine carbon paper. Total staff: me and my wife, Revella. We phoned all New York dailies, called major local radio and TV stations. No one interested. Luckily, we had accumulated one bit of capital: ***Union Democracy in Action No. 18***. The issue had just arrived from the printer, only a 4-page newsletter; but it reported the first full account of Wilson's battle in California.

Press releases! With that old typewriter and onion skin, six near- legible copies could be tediously tapped out at a time if you hit the keys hard enough. But it didn't have to be long: "Dow Wilson murdered in San Francisco. For background and significance, see enclosed issue of Union Democracy in Action. Call for more information." We mailed the crude release, along with UDA No 18, to the dozen leading national dailies whose addresses were readily available. All ignored us, except one. But that was a big one.

Somehow, the amateurish product reached the city editor at the **Washington Post** who passed it on. "Frank, this may interest you," he said to Frank Porter, the paper's labor editor. [Later, Porter told me and Schonfeld that he had been a seaman in his youth and could understand the battles of unionists for justice.] Porter phoned the Post's office in San Francisco, verified the accuracy of the murder report, and flew to New York City to meet with me and Frank Schonfeld. Three weeks later, he broke the story in a long four-part major series, April 24-27, beginning on the first page of the Post's Sunday edition. The story of Dow Wilson, Frank Schonfeld, and the painters' battle for reform now was national news. And just in time.

A few days later, on May 8, Lloyd Green, leader of Painters Local 1178 in Hayward and Dow Wilson's close collaborator, was the next to die. As Green sat in his office, the killer fired through the window and blasted him to death with a shotgun. Again, it was horrifying and frightening. Again—what to do? what to do? what to do? The murderers were still unknown and at large.

There was Norman Thomas, still with us. He agreed to sponsor a "Citizens Committee for an Investigation of the Wilson-Green Murders and of Racketeering in the Painting Industry." In 1959, for the two expelled machinists, we had managed to enroll a tiny support committee of three. By this time, however, ***Union Democracy in Action*** had been at work for more than six years and now had a following, small but respected. With the help of Rochelle Flanders, a close friend, not working, we enrolled more than 20 co-sponsors in addition to Thomas, including Algernon Black, Irving Howe, Mike Harrington, Msgr Charles Owen Rice, Father Philip Carey, Meyer Shapiro. The committee called for an investigation by the U.S. Department of Justice. Gordon Haskell, then ACLU development director, and I became committee co-coordinators. [Soon thereafter, Flanders was hired by the United Federation of Teachers to help edit its newspaper.]

Late in May 1966, the case cracked open when Norman Call and Max Ward, two employer insurance fund trustees, were indicted in state court for the murders, along with three fund administrative employees, revealing a conspiracy to defraud the funds of hundreds of thousands of dollars. Two days later, Sture Youngren, the fund administrator, committed suicide after confessing to stealing $60,000. In September, Ward and Call were convicted of murder; the charge against the other three was reduced to embezzlement.

In the San Francisco Bay Area, local unions mourned the deaths and marched in protest. But, despite the mounting pressure of publicity, not the AFL-CIO under George Meany, nor the Painters international, nor any AFL-CIO affiliate bothered to note these events or to express horror at the assassination of two labor leaders. When pressed, Frank Raftery, painters international president, shrugged it off, "Those who live by the sword," he told one reporter "die by the sword," an enigmatic remark— really stupid — because it was Rasnick who lived by that sword!

The AFL-CIO national Building Trades Department commented, but only to clear its skirts. It affirmed vehemently that no one in "labor" was responsible, that "labor" was clean. But its public relations reassurance and self-consoling stance was brutally upset when Norman Call, convicted of murder, came up for sentencing in September. Anxious to avoid the death penalty, he confessed that after Wilson had beaten off the slander charges at the union trial, Rasnick had ordered the murder. He revealed that after the internal union charges against Wilson had bombed, Rasnick directed the two "to go ahead and make plans for him to be killed." And there was more. Ward's wife had been sleeping with Rasnick. She testified that, in a moment of unguarded intimate indiscretion, Rasnick had admitted ordering the killings. He was convicted and sentenced to life.

The story was now wide open. On July 6, 1967, the *Wall Street Journal* ran one of its major investigative pieces on the Painters union, reporting on reform movements and corruption scandals not only in New York and California, but Buffalo, Minneapolis, and Washington, DC. *Business Week* and *Time* published stories. Even the *New York Times* broke down and ran a small notice.

In Washington DC, Painter reformers exposed widespread cheating in the painting of government buildings. The ***Washington Post*** reported, "One coat instead of two was used on a repainting job last year at C.I.A.'s headquarters in Langley. That job was done at night under such secrecy that union stewards were not allowed to make sure that the painters contract was not violated." A fine example of C.I.A. vigilance!

Meanwhile, back in New York City, events were coming to a head. Martin Rarback, secretary treasurer of District Council 9 in New York had been indicted for bid-rigging. The international imposed its mock trusteeship over the council which left the corrupt status quo unmoved.

With Ben Rasnick indicted for murder, the pretense that the killing was unrelated to the battle for union reform could no longer hold water. An AFL-CIO executive council meeting was scheduled for February in Florida. In preparation for the sessions, reformers in New York and in California drafted an appeal to the AFL-CIO Ethical Practices Committee, outlining the long history of corruption, blacklisting of critics, stolen elections, beatings and murder of dissidents, sweetheart deals with employers. They asked the AFL-CIO to remove the top officers of the Painters union and restore democratic rights in the union. Evenson and Schonfeld flew down to Florida to deliver their message. But their appeal never reached the EPC; by that time the committee was defunct and the Ethical Practices Codes were a dead letter. But they did get national attention. The ***Miami Herald*** ran a front page, full-sized, photo of George Meany receiving the text of the appeal from the hand of Morris Evenson.

Meany, now under mounting public relations pressure to do something, appointed a committee. It performed its expected servile service. After a cooling off cycle, and without bothering to interview even a single complainant, it advised Meany that there was nothing to do, which he did.

Postscript: In California, the battle culminated in an uneasy stalemate. With Wilson gone, his friends held on in District Council 8, but only as an island, as a redoubt of independence from a suspect international office. Without his driving force, his talent for mobilizing support in the union and in the community, they lacked the ability and the fervor to use their local strength as the springboard for a national reform movement. With the murder of Wilson and Green, the reform lost its vital spark and the impetus for a national reform movement was dissipated.

However, that ten-year reform record, in New York, California and elsewhere, remains as evidence of the potential for democracy and reform in the labor movement. And, in this case, it had a more immediate and more lasting effect. The painters battle shaped union democracy law through the decision in *Salzhandler*, which established a firm statutory base for civil liberties in unions. And their ordeal prompted the formation of the Association for Union Democracy. Many of those who had joined the Citizens Committee for Wilson and Green as an ad hoc formation in 1966 agreed to sponsor AUD as a continuing organization in 1969.

Chapter 6: Early Activities of the Association for Union Democracy

When I started publishing *Union Democracy in Action* in 1960, I was under the illusion that the time was ripe for something bigger. Once UDA disclosed the existence of all those union reformers and publicized their need, surely, someone, somehow, somewhere, among all those civil libertarians, those prominent academics, those concerned political leaders, who were verbally preoccupied with the idea of union democracy, would do something to fill that need. But it didn't happen. The gap between word and deed, between analysis and action, persisted.

The most likely rallying center for civil liberties in unions seemed to be the American Civil Liberties Union. In 1958, it had initiated the call for federal legislation with its proposed Bill of Rights for union members; its declaration on Democracy in Labor Unions, written by Clyde Summers, inspired the Bill of Rights section of the LMRDA. But the ACLU never went much beyond publishing a statement of principles and later a handbook on labor law.

In 1960, when democracy was in crisis in the United Steel Workers and dissidents were threatened with wholesale expulsion, I was assigned by the ACLU Labor Committee to report on the union's convention that year in Atlantic City. There, I saw Don Rarick, the opposition leader, beaten right on the convention floor while at that precise moment Arthur Goldberg, at the podium, was extolling the union's great contribution to industrial democracy. I met with unionists from locals around the country who described exactly how elections were stolen and how opposition members were physically threatened. In my report to the ACLU, I proposed that it sponsor a project to monitor events in the union. But it chose to do nothing. Around 1972, after big events in the miners union, the ACLU received a foundation grant of $25,000 from the Kaplan Fund for a union democracy project. After reconsidering, the ACLU returned the money, an extraordinary act of self-denial.

The ACLU would resist violations of civil liberties by government but not by unions. That basic policy was not always rigidly observed. Occasionally, one of its attorneys or one of its chapters would deviate from the line and briefly take on a union democracy issue, or file an amicus brief. But, regrettably, the ACLU would not fill the need for sustained support of union democracy movements. For a time, I served on the ACLU Labor-Business Committee. At one point, unaccountably, Anthony Scotto, Brooklyn leader of the International Longshoremen's Association, was added to the committee but never attended meetings. Later, he went to jail as an organized crime capo. The committee atrophied and was finally dissolved.

In 1969, the Association for Union Democracy was chartered as a non-profit New York corporation. Norman Thomas had died the year before. If he had still been alive and active, AUD would have been off to a faster start. Those who had joined the Wilson-Green committee were sympathetic but not rich. Lewis Mayers filed the corporation papers and arranged for IRS tax-deductible status as a 501(c)(3) organization, but AUD remained in limbo, without resources, a paper shell.

The painters' battle and the revulsion against the two murders had goaded us to begin, but it is hard to say how long it would have taken to get going, starting with nothing more than the UDA mailing list.

At that point, the Association for Union Democracy was still a non-profit corporate shell with a skinny bank account. I was still publishing *Union Democracy in Action* as a one-man band, without rigid schedule, with occasional assistance from Gordon Haskell, still on the ACLU staff; from Jim Peck, pacifist and Freedom Rider; and Lewis Mayers. UDA operated out of a tiny $25/month office on Union Square in Manhattan; no staff, paid or unpaid. I held down a part time job, sometimes two, to contribute toward the family income, while my wife carried the main burden. My unpaid part time was devoted to union democracy business. Financing was hand-to-mouth. The appearance of each issue of UDA was followed by a pause, awaiting donations to finance the next. Still, when UDA ended 14 years of publication in 1972, to make way for *Union Democracy Review*, its union printer had been paid in full, no bad debts left behind, which is probably a record for offbeat newsletters in the days before computerized self-publication.

By 1971, I had a problem. Fourteen years of *Union Democracy in Action* and an increasing response to UDA from grassroots unionists had proven that the potential was there but without any resounding echo from the liberal-labor-civil libertarian "community," It was a discouraging moment. Without money, without a supporting staff, there seemed no prospect of any big step forward. The first wave of hopeful insurgency that followed the adoption of the LMRDA in 1959 had subsided. The victory of the Miners for Democracy in 1972 was still to come. What was the point of grubbing along in the same narrow groove? The question began to nag at me. But unexpectedly, just around the corner, help arrived. A cliffhanger!

"What would you do if you had some real money?" a close friend asked. We had first met as comrades in the old Independent Socialist League. Luckily in the intervening years, unique among my friends, he had made some money. He shared and respected my views on union democracy. No need for me to agonize over the answer, the question had haunted me for years: "We could transform AUD into a real institution." His question was not rhetorical. He came through with a grant of $30,000. Then he added another $7,500 to hire Judith Schneider as full time legal director. At last, the catalytic agent!

A functioning Board of Directors was established. My old *Union Democracy in Action* was supplanted by AUD's new *Union Democracy Review*. It was more than a name change. The new publication was enlarged and came out regularly, first as a quarterly, then as a bi-monthly. I continued as unpaid editor, but the contents now had to conform, not to my own personal whims, but to non-partisan AUD standards.

Introducing the Association for Union Democracy, UDA reported, in its final issue in May 1972, that AUD "will not advocate any special platform of its own within the labor movement or for it. The organization will not be identified with any particular faction or tendency. It takes no position on questions of collective bargaining policy or national politics...It will not lobby for legislation or support candidates for any office." As we put it later: AUD supports the rights of all unionists, left, right, or center, from abuse from any source, right, left, or center.

Activities. Early Board of Directors

The scope of AUD's work and the direction of its policy is partially expressed in the careers and contributions of the members of its early Board of Directors:

When AUD came alive in 1972, the six who constituted its Board of Directors were: Herman Benson, Gordon Haskell, Irving Howe, Lewis Mayers, Al Nash, and Clyde Summers.

Howe, eminent and preoccupied as teacher, literary critic, and **Dissent** editor, agreed to serve but only temporarily to afford AUD a certain distinction. He soon begged off the board but remained as an Advisor.

Summers, as a young professor at Buffalo Law School in the mid-forties, was already one of the leading authorities on union democracy law even before the adoption of the LMRDA. He wrote the ACLU declaration on union democracy and helped draft the LMRDA Bill of Rights. From Buffalo he went to Yale and then to the University of Pennsylvania Law School in Philadelphia. In 1958 he was one of the three sponsors of the committee to defend the two machinists expelled from the IAM in Chicago. In 1966, he joined others in calling for a federal investigation of the murder of two painters union insurgents.

When I first approached Summers, rather diffidently, to join the AUD Board, he asked, "Do you want a figurehead or someone to really participate." Of course we preferred him as an active director; but I evaded, not certain of his level of interest. But he was way ahead of me. "If you want a real Board of Directors, O.K." I realize now that he was probably willing either way to help the cause. Since then, he has been AUD's pillar of strength, authoring amicus briefs, available to embattled unionists and their attorneys for expert advice. Ask him a tough question and get a brilliantly formulated answer, sometimes in words, just as often in a scrupulously worded written reply.

Nash had worked sometimes as organizer, sometimes as educational director, for several unions; Textile Workers, ILGWU, AFSCME. In the 1940's, he worked on the assembly line at the Chrysler-Jefferson plant in Detroit where he served as a UAW shop steward and international convention delegate. He enrolled as a student in Cornell in New York, emerged with his doctorate, and taught at the Cornell labor studies school in New York City. He remained on the AUD Board until his death in 1996 from Parkinson's disease.

Mayers was a retired attorney and law professor and already in his 80's when he joined the board. He was the author of "The American Legal System" once widely used in law schools as a text book. Back in 1943, as a member of the ACLU, he was one of the signatories on its early statement, "Democracy in Labor Unions." He incorporated AUD as a non-profit organization and established its status with the IRS as a 501(c)(3) tax-exempt foundation. He remained on the board until his death in the late 1970's.

Haskell was AUD's founding president. His labor career began shortly after he graduated from college in 1939, when he went to work in California for eight years as a locomotive engineman. In that time, he organized the

Railroad Workers Joint Action Committee, a cross-craft rank and file caucus to promote the idea of unifying the many rail unions. (Since then rail union amalgamation has been widely effected) After moving to New York, he became my colleague at *Labor Action.* When the paper folded, he was hired as assistant director of the New York Civil Liberties Union and then as development director of the ACLU. Between 1980 and 1984, working full time for AUD, he induced a consortium of foundations to sponsor a three-year, $100,000 AUD expansion program, a project which gave AUD a temporarily secure base. He died in 2002.

In the early years, others joined the board.

Judith Schneider joined the board in 1980. She was a law student at NYU when she first came to work for AUD in 1972 as a work-study student. She organized two four-person teams of NYU law students to drive into the mining areas of Pennsylvania to observe the government-supervised balloting in the United Mine Workers election that year. Their experience was reported in *Union Democracy Review* and at a public meeting at NYU Law School. In a detailed account, one of the students wrote, "Ed Monbourne, Arnold Miller's campaign manager, who… is running for District 2 president, kept saying how wonderful we were to come and help. I felt the praise was misdirected; I considered it a privilege to be there, and I could not thank them for it except by doing what I was there for."

When Schneider graduated from law school, she came to work full time for AUD and was soon admitted to the bar. In one of her earliest assignments, she represented members of the Civil Service Employees Association in New York State who had been denied the right to run for statewide convention delegates. With her help, they were successful, a small victory; but later, the incident had important repercussions. In 1978, 50,000 members of the CSEA Professional and Technical unit, split away and formed their own Public Employees Federation. But when PEF came under the domination of a crooked and authoritarian president, an opposition rank and file caucus organized to oust the offending president. The insurgent leaders, recalling Schneider's earlier assistance, appealed for guidance to AUD, which publicized their campaign in ***Union Democracy Review***. With the help of John Harold, an AUD director, who represented them privately without fee, they won their battle and turned PEF into a model democratic union.

Schneider continued as AUD legal director for the next six years, usually at the same minimal salary of $7,500. In the mid-1980's, after Gordon Haskell stepped down, she took over the unpaid post of AUD president and serves on the AUD Legal Review Committee. She is now an administrative law judge in New York State.

John Harold: Back in 1959, one of the first to welcome my "Intellectuals and the Lonely Union Reformer" was John Harold then a young attorney and chief counsel of the Association of Catholic Trade Unionists. At that time, ACTU in New York offered the same kind of support to union reformers that later was provided by AUD. As ACTU attorney, he represented, without fee, a group of licensed marine deck officers who had been expelled from the Masters, Mates, and Pilots in the early fifties for forming an opposition caucus and won their reinstatement. By the time he joined the AUD Board, ACTU had gone out of business. In 1982, he volunteered as pro bono attorney for the State Coalition for a Democratic Union inside the Public Employees Federation, providing the legal and practical guidance that helped them overthrow a corrupt leadership. He remained on the board until his death in 1995.

Arthur Fox and Paul Alan Levy: When the Public Citizen Litigation Group, a Ralph Nader offshoot, established its union democracy project in 1980, it was a great day for the cause because it brought into the "movement," and then on to the AUD board, these two dedicated and talented young attorneys.

In 1971, Arthur Fox enrolled truck drivers into the Professional Drivers Council. Later, when PROD merged with the Teamsters for a Democratic Union, Fox served pro bono as a PROD-TDU attorney. During his early years on the AUD Board, after leaving Public Citizen for private practice, he represented insurgents in the National Maritime Union in a successful suit to dissolve the crooked and bureaucratic merger with the Marine Engineers Beneficial Association. On behalf of a local of the National Rural Letter Carriers Association, he sued the national union and won the right of dissidents to space in the union's magazine to voice their opposition to a proposed collective bargaining agreement.

Paul Alan Levy, together with Arthur Fox, initiated the union democracy project of the Public Citizen Litigation Group. He joined the AUD board shortly thereafter and went on to become one of the most effective union democracy attorneys in the United States. He helped AUD build a solid reputation as an advocate of the rights of union reformers. Representing ironworkers in federal court, he compelled the union to remove a clause in its international constitution which forbade locals from communicating with one another on union business without permission of the international executive board. Representing members of the International Brotherhood of Electrical Workers, he forced the union to reveal that it had spent hundreds of thousands of dollars on court costs, legal fees, and damage awards in a vain attempt to suppress the democratic rights of Dan Boswell, an insurgent electrician. In ***Doyle v. Brock***, (1986) Levy successfully sued the U.S. Labor Department in a major case that strengthened union democracy law by extending the right of unionists to run for office. Until Levy intervened, many unions were enforcing constitutional provisions which barred from the ballot members who had not attended a prescribed number of union meetings. In practice, because so few members actually attend meetings, these rules disqualify over 90% of the membership and permit a tiny clique to remain in power without challenge. In 1977, the Supreme Court had invalidated precisely such a Steelworkers rule; but for more than 20 years thereafter, the U.S. Labor Department discovered (more accurately, invented!) loopholes in the decision and continued to permit unions to enforce such restrictive provisions. When the Labor Department upheld an IBEW attendance rule which disqualified Tom Doyle from running for office in IBEW Local 6, Levy sued the Labor Department on his behalf. Although the Department resisted stubbornly, dragging the case out for many months, Levy was upheld in both the federal district and appeals courts, forcing the Labor Department to amend its regulations to discourage the offending provisions.

William Kornblum joined the Board of Directors in 1981. Earlier he had worked in the steel mills of Chicago where he met Ed Sadlowski and joined his insurgent caucus in the United Steelworkers union. Fluent in French, he campaigned for the Sadlowski slate in Quebec. After leaving the mills, he wrote a sociological study of Chicago steel workers. He became a professor of sociology in the City University of New York.

James McNamara was an organizer for the Hatters union under Alex Rose. New York Mayor Koch appointed him chairman of the city's Construction Industry Employment Committee, an agency established to monitor hiring discrimination in the industry. After the committee was dissolved, he became a consultant for the division on racketeering of the Manhattan district attorney's office under Robert Morgenthau. He became an AUD director in the late seventies. Upon retirement from government service, he was elected to the (unpaid) position of AUD Research Director, specializing on issues of corruption and racketeering in unions. He has worked with carpenters, plumbers, service workers, public employees, and others who face corrupt or mob-ridden officials.

Benjamin F. McLaurin had been a vice president of the Sleeping Car Porters union under A. Philip Randolph. New York Mayor John Lindsay, who established a Committee on the Exploitation of Labor, appointed McLaurin as chairman. Dealing with complaints of hiring discrimination against minorities, he became aware of problems of democracy in the city's unions. He joined the AUD board in 1980, spoke at all our national conferences, and remained on the board until his death in 1989.

Barbara Harvey was elected to the Board of Directors in the late 1980's after an impressive record as a workers' rights attorney. She had been a professor of law at Wayne State and a volunteer attorney for the American Civil Liberties Union in Detroit and became "hooked" on the union democracy cause after representing some rank and file Teamsters in the early days of TDU. One of those rare, dedicated, effective union democracy attorneys, she has represented Teamsters, Electrical Workers, Auto Workers, Postal Workers, Steelworkers, Public Employees...the list goes on.

Alan Hyde joined the board in the mid-1980's. After graduating from NYU Law School, he became a professor of law at Rutgers University, concentrating on union democracy law and later on the broader subject of employment law. His familiarity with the LMRDA make him a valuable board asset. He wrote AUD's amicus brief before the Supreme Court in one case; he wrote a law review study on the possible application of the LMRDA to union democracy issues in Canadian locals affiliated to U.S.-based internationals. His study "Democracy in Collective Bargaining" is an important addition to the AUD reading list.

Over the years, by phone, mail, in person, and in later years via the internet, AUD has provided advice and guidance to thousands of unionists, in most major unions, on exercising their democratic rights in their unions. Where appropriate, they have been referred to cooperating workers' rights attorneys. After conferring with AUD, many formed caucuses and issued independent newsletters in their unions. Back in 1962, Union Democracy in Action brought together the reform leader, the painter complainant, and the attorney leading to *Salzhandler v. Caputo*, the landmark case establishing basic civil liberties in unions. It initiated *Boswell v. IBEW*, the case which opened the way to democracy in that union. It supervised the Steel Workers Fair Elections Project in the late 1970's. It forced the Ironworkers, the Plumbers and Pipefitters, and the International Longshoremen's Association to remove repressive clauses from their constitutions. It intervened successfully in Federal Court to assure a fair election in the Teamsters union in 1991. Its cooperating attorneys initiated suits in Federal Court compelling unions to comply with LMRDA Section 105 which requires them to inform members of their union democratic rights under Federal law. With AUD, union reformers were still embattled, but no longer quite so lonely.

Where does the money come from?

In sum, AUD has worked to strengthen democracy in most major unions in the United States. It is the scope of these activities, and the achievements, perhaps, that have induced friends and critics alike to express curiosity about AUD's financing over the years. How do you manage? Where does the money come from? Since AUD is a 501(c)(3) tax-exempt non- profit organization, the basic figures are publicly available in Form 990 filed with the IRS. But the raw arithmetic cannot tell the full story.

AUD has been sustained throughout by the same magic formula that made possible the success of capitalism in its formative years: unpaid and underpaid labor. Its major resource has always been the donated services of its supporters, especially its board of directors, including the attorneys and law professors who provide legal advice, prepare briefs, and provide legal representation in union democracy cases. And of course, the underpaid work of a tiny staff.

At the beginning, in the early seventies, AUD managed on less than $30,000 a year. With foundation support, it ran the Steelworker election projects on about $125,000. In the following years, omitting peaks and valleys — once or twice, we hit the $200,000 mark — AUD has received an average of about $150,000 a year. Its paid staff numbered from zero in 1971 and soared to a momentary height of five: one on full time and the others on part time.

As for me, in the twenty years between 1960 and 1980, my work for Union Democracy Review and AUD was unpaid. From time to time, I could count on one minimally paid assistant, like Judith Schneider who served as legal director at $7,500 a year. In 1980 when I retired from remunerative private employment, AUD paid me a salary that ranged from $5,000 a year to $10,000, except for a few short glorious years when I reached the summit of $15,000. The U.S. government involuntarily and unconsciously subsidized the work of AUD by paying me social security. I went off the AUD payroll in 1996 and rejoined the unpaid staff as UDR editor and general factotum. Susan Jennik, an attorney, worked for AUD for some five or six years, part time, then full time as executive director, at the customary pay level, until 1991 when she was retained as an attorney for Teamsters Local 966.

In earlier years, about 1/4 of the income came from small individual donations and the balance, in shifting amounts, from foundations: notably, the Rockefeller Family Fund, Kaplan Fund, Field Foundation, Veatch Fund, Stern Fund, and Scherman Foundation. Individual grants ranged from $10,000 to $20,000, with a single one-time unusual grant of $50,000 from Kaplan.

However, no foundations ever gave union democracy a high priority. (Most, no priority!.) In time, some went out of business, others decided they had supported AUD long enough, and others lost interest. The Kaplan

Fund, now under the administration of a new family, noted, in its final grant to the organization that AUD was dedicated to promoting democracy in "what's left of the labor movement." AUD has built a firmer financial base of donations from its own individual supporters, including 30 people who donate at least $1,000 each year. In recent years, the source of AUD's income shifted drastically. Some 3/4 comes from individuals and only 1/4, or less, from foundations.

For a time, while it was still active as a private foundation, the Rockefeller Family Fund was one of AUD's main supporters; and AUD's adversaries hoped to frighten away unionists by waving the Rockefeller name as a bogey man, presumably portraying AUD as a tool of reactionary corporate interests. In the mid-1980's, when Joe Samargia, president of a metal miner local, ran as an insurgent for director of the Steelworkers in Minnesota, the union officialdom succeeded in bringing him down by pointing to his collaboration with AUD and "exposing" it as a Rockefeller-backed beneficiary. Later in Detroit, one establishment labor attorney, brandished the Rockefeller name against Teamster reformers.

But, apart from its momentary success against Samargia, the Rockefeller scare never went anywhere. In a piece in Union Democracy Review entitled "Beware — not Jabberwocks — Rockefellers!," AUD set the record straight:

In the 1980's, the Coalition for Labor Union Women accepted $81,482 from the Rockefeller Family Fund; and the A. Philip Randolph Institute got $10,000. Both are official AFL-CIO institutions, and no one in labor ever noticed anything amiss. For a time, Lane Kirkland, then AFL-CIO president and Eleanor Holmes Norton, once a member of the UAW Public Review Board, both served on the Board of Trustees of the Rockefeller Foundation, despite its awesome name. In 1970, Arthur Goldberg ran for governor of New York. Even though he had been general counsel of the Steelworkers and of the CIO and the architect of the AFL-CIO merger, the New York State AFL-CIO endorsed his opponent: Nelson Rockefeller. A few years after denouncing reformers for accepting grants from foundations like the Rockefeller Family Fund, the Teamster magazine featured a photo of a Senator with his arm around to top Teamster officials. The Senator's name? John D. Rockefeller. And when Senator Rockefeller ran for governor of West Virginia, the AFL-CIO supported him. In 1982, when Rich Trumka was sworn in as president of the United Mine Workers, Governor Rockefeller, elected with labor support, told the audience at the ceremony, "A great new president! God bless, Rich Trumka."

With that, UDR concluded, "So our labor officials accept Rockefeller money. They support Rockefellers for high office. They welcome

Rockefeller support. But their eyebrows lift with affected horror only when checks are made out for union democracy. What bothers them is not who gives the money but for what...They are sure to object whether the donor's name is Rockefeller, Smith Brothers, or Cough Drops whenever the object for support is the rights of members inside their unions."

Since then, AUD has heard little more about those alarming Rockefellers.

Section III
Battles for Union Democracy

Chapter 7: Victory of Miners for Democracy and its repercussions

The first flush of optimism inspired by the AFL-CIO Ethical Practices Codes and the adoption of the LMRDA had called forth movements for union democracy and reform in the years immediately following 1959. But soon, with the sobering realization that the new federal law would not be vigorously enforced and would produce no miracle and that change would not come easily, those trends were subdued.

Then, in 1969 came a powerful impulse from a new source, bringing new hope and stimulating a new wave of insurgency: Jock Yablonski's challenge to Tony Boyle for president of the Miners' union and the victory of the Miners for Democracy in 1972. In the previous decade, a new spirit of democracy was beginning to penetrate the labor movement, but so slowly that no change in atmosphere was yet apparent. The miner's revolt forced the subject, bluntly and explicitly, into the open.

"Union democracy is the single most important issue...," wrote Jock Yablonski in 1969 just weeks before he was murdered. Yablonski had been a top officer of the United Mine Workers under John L. Lewis and was a member of the union's international executive board when he announced his campaign for union president against incumbent Tony Boyle. According to the official union tally, Yablonski received 37% of the votes in a membership referendum; but the election was riddled with fraud and voided many months later after the U. S, Labor Department sued in federal court. Yablonski himself, however, never got a second chance; on the night of December 30, 1969, three murderers broke into his house and shot him to death along with his wife and daughter. (Later, UMW president Tony Boyle, convicted of hiring the killers, was sentenced to life and died in prison.)

Yablonski's death did not demoralize the reform movement. His supporters, organized into the Miners for Democracy, continued the battle, elevated now into a moral crusade. In an election supervised by the Labor Department in 1972, the insurgents ousted the Boyle machine. At the first union convention under the new leadership, the constitution was rewritten to reestablish autonomous rights to the districts, to guarantee fair elections, and to establish the right of miners to vote on contracts. Some years later, protected by that new constitution, Rich Trumka was elected UMW president.

The victory of the MFD inspired a new wave of public support for democratic rights in the labor movement. For one thing, it demonstrated in action the kind of tri-partite combination that could rescue a union from the hands of corrupt and unscrupulous autocrats. First, there was an organized movement of union members determined to fight for their rights. Second, there was federal law which protected those rights and provided the basic tools of democracy: civil liberties and fair elections in their union. And finally, there were the supporters of democratic unionism outside the labor movement in the larger society: the civil libertarians, the workers rights attorneys, the liberal and pro-labor foundations who came forward with the talent, the legal aid, and the money so necessary to even the odds in any battle against an entrenched officialdom.

Under the direction of Joe Rauh, one of the most effective of the nation's civil liberties and pro-labor attorneys, a group of lawyers were recruited to give legal aid to the Miners for Democracy. In federal court, they compelled the UMW to release its autocratic grip over the districts and open them up to democratic contest. They intervened in the Labor Department's election suit in federal court and induced the judge to order the most far-reaching conditions for democratic procedures ever devised in any union election.

Joe Rauh's decision to represent Yablonski, then the murder of his new client and friend, and the crusade of the Miners for Democracy, changed his life. From that moment, until his death in 1992, Rauh worked closely with the Association for Union Democracy and remained preoccupied with the cause. Beginning with AUD's first national conference in 1980, Rauh was a featured speaker at all its conferences as long as he was able to get around. He made his last appearance, leaning for support on a cane. In 1994, President Clinton awarded him, posthumously, the nation's Medal of Freedom, recognizing that "he dedicated his considerable talents to battling segregation and racial injustice and to promoting democracy in the labor movement."

From the very beginning of his career, Rauh was a fighting attorney for the underdog. He represented the UAW, the Sleeping Car Porters, and served as attorney for the civil rights movement. He was the lead attorney for a whole consortium of major unions in a suit against the National Right to Work Committee. But after he served Joseph Yablonski and later Ed Sadlowski, he became persona non grata among labor officials and was removed as their attorney in the Right to Work case.

I first realized that he was one of us when the Yablonski murders hit the front pages. Speculation was rife: who did it? After the killings, labor leaders, interviewed by the press, were evasive. Albert Shanker told me not to jump to conclusions. He suggested that Y. might have been fooling around with someone else's wife. *New America*, the prounion social democratic paper, ran a rambling piece ascribing the murder to traditions of violence in mining as though sociology was the disembodied perpetrator. But when reporters asked Rauh if he thought that the murders were connected to the internal union battle, there was no equivocation in his reply, "Of course!"

In 1984, after requests from a several leaders of construction local unions in Canada, AUD was preparing for an international conference in Toronto. At the time, there was so much interest in Canada that we were sure the sessions would be packed. But we received an annoyed call from Dennis McDermott, the head of the Canadian Labor Congress. He insisted that we call off the conference because, he claimed, it would be attended by all varieties of malcontents and somehow would undercut his plans for a unification of the auto, steel, and machinists unions of Canada into a single metal federation. (PS: The unity never jelled.) If we went ahead, he threatened, the CLC would have to repudiate us. He also added something irrelevant about you Americans with your Viet Nam War. I immediately called Joe Rauh who would have been a keynote AUD speaker. "You can count on me," he said, "I'm not intimidated by labor bureaucrats here; and I'm sure not going to be intimidated by them there." We did abandon the conference, but not because of the threats. Our Canadian friends, mostly construction workers, like Barry Fraser in the IBEW and John Donaldson in the Ironworkers, had to bow out because they desperately needed CLC support in a big battle then in progress between the CLC and the U.S.-based Canadian construction unions which had just pulled out of the CLC to set up a rival federation.

Yablonski's murder taught Rauh a bitter lesson. Back in 1966, when I was racked by uncertainty over how to respond to the murder of Dow

Wilson, I called Sam Fishman, an old friend and comrade who was then an aide to Walter Reuther and was close to Rauh. Fishman relayed Rauh's advice to me: Go to the U.S. Justice Department. Three years later, when Joe tried to follow his own advice, it was tragic failure. After Yablonski, had been viciously assaulted, Rauh appealed to Secretary of Labor George Shultz to intervene. "Somebody's going to get killed," he wrote. Shultz turned him down. Neither the DOL nor the Justice Department would show presence. After the killings, Rauh charged that the Department's "icy indifference" had "contributed to the death" by leading "the most lawless elements to believe that the Yablonski group was defenseless." *Union Democracy in Action* reminded readers that the same icy indifference had preceded the murder of two painter reform leaders in California three years before. UDA called for a full investigation of the Labor Department's LMRDA enforcement record.

In 1970, Karl Kafton, one of the leaders of the Miners for Democracy, discovered *Union Democracy in Action* through press notices and distributed copies among his colleagues. Later, Kafton chaired the Miners for Democracy convention which nominated Arnold Miller and opened the campaign against Tony Boyle, who had not yet been indicted for murder. Upon invitation, I attended that convention, which event marked the beginning of a long collaboration of AUD with Joe Rauh and attorney Joseph (Chip) Yablonski, son of the murdered miners' leader.

The miners battle forced unionists and labor intellectuals to reevaluate their views on the meaning of democracy in unions. It exploded the notion that democracy was unnecessary in unions as long as they were run effectively by benevolent dictators. Up to then, a common conception, perhaps the prevailing ideology, held that democracy was somehow irrelevant in a labor movement whose objective was to make practical gains for workers by whatever means, preferably legal. When we formed the Association for Union Democracy in 1969 some of our best friends suggested that we were wasting our time in efforts divorced from reality. John L. Lewis was always offered as crushing proof. He was autocratic, contemptuous of democracy, and preoccupied presumably with providing "eating money". Guided by that philosophy of power he had wiped out democracy in the miners union; but, our critics insisted, he had built a powerful union which served its members well. The miners reform movement tore away that lovely veil. Behind that not-so-benevolent autocracy, the union and its officialdom had been degenerating. After Lewis retired in 1960 and Boyle took over in 1963, the decay was manifest: dictatorship, beatings of delegates, union money pilfered, insurance funds dissipated, miners health and safety ignored. And what was the missing ingredient, what the weapon to cure the rot? In Yablonski's words: "union democracy."

Once the miners lit the torch, others were moved to take it up. With the support of civil libertarians, with their legal rights defended by cooperating attorneys, and with a fair election count assured by government authorities, the insurgent miners had triumphed in a union dominated by thugs and crooks. It was possible! Their success encouraged reformers in other unions and motivated young attorneys, looking for a worthy cause, to volunteer their services.

A kind of union democracy "movement" began taking shape, not as a formal organization but rather as an unplanned collaboration of democratic-minded unionists and civil libertarians. No longer were insurgents lonely union reformers, morally and physically isolated from one another. There was now an informal bond, not any centrally directed organization, but a loose network based upon a sentiment of solidarity. But there it certainly was, and its existence and its activity was beginning to influence thinking in the labor movement, releasing a flood of dissent. The next 20 years can be viewed as preparation for the great watershed event which helped shake up the whole labor movement: the defeat of the corrupted and racketeer infiltrated officialdom of the Teamsters union.

The Association for Union Democracy, superseding the 10-year old publication *Union Democracy in Action*, founded in 1969, had already established some slender ties with the miners movement. By 1972 it was providing advice and assistance to reformers in many unions. Several magazines focussed on labor but independent of any union officialdom began publication. There was *Labor Notes*, which called for more militant labor policies; it reported widely on union democratic reform groups. Within a few years, it was holding annual conferences which attracted 1,000 union activists. The Midwest Center for Labor Research introduced its independent **Labor Research Review**, reaching an audience of local leaders, rank and file activists, and labor educators, providing a discussion platform free from the control of any labor establishment.

And there were the attorneys. To defend the legal rights of miners, Joe Rauh and Chip Yablonski, the murdered miner's son, brought together a group of lawyers in the Washington Project, which disbanded after the election. A few older and experienced union democracy attorneys renewed their interest: Paul Tobias, who later founded the National Employment Lawyers Association; John Harold, formerly counsel for the Association of Catholic Trade Unionists; Burton Hall, a pioneering union democracy attorney. Younger, newly motivated lawyers come forward. Michael Goldberg led a non-profit union democracy support group in Seattle. There was Leon Rosenblatt in Connecticut; Robin Potter in Chicago; Mark Stern in Boston; Arthur Schwartz, Dan Clifton, and Amy Gladstein in New York. Judith Chomsky in Pennsylvania; Barbara Harvey in Michigan; Naomi Baden, Dan Siegel, Jonathan Siegel in California, Judith Schneider and Susan Jennik for the Association for Union Democracy; Robert Gibbs in Seattle; Rick Macpherson in Minnesota. Ellis Boal in Detroit who began by representing the newly formed Teamsters for a Democratic Union. Alan Hyde joined the AUD Board after graduating from law school, became a law professor at Rutgers, and wrote amicus briefs for AUD in high profile union democracy cases in federal court. They could all count on advice from Clyde Summers,

The Naderite Public Citizen Litigation Group initiated a union democracy project headed by Paul Alan Levy and Arthur Fox who both joined the AUD Board of Directors and helped shape union democracy law in the years that followed.

Some of these young lawyers were associated with the National Lawyers Guild which in 1980, in the spirit of the times, established its own National Labor Law Center to defend the rights of union dissidents; for three years it could be counted on by reformers; it published a stream of helpful guides on union democratic rights.

In those heady years, in that first flush of optimism and enthusiasm that followed the victory of the Miners for Democracy, it was accurate to speak of a "union democracy bar," not an organized group but a fraternity loosely cooperating in a common cause.

In the inexorable hurrying of Time's winged chariot, we all grew older and matured into family responsibilities. Some found it simpler, more secure, and less nerve-wracking to serve the union establishment in combatting the corporate establishment. After three years, the National Lawyers Guild abandoned its union democracy project under pressure from union officials who threatened to withdraw support if the Guild persisted in defending the rights of union insurgents. Dan Siegel, a Guild workers rights advocate who opposed the project's dissolution, explained, "It's not easy to make a living representing rank and file members and their caucuses; and few unions — even progressive ones — are willing to hire lawyers with a reputation for suing unions."

But some remained steadfast in the years that followed, cooperating with The Association for Union Democracy and with the Teamsters for a Democratic Union, to provide formidable legal support to the battle for union democracy and reform. A few Guild lawyers continued their own personal support to union dissidents. The cause did get continuing reinforcement from that one-man army, Joe Rauh.

And there were the foundations. In the spirit of the times, a group of liberal and civil libertarian foundations provided substantial support for the defense of democracy in unions. They helped finance the Washington Project, Joe Rauh's miners legal support group. They supported the Teamster reformers, they bankrolled an AUD project to monitor the Steelworker election in 1977. They financed a three-year expansion program for the Association for Union Democracy in 1980.

Enthusiastic support by attorneys and foundations was crucial in propelling forward the union democracy "movement". But, anticipating a quick fix, the expectations of some were too high. When the dramatic miners' victory was followed by stalemate in steel, and it became clear that no spectacular change in the labor movement was immediately at hand, and the prospect was not for brilliant battles but for slow slogging campaigns, the interest of some of that band of liberals, civil libertarians, labor attorneys, and progressive foundations dwindled. Joe Rauh put it this way in 1984, "After helping to clean up a union [the Miners] and turn it back to the membership, you get an overblown reputation. Everybody thinks you can do that kind of thing over and over again, but it's not easy to repeat." But the fervor of reformers in unions did not chill. Movements for democracy and integrity proliferated. Even our inadequate partial listing here tells the story;

Marine engineers: In the years of doldrums that becalmed the Marine Engineers' Beneficial Association, after the earlier dissidents had been quelled, the top MEBA officials turned the union into a cash cow. Headed by international President Gene DeFries, they concocted an abortive merger with the National Maritime Union. After creating what they defined as a "new" union, they extracted millions of dollars in severance pay and pensions from the "old" union but continued as paid officers of the new. As an added insult, the merger threatened to undermine the stability of the engineers pension fund. In 1989, rank and file engineers organized a reform caucus, Members Against DeFries (MAD, later renamed Members Advocating Democracy.) Larry O'Toole, one of the caucus founders, had preserved 1972 press clippings on the Miners' battle; their references to the Association for Union Democracy brought him to the AUD office. After a bitter two-year battle, the insurgents ousted the old leaders and voided the merger. Soon after, former MEBA officials were convicted in Federal court on corruption charges.

Musicians: The movement for democratic reform in Musicians' Local 802, New York, stalled and then dissolved in 1967, revived with enhanced power by 1980. In 1982, the reformers won a sweeping victory in local elections, electing as president John Glasel, one of the leaders, fifteen years earlier, of the Musicians' Voice group. That same year, the Recording Musicians' Association, like the symphony musicians years before, won recognized "conference" status in the American Federation of Musicians.

Postal Workers: LMRDA-protected democratic rights were extended to postal workers in the Postal Reorganization Act of 1970.

In the National Association of Letter Carriers, after a rare strike of postal workers in 1970, Vincent Sombrotto, campaigning as an advocate of democracy and militancy, defeated the incumbent for president of Branch 36 in New York. He parlayed his status in this big local into a successful insurgent run for president of the national union in 1978.

In the American Postal Workers Union, the union of clerks, Moe Biller, the president of the New York Local, won national recognition after leading a protest against the contract accepted by the national president in 1978. Two years later, as an opposition candidate, he was elected national president in a four-way race.

The National Postal Mail Handlers' Union, which represents those who do the heavy lifting and shifting, is a division of the Laborers' International Union (LIUNA.) For 20 years, 1968 to 1988, it remained a subservient unit, dominated by the LIUNA national office, denied the right to elect its own officers or negotiate their own contracts. In defiance of the LIUNA hierarchy and with the backing of a Federal court, mail handlers assembled in convention where the delegates asserted their autonomous rights, adopted a new constitution providing for the direct election of their officers, the right to vote on contracts, and for control over collective bargaining. In February 1989, taking a cue from Teamsters for a Democratic Union, an insurgent caucus, Team for Union Democracy, elected all officers of the Mail Handlers division.

Public Employees Federation of New York State: In 1976, the 50,000-member statewide unit of professional and scientific employees, in quest of a union which provided more extensive democratic rights, broke away from the 250,000-member Civil Service Employees Association to affiliate with both the American Federation of Teachers and the Service Employees. By 1979, convinced that John Kraemer, their president, had turned into an intolerant autocrat, a vigorous opposition caucus formed, the State Coalition for a Democratic Union (SCDU.) In an election supervised by the American Arbitration Association, Kraemer was badly defeated and SCDU took over. (Later, Kraemer pleaded guilty of embezzling $40,000 from the union.) The insurgent rank and filers, now in control, turned PEF into a union where democratic rights are respected and frequent contests for office are expected, and accepted, as normal.

Hospital Local 1199 in NY: After Leon Davis, the pioneering founder and president of the 70,000-member District 1199 in New York retired in 1982, the union presidency was bequeathed to Doris Turner who soon revealed herself as a ruthless manipulator, purging the union of independent-minded staffers. In 1984, she led a disastrous 47-day strike during which the members remained uninformed and confused; and many drifted back to work. After the strike was called off, she falsified the terms of the settlement. When she ran for reelection in 1984, she faced active opposition from a full "Save Our Union" slate. She was declared the winner in an election riddled with outright fraud. Thanks to the LMRDA, the opposition had recourse under Federal law. In a rerun supervised by the U.S. Labor Department, the opposition triumphed by 19,300 to 17,000. Jerry Brown, then secretary of the National Union of Hospital Workers, said, "A key factor in the election victory was the growing conviction among unionists that there was a close connection between free democratic unionism and effective unionism."

The Graphic Communications International Union was racked by a bitter battle between two factions, each supported by strong local leaders, and each accusing the other of electoral fraud. The conflict was resolved only after the Labor Department, exercising its authority under the LMRDA supervised a rerun election for most top posts, an election won by the incumbent national administration.

In the United Food and Commercial Workers irony mixed with drama in the search for reform. Lewie Anderson first achieved minor celebrity status as the UFW national representative assigned to quell the rebel leaders in Packinghouse Workers Local P9. They had led a bitter strike for ten fiery months at the 1,500-worker Hormel plant in Austin MN in 1986. But in 1989, after Anderson criticized the international for continuing to sign concessionary packinghouse contracts, he was removed as director of the Packinghouse Division. In March that year, with the support of 13 local union presidents, he announced the formation of a new reform caucus called Research, Education, Advocacy, People (for short: REAP). In April 300 members from 20 locals, came to REAP's founding convention in Sioux Falls, SD.

"Democratic Reforms Needed Within the UFCW" read the main headline in one of REAP's regular newsletters, the *REAP News and Views*. The group called for the direct election of international officers, the election of directors of regions and of trade divisions by vote of their respective memberships.

In the United Auto Workers, The international leadership had not faced organized opposition for decades. Its administration caucus held sway unchallenged in what the UAW Public Review Board defined and accepted as "one-party government." But in 1986, that changed when it faced opposition led by Jerry Tucker. As assistant director of Region 5, encompassing Missouri and four other states, Tucker had been a partisan of the administration caucus. However, prodded by some members and local leaders, he agreed to run for regional director against the administration's choice, incumbent Ken Worley. But in timing the announcement of his candidacy, the administration charged, he had violated an obscure rule which limited the right of staff appointees to run against an incumbent without giving extended notice of his intentions. The rule had been adopted by the ruling administration caucus; and no solid proof could be advanced to demonstrate that it had ever been actually approved by the union itself. In any event, Tucker was fired from the staff, and the administration went all out to defeat him. Consequently, despite himself, Tucker's race was transformed from a mild expression of independence to an outright insurgent campaign against the top leadership.

UAW regional directors are elected at conventions by the local delegates from their respective regions. Worley eked out a razor-thin majority. But the Department of Labor, ruling that some delegates had been improperly elected, voided the result. In a DOL-supervised rerun, Tucker won by a comfortable majority. At the next convention, the administration rallied its forces and succeeded in defeating Tucker's bid for reelection. The international board reverted to its "one-party" status.

But Tucker would not go away. His followers, backed by Victor Reuther, now a retired UAW elder statesman, by Chip Yablonski and Joe Rauh of miners fame, and by a sprinkling of supporters of the publication, *Labor Notes*, set up New Directions as a formal caucus campaigning for militant union resistance to contractual concessions, for the election of officers by direct membership vote instead of by convention delegates, and for an end to collaboration with employers in quality of life programs. Bolstered by a series of national conferences over the years, New Directions maintained a continuing national opposition network. For several years, the voice of organized dissent was heard throughout the UAW. As a watchword, "New Directions," became a popular insurgent trademark, adopted by caucuses in the Masters, Mates, and Pilots and in the Transport Workers Union.

Steel Workers: Earlier, in the period of expectation that followed the Miners victory, Joe Rauh, Chip Yablonski, liberal foundations, and the Association for Union Democracy were called upon to support the rights of an insurgent movement within the United Steel Workers of America, one of our largest and most powerful unions.

Chapter 8: The Quest for Honest Steel Worker Elections

From Chicago, Ed Sadlowski phoned me at home on the evening of February 23, 1973. He had just run as an insurgent for director of the 125,000-member district of the United Steelworkers of America, the union's largest. Victory would give him a spot on the ruling international executive board where votes of the board members are weighted according to their district membership. Members had already cast their ballots, but the results were not yet officially tabulated. With the count almost completed, his observers' informal tally showed him leading comfortably by about 4,000 votes, enough to guarantee victory. But this was an election in Chicago, the fabled land of miraculous late returns where the Daley Democratic machine ruled. Steelworker officials, close to the machine, had learned its lessons well. A few big locals were holding back their returns. Sadlowski, fearing that the well-honed Chicago skill, would rob him of victory, was wondering what to do. I suggested that to prepare an election appeal, he compile a written record of all that went wrong and get an attorney.

It went just as he had feared: Ed went to sleep that night, the certain victor, only to discover next morning that those late returns had done him in. From an expectant winner by 4,000, he was transformed into a loser by about 1,800. The tally announced by the official union tellers went 23,394 for Sam Evett, the administration's "Official Family" choice, to 21,606 for Sadlowski. He followed through and retained Leon Despres, a prominent Chicago civil liberties attorney, the founder of Independent Voters of Illinois, the state equivalent of the Americans for Democratic Action.

After going through the constitutionally required but futile internal union appeals, attorney Despres gathered extensive evidence of election fraud and forwarded Sadlowski's complaint to the U.S. Labor Department, only to discover that the department was dragging its feet. And so he called upon Joe Rauh, whose legal skills had served the miners so well. Rauh's entry electrified the atmosphere. He demanded that the Labor Department speed up its investigation. He insisted that it remove from the case one Labor Department official who had worked for the Steelworkers union. Under drumfire pressure from Rauh, the department upheld Sadlowski's complaint; and, when the Steelworkers rejected demands for a rerun, the Labor Department filed suit in federal court to void the 1973 election.

On January 27, 1974—already almost a year after the suspect election—1,000 Steelworkers attended a rally for Sadlowski in Chicago. It was standing room only at the hall of U.S. Steel Local 65. At Rauh's invitation, Judith Schneider attended the rally for AUD. Joe knew that the Steelworkers would resist stubbornly in court and that the Labor Department could not be counted on for an effective defense of Sadlowski's rights. In support of the Miners for Democracy, in *Trbovich v. UMW* at the Supreme Court, Rauh had won the right of complainants to intervene in election suits brought by the DOL. He intended to intervene in the DOL Steelworkers suit. He asked AUD to assign Schneider, who had just been admitted to the bar, to help. AUD agreed. Her salary of $7,500, meager by any standard, was covered by a special grant which kept her going on a subsistence level. It was the beginning of a long collaboration between AUD and Rauh which lasted until his death in 1992. For Rauh it led to eight years of preoccupation with the battle for democracy in the Steelworkers union.

And it meant, despite his years of dedicated service to the labor movement, that he would excommunicated by the union establishment. "I have had more obloquy and more scorn from the labor movement for representing Yablonski and Sadlowski and helping reformers in the Laborers and other unions," he told an AUD conference in 1984, "than I ever got from representing people under attack during the McCarthy period in the 1950's. The problems we went through in the McCarthy period were as nothing compared to labor's recriminations against those who have become spokesmen for union democracy."

In federal court as intervenors, the team of Rauh, Despres, and Schneider presented evidence of election misconduct so overwhelming that the Steelworkers officialdom finally backed down and agreed to a new election under DOL supervision. In the November 1974 rerun, 21 months after the original election, with his rights now assured, Sadlowski defeated

Evett by a margin of almost 2 to 1: by 39,637 to 20,158. No mistaking what the members wanted.

Ed Sadlowski was 35 and a second-generation steelworker when he ran for district director in 1973. His father had retired as a member of the Steelworkers union. Ed rose from the ranks and from within the union leadership, not in opposition to it. He went into the mill early, worked for 12 years at a U.S. Steel plant in Chicago as a laborer and then as a machinist. At 25, he was elected president of the 10,000-member Local 65 and then was appointed to the staff as an international representative. The district's first director, Joe Germano, had held the job for 30 years, one of only three men who had served on the international executive board continuously since the union was founded in 1942. When the administration backed Evett as Germano's successor, Sadlowski broke ranks to run against him.

Sadlowski's platform was simple and down to earth, emphasizing straight union issues: pensions, scrupulous attention to grievances, the right to vote on contracts, all summarized in his basic plank, "Rank and file control over basic union policy." He knew he could break through the official apparatus because Steelworkers elected officers by direct membership vote, and he could count on enthusiastic support from the rank and file. He and never been the familiar predictably inveterate oppositionist; he was a rank and file leader at heart whose natural instinct was to represent workers in their battle for fair treatment. His main beef was not against union officials but against abusive employers. He was never infected with that occupational egomania so prevalent in labor leadership. The rank and file, those who knew him, saw one of their own whom they could trust. And he felt under enormous pressure to give voice and representation to their desire for a new responsive leadership.

Liberals and pro-labor intellectuals on the outside, encouraged by the victory of the Miners for Democracy, were also looking for new labor leadership that could shake the labor movement, and then the nation, out of its doldrums. (Twenty years later, John Sweeny would respond to that sentiment. When Sadlowski announced for Steelworkers president in 1976, he was a premature John Sweeny.)

Discontent with the union leadership was widespread, obvious ever since Donald Rarick, the unknown mill worker, came close to toppling David McDonald in 1957 and still ominously evident even after I.W. Abel defeated McDonald in 1965. In one district after another incumbent directors had faced serious opposition. Repeatedly, in national contests, the administration was outpolled by insurgents among workers in basic steel.

By the time Sadlowski was installed after the special supervised election in 1974, two years of his term had already elapsed. By 1976, it was time for new elections to fill all top posts. He decided to run for the top position of international president at the head of a slate in open opposition to the incumbent administration. It was not a decision taken lightly.

Steelworkers elect international officers by direct membership ballot. Votes are cast and counted in each local, and a simple tally sheet is sent to the national center where the reported—or reputed—results are not verified but merely added up. It is impossible for any rank and file opposition, outside the official machine, to recruit observers enough to police the casting and counting of ballots at those 5,700 voting sites in the 5,400 locals. In the 1976 election, fraud, more than a mere possibility, seemed inevitable, because the Steelworkers had a long history of fraudulent elections.

As former Steelworkers president David McDonald, waxing nostalgically, told a New York Times reporter in 1976, "I know how to run elections. I stole four elections for Joe Germano as director of District 31." In 1965, McDonald himself faced the same technique when he was defeated for reelection by I.W. Abel. At that time, David Feller a distinguished labor attorney, was chief counsel of the Steelworkers union. Seventeen years later, in March 1982, when he was a professor of law at the University of California Law School, he spoke his mind at a seminar at the New York University Law School:

"If you want to talk about the Abel-McDonald election, I don't know who gained the most votes...where the district director favored Abel and there were no McDonald observers at the polls, then you find in one local something like 1100 for Abel and two for McDonald. You go to the locals that McDonald had in Florida and it came out equally unbalanced in McDonald's favor, except they were smaller locals." Feller was just as dubious about an earlier election: "In the election of the Steelworkers president in 1956, I think there is grave doubt whether the man who was declared the winner actually won, I'm talking about the time that Don Rarick ran against David J. McDonald...in 1956 [Rarick] was reported to have gotten a majority. There was no Landrum-Griffin, so there is no way of knowing how many votes he really got."

In his own District 31, Sadlowski was supported by an organized following, who could not only get out the votes but could be sure that they were counted and recorded honestly. But nationally? Who would oversee the count at all those voting sites, scattered all over United States and Canada?

Joe Rauh, still riding the wave of optimism generated by the miners' victory, set out to crack that nut. For the miners, he had assembled a team of attorneys and raised money for extensive legal work and campaign funds. Representing Sadlowski without fee, he hoped to do the same for steelworkers. How to guarantee a fair Steel election in 1977? Joe Rauh asked AUD to administer a major project to monitor the Steelworkers' election. If AUD would run the project, he would raise the money.

For Rauh, AUD was a logical choice. By this time, I had been campaigning for union democracy for more than 18 years. We had publicized the miners' battle. Our Board of Directors, included top experts in union democracy law. Judith Schneider, AUD legal director, already had Steelworker experience in District 31. With its 501(c)(3) standing, AUD could assure tax-exempt status for donors. With Judith Schneider admitted to the bar, AUD was geared for participation in Steel-related projects. At that point, however, AUD was a little-known entity. Joe Rauh, eminent and respected as a crusading civil rights and labor attorney, was instrumental in raising money from a group of liberal foundations. Earlier he had recruited foundation backing for the Washington Project in defense of miners' rights. I was not involved in that project, but I assume that he went back to the same group for the Steel projects.

But before agreeing to sponsor the project, we had to consider its implications. As a nonpolitical, nonpartisan organization, AUD defends the right of candidates to a fair election, but we do not support candidates for union office. That distinction, was a fine line that could not be crossed. It went to the heart of AUD's role as a nonpartisan civil liberties organization. In assigning Schneider to run the project, the AUD board was careful to define her role:

"Her assignment is to help protect the rights of Sadlowski to a fair election rather than his interests as a contender for office. Put differently, her objective is not to help elect Sadlowski but to help him win a fair chance to campaign for office and an honest count. This distinction may sometimes seem like a fine one, but it is essential to keep it in mind. The Association does not take partisan positions in union elections; it does not support any candidate for office. It does defend the right of all candidates to a fair election. This role is not only prescribed by the Association's charter but it is the only kind of role that can preserve its effectiveness in its chosen field of activity."

Later, the Steelworkers' union challenged our position, insisting that, by providing legal assistance to defend insurgents' rights, we freed up resources for campaigning that they would otherwise have had to spend defending themselves. But that argument missed the whole point. The role of any civil libertarian group is precisely to relieve the victims of repression of the obligation of defending their right to free expression so that they can actually exercise that right. If insurgents could be pauperized by the costs of defending the right to speak, they could never actually enjoy that right.

Schneider opened an AUD office for the Steel Workers Election Project and remained in Chicago until the election was over. Eleven foundations donated a total of approximately $107,000 to finance the project. Among the major donors, the Field Foundation and the Kaplan Fund were already familiar with AUD and had made modest grants to it in previous years. But for others, AUD was still an unknown quantity; they trusted us only because they admired and trusted Joe Rauh.

Schneider organized the program into three distinct phases: * the writing, printing, and distribution of a manual for election observers; * legal action to assure the equal right of candidates to get on the ballot and to campaign; * recruitment and assignment of observers to watch the balloting and monitor the vote tally on election day.

A 15-page manual for observers advised them how to guard against fraud and assure that accurate results were transmitted from the locals. Twenty thousand copies were distributed around the country. The manual warned observers to keep their eyes open everywhere every moment. I learned the tricks of the trade back in 1960 at the Steelworker convention where insurgents explained how it was done: During the Rarick-McDonald race in 1956, they managed to avoid a major swindle in one big local where they had observers enough to scrutinize every phase of the election. They watched when the back panel of the voting machine was opened; and, reading off the results, one official teller called out the actual count: some 3,000 for Rarick and only 1,000 for McDonald.

But at another table, several feet away, a second official teller entered the results on the sheet to be sent to Washington. An observer for the insurgents insisted on inspecting the tally sheet, discovering that an "error" had been made. The recorded results had been reversed: 3,000 for McDonald; 1,000 for Rarick. In that instance the "error" was corrected. But there were thousands of other sites where, unobserved, the tellers were free to make similar mistakes.

Three lawyers, assisted by a secretary, made up the full project legal team: Joe Rauh, Judith Schneider, and Tom Geoghegan. In the early weeks of the campaign, they pursued four major actions in federal court to defend the insurgents' campaign rights. But the overwhelming task was to police the count at 5,700 voting sites. The 1977 election was conducted, as usual, by the official family union staff which knows what results are expected. Who, in a union with a record of election fraud, would watch over their shoulders? Without a network of observers, independent of the administration, it would be impossible to fulfill the law's requirement for "adequate safeguards to insure a fair election." It was Schneider's heavy responsibility to drum up observers to serve at the polls and at the count. With limited resources, and under time pressure, she had to find and organize recruiters to go out into the field, visit locals and ask for volunteers. It would never be possible to cover all 5,700 sites; she could do only what she could.

Forty-seven union members, hired as recruiters, averaged three days a week during the pre-election period and were each paid a total of about $700. They signed a declaration pledging to refrain from any campaign activities during the time they were on the project payroll. At the polls, observers served as unpaid volunteers.

On election day, the project succeeded in monitoring the count in about 800 locals. The Sadlowski group itself covered perhaps an additional 200 in the Chicago area. In over 4,000 locals, then, election officials were free to exercise their unsupervised imagination. As democracy in action, this election was imperfect, even fatally flawed. But not at those 1,000 local sites. For that reason, ironically enough, even with all its defects, this election came closer to an honest count than any before. In their post election report, the official international tellers wrote, "...this was the best run election that we have had the privilege of supervising." For that, the AUD project deserves credit. Still, our best was not good enough.

After the official tellers added up tallies recorded on sheets mailed in by the locals, Lloyd McBride, administration candidate, was declared the winner by 328,861 votes to Sadlowski's 249,281, a margin of 79,850 of the 580,00 cast. A switch of an average of only 8 votes per local could have shifted the balance in this union with its 20-year tradition of suspect elections. (Four years earlier, in district 31 alone, Sadlowski had been fraudulently counted out by 1,688 votes; in the supervised rerun, he won by 12,479.)

Who really won the election? No one really knows. As in 1957 when Rarick ran against McDonald, and in 1965 when Abel ran against McDonald, so in 1977 when Sadlowski ran against McBride, no one, in this union of stuffed ballot boxes, can be certain of who actually got a majority. Election irregularities were widespread enough to justify a challenge to the results. Before the AUD election project was terminated, it helped prepare an election appeal, first within the union, and finally in Federal court. Meanwhile, AUD had to fight off a legal and administrative attack that threatened its existence.

AUD Survives a Steel Worker Attack

Election victory was not assurance enough to allay the official family's nervous misgivings over the uncertainties of democracy. Seeking more reliable guarantees against future shock, they initiated a three-pronged campaign to guard against serious challenge:

* They sued AUD in federal court along with eight foundations that had financed the steel election project.

* They lured the IRS and the NYC Attorney General to challenge AUD's status as a tax-exempt foundation.

* And, finally, they amended the union's constitution to make it difficult for any future challenger to raise enough money for an effective national campaign.

First came the Steelworkers legal attack on AUD: On April 19,1978, the union sued in New York Federal District Court before Judge Cannella against AUD, the Rockefeller Family Fund, the New World Foundation, the Field Foundation, the Samuel Rubin Foundation, the J.M. Kaplan Fund, Ottinger Foundation, Community Funds, and the Youth Project charging that they were "employers" who had contributed money "on behalf of candidates for USWA offices [the Sadlowski slate] in blatant violation of Section 401(g) of the [LMRDA]." In short, the union accused the foundations of "laundering" money through AUD to support the Sadlowski slate. The law forbids "employers" from supporting candidates for union office. The union asked that all defendants be enjoined from such actions "with respect to a any USWA election'" and that it be awarded damages and legal fees.

From the simple standpoint of law, the suit was a dud. The LMRDA restricts the right of private parties to sue in union post- election cases and provides recourse only by complaint to the Secretary of Labor, who alone is authorized go to court. On that basis, in April 1979 a year after it was filed, the judge dismissed the complaint, making an actual trial unnecessary. Still, the union dragged out the case for two years, losing at every level but not before piling up the mountain of procedural documents familiar in such litigation. Oral hearings were scheduled at the Appeals Court on October 31,1979 where the judges needed only a single day and 2 1/2 pages to dismiss the appeal on November 1. Still, the union pressed on up to the U.S. Supreme Court which, in 1980, refused to take the case.

For AUD, however, it was a dangerous moment, even though, obviously, the union's case was fatally flawed. Extended legal proceedings could bankrupt a small impoverished group like AUD whose total annual budget fluctuated around $100,000. We were afraid, too, that win or lose in court, the foundations that backed AUD would be scared off. They had begun, innocently enough, to support a worthy cause only to be embroiled unexpectedly in expensive litigation. Our fears proved to be well founded, but only in part. After the case was finally litigated to the end, half the foundations did back off, never to be heard from again. But not all; some of the foundations now viewed AUD with a new, reinforced respect. Up to that point, they knew little about AUD and supported its project only because it was endorsed by an eminent civil libertarian like Joe Rauh. If AUD's activities were taken seriously by so powerful an adversary as the Steelworkers, it must be doing something right, and significant.

AUD was spared the lethal financial burden of financing a legal defense against the Steelworkers suit by an imaginative formula worked out by Bob Scrivner of the Rockefeller Family Fund. He convinced the defendant foundations that costs should be apportioned among the participants according to their assets. We were easily persuaded to agree.

In the end, ironically, the Steelworkers assault on AUD had an opposite, unintended effect. Instead of putting AUD out of business, it put us on the map. A few foundations continued to support AUD generously for years. And just in time. We were suddenly faced with challenges to our tax-exempt status from the New York State Attorney General and the IRS.

Enter the NYS Attorney general: On May 11, 1978, just one month after the vexing Steelworkers suit hit the hopper, AUD faced an unexpected demand letter from the New York State Assistant Attorney General, Sherman Oxenhandler, requesting AUD annual financial reports since its incorporation in 1969. In all those years, instructed by our accountant, AUD had been submitting the required reports to the New York Department of State. For nine years nobody in the AG's office noticed that we were not there. Now, just as the Steelworkers were breathing down our neck, the AG was alerted. Naturally, we suspected the Steelworkers; events promptly vindicated that nasty thought.

Oxenhandler was right on target. In September he wrote that he had "carefully reviewed" our records only to discover —surprise! — "certain extremely difficult problems…to be resolved promptly before any further difficulties should arise." A week later, he defined the scope of his interest, asking for all financial records, minutes, documents, et. al. for the period of 1976 and 77, precisely the dates of our Steel Election Projects.

Oxenhandler admitted that he had been alerted to AUD by the Steelworkers' suit and that his concern had been aroused by reading its complaint. But he put the case on hold because AUD promptly faced a more disturbing challenge. The AG could simply wait and see how that one evolved. The next reel showed AUD perilously poised over the cliff.

Enter the IRS: In the eight years since AUD had been granted tax-exempt status by the IRS, it had audited our books only twice, briefly and routinely. No problem. There was nothing much to find. The top salary in those days was $7,500, pitiful even then, to a total staff of one. And, after the events here chronicled had run their course, the IRS audited us only once. But early in 1979, soon after the Steelworkers had filed its suit and the Attorney General had sniffed out our trail, the IRS dispatched a Mr. Milton Schreiber for an audit, initiating proceedings that dragged out for two years and cost us over $15,000 in legal fees and the agonizing hours of assembling documents, attending conferences, preparing briefs — all the tedious paper-consuming accumulations conventional to administrative, legal, and paralegal processing.

Mr. Schreiber entered our office early one day in January 1979 for the crucial audit, but he didn't stay long. In preparation for his visit, we had spread out on the table an enormous pile of relevant books, ledgers, time sheets, minutes, cancelled checks, and bank statements; but within a few minutes, Schreiber's eagle eye had spied out his prey. "What's this?" he asked, zeroing in on references to the AUD Steel Election Projects. We explained, or tried to. In one leap of instantaneous analysis, he had already reached a confident conclusion: Our projects, he insisted, were suspect because they supported the candidacy of Edward Sadlowski for Steelworkers president. Our aim, we explained, was not to support the candidate but to defend his right to a fair election and thereby to protect the right of steelworkers to choose their own leaders in honest balloting. When the ACLU defended the right of Nazis to march, we said, it was not defending Nazism. When it defended the right of Communists to get on the ballot, it was not defending Communism. Similarly, when AUD supported the rights of the candidate, it was not supporting his candidacy for office, etc. etc. etc. But he wasn't listening. Not to be confused by facts, everything was already clear to him. That ended the fleeting "audit" and he left, satisfied to remain unsatisfied.

On February 27, 1979, he sent us his formal 2-page "statement of facts and issues" to be forwarded to the IRS National Office for "technical advice." In a letter to the IRS in Washington, I wrote, "What makes this ill-founded finding of 'fact', and this biased framing of the 'issue' somewhat puzzling, even disquieting, is its remarkable similarity, almost identity, to one baseless charge among others levelled by the United Steelworkers of America against the Association for Union Democracy and several foundations in a suit which is still pending in Federal District Court in New York. This suit is a harassing retaliation against the Association for Union Democracy for its activities for a fair and legal election of Steelworkers officers...The difference between supporting democratic rights and supporting candidates or causes is well known...Mr Schreiber ...adamantly resisted that distinction..."

The issue as he framed it was loaded: "Whether the organization's participation in the Steelworkers' election constituted the defense of 'human and civil rights secured by law'...and whether the organization is serving private rather than public interests in its support of the Sadlowski candidacy for international president of the United Steelworkers of America." We were given ten days in which to challenge Schreiber's finding of facts and his formulation of the issue, which I did in a detailed reply submitted to the IRS national office. But that was only the beginning. Gordon Haskell and I were now summoned to a meeting with IRS representatives in Washington, set for July 11, 1979.

We didn't realize it right away, but after conferring with people expert in IRS and non-profit law (we were steered to them by that wonderful, ubiquitous Joe Rauh) we learned that it would be foolhardy to proceed without expert counsel. The reality, they said, was that an IRS notice to appear was almost always a sign that the IRS had already decided on an adverse determination and was simply going through due process formalities.

Tax-exempt status was at stake and with it the very existence of the Association for Union Democracy. Foundations invariably require IRS tax-exempt status before making grants. It is difficult enough for AUD, even with tax-exemption, to find willing foundation donors for so unfashionable a cause as union democracy; without it we would be dead. And so, again with the help of Joe Rauh, AUD retained the services of the firm of Caplin and Drysdale who assigned two attorneys, Tom Troyer and Frank Chapper, to the case. They were tops in the field and did an impressive job. One flaw, however. We had to come up with an initial payment of $10,000, for the firm, an inconsequential token payment; for us a small fortune. (Later, we came up with $5,000 more in monthly installments paid over a four-year period. They were worth every penny and more.)

In fact, we didn't have $10,000. To the rescue came Bob Scrivner of the Rockefeller Family Fund, one of the few foundation directors who fully understood what we were doing and knew it was important. Whenever I would express gratitude, he would say, "Don't thank us. We thank you for the great work you are doing." The RFF came through with a grant of $10,000 to cover the first fee installment. (When Bob died of cancer a few years later, still young, it was a terrible loss for AUD.)

In Washington on July 11, we got the bad news, worse than we thought. Leon Kaplan and Edwin Brown of the IRS informed us that the critical decisions were a fait accompli. The service had already made two determinations that fatally affected AUD. It was a double blow:

IRS regulations did specify that activity in defense of "human and civil rights secured by law" was one valid basis for tax-exempt status. But — and here came the new hook — the provision applies, we were informed, only to "constitutional" rights which derive from the 13th and 14th amendment and not to "statutory" rights which flow from legislation. And since the rights of union democracy were founded in law, the Landrum-Griffin Act (LMRDA), AUD could not pass muster. It was a crabbed ruling, but even that was not all: Under another IRS regulation, tax-exempt status could be conferred only on organizations which serve the broad public interest. But, we were told, the IRS had already decided that Landrum-Griffin rights (to union democracy) serve essentially "private" not public interests.

These, we were told, were already "settled" IRS positions; but before publishing its rulings and making them final, the service was ready to listen to arguments and consider "new information" although, they said, it had already reviewed all relevant court decisions and the legislative history of the Landrum Griffin Act. More meaningless "due process." It looked hopeless. If we wished, we could present a brief. And so we went through the motions.

In my little cabin in the woods, I invested most of that summer compiling the records: AUD's history, our finances, statement of objectives, comments by congressmen on the public interest at stake — at least a hundred convincing (certainly to me) pages. By September, Chapper and Troyer came up with a brilliant 49-page brief addressing every issue raised by the IRS. Our case, I am really convinced (naturally), was overwhelming: the text of the law itself settles the "public interest" dispute when it notes that the law "will afford necessary protection of the rights and interests of employees and the public generally" and the U.S. Supreme Court had noted "Congress emphatically asserted a vital public interest in assuring free and democratic union elections"; the strained distinction between statutory and constitutional rights seemed facially absurd; AUD's board minutes, statement of principles, and practical actions demonstrated AUD's nonpartisanship.

By now, it was obvious that our little AUD was carrying the ball for others. If the dubious distinction between constitutional and statutory rights and between public and private interests could be sustained, the status of a whole army of public interest groups would be undermined along with AUD: environmentalists, peace groups, civil rights advocates, women's groups, and many others. And so, some did back AUD with letters of support to the IRS (but, sadly, no money!) "...no valuable distinction can be drawn," wrote the Council for Public Interest Law, "...between organizations which defend human and civil rights rooted in the Constitution and such rights when they are rooted in the statutes. Defense of such rights all serve the public interest..."

Abruptly, the IRS changed its position. Cogent as our arguments surely were, I doubt if they could have moved the presiding IRS bureaucrats. It is hard to understand how the IRS ever came to its original view. If true believers know that a purple space ship will descend from the skies in a blast of fire and carry votaries up to heaven, I don't think that a 49-page irrefutable scientific treatise could change their minds. To this day, I can't understand what quirk originally motivated the IRS, except a push from the Steelworkers. But it seems clear that more than logical arguments impelled their change of heart. Federal judges made the difference.

In reversing its original stance and clearing AUD, the IRS memorandum noted that its new position was "in accord with the trend of recent court decisions," which rejected the IRS narrow definition of "human and civil rights secured by law." In one of those decisions in December 1979, a Federal District Court in North Carolina upheld a suit by the National Right to Work Committee against the IRS. The IRS had cancelled the NRTW tax-exempt status on grounds similar to those cited against AUD. The court rejected the IRS position and restored the NRTW tax-exempt rights. The NRTW v. IRS case is textbook example of the benefits of democracy. Here was a conservative far-right, anti-union (fill in your own pejoratives) institution, one whose aims run counter to most public interest social movements, certainly counter to AUD; and yet, in defending its own rights it strengthened the democratic rights of its adversaries.

Denouement: And so, more than two years after the IRS first knocked on our door, it decided that AUD's exemption under section 501(c)(3) should not be revoked. It noted that AUD's "activities to insure that the steelworkers election was conducted in a proper fashion, as mandated by Congress in LMRDA, constitute the defense of human and civil rights secured by law...its intent and purpose was to serve the broad public interest of union democracy generally rather than the private interests of any particular candidate for elective office."

Sadlowski's election appeal

Sadlowski observers could monitor the election in only 1,000 of more than 5,000 Steel locals. But it was enough to suggest that something was seriously awry. After going through the motions, futile but requisite, of appealing first to the official tellers committee (administration supporters) and then to the international executive board (his election opponents!) Sadlowski, represented pro bono by Joe Rauh in an appeal to the U.S. Labor Department, challenged the validity of the election and asked that it be declared void. The Department dismissed the appeal and upheld the election, but nothing in its investigation or in its findings can create confidence in the integrity of this election. Quite the contrary. Sadlowski was about to undergo what so many reformers in other unions, earlier and later, experienced: the unpredictable, reluctant, erratic quality of DOL enforcement of its authority under the Labor-Management Reporting and Disclosure Act.

To invalidate a union election under LMRDA standards, it is not enough to demonstrate that the law has been violated during an election. Sadlowski could easily demonstrate a plethora of violations. But before moving to invalidate an election result, the Labor Department must decide whether those violations could have "affected the outcome."

In general, the DOL is most comfortable with simple bean counting. If a candidate has won an election with a majority of, say, 100 votes; and you can prove that 101 votes or more were clearly tainted, that should settle it; because, by discounting those 100 votes, we wipe out the winner's majority. However, suppose those violations involved only 60 votes? If, like the DOL, you simply deducted those 60 votes from the winner, he would still have a 40 vote majority. Election sustained! But, if you not only deducted those 60 suspect votes from the winner but also credited them to the loser, the putative winner would become the actual loser. Deducting 60 from one side and adding 60 to the other shifts the balance by 120 votes, enough to wipe out that original 100 vote majority. That kind of calculation makes sense, because obviously 60 fraudulent votes could have been stolen from one side and shifted to the other, which is precisely the kind of trick those Steelworker insurgents had mentioned back in 1960. But for reasons unknown, the Labor Department rejects that simple calculation.

And there are other serious problems. How can every violation be translated into voting arithmetic? As Paul Levy, asked: If an oppositionist candidate is beaten, how many votes is a punch in the nose worth? And so, in interpreting that magic question, "affected the outcome?" the department has an almost unlimited scope for the exercise of judgement, or imagination.

On June 1,1977 Joe Rauh submitted Sadlowski's appeal to the Labor Department charging widespread fraud. In some of those 1,000 locals where Sadlowski could post observers, he could point to outright fraud, no secret ballot, a few instances of violence against Sadlowski supporters, including one shooting. And assorted other charges.

In rejecting Sadlowski's appeal in an 83-page statement of reasons, the DOL concluded that "On the whole, the election was conducted in accordance with the law and with the union constitution." That confident sounding conclusion conceals a serious defect: by DOL standards of what might "have affected the outcome," a union election can be unfair, undemocratic — even riddled with fraud — and still be "in accordance with the law." A close study of the 83-page document tells us more about the chronic shortcomings of the Labor Department than about the validity of the election.

Attorney Rauh, for Sadlowksi, had proposed that, in investigating the quality of the election, the department require every local to answer a detailed questionnaire. The department turned him down, arguing that "the questionnaire method would make it impossible to complete the investigation and evaluate the results within the 60 days permitted by the act." But in the end, with the agreement of the union, the department devoted not 60 days but five months to a limited investigation. The limited nature of the investigation was not its only defect; the department's analysis of what it discovered was curiously warped. The investigation covered only 712 of the union's 5,125 locals. Those locals, with a membership of 351,000 of the 1,400,000 Steelworkers membership, had cast 30% of the total vote. Locals which cast over 2/3 of all the votes were never covered by DOL investigators. (Because of assorted complexities, the DOL did not take Canadian votes into account. These figures relate only to votes cast in the United States.)

When the department completed its intricate system of counting and evaluating ballots it estimated that 17,096 of McBride's U.S. margin could have been affected. Not enough, it concluded, to affect the outcome, because McBride still enjoyed a comfortable 27,730 margin even after deducting that suspect 17,096. On that basis it concluded: "These figures demonstrate to the satisfaction of the Department that the violations which occurred could not have affected the outcome of the election in the United States." It was a curious conclusion.

The DOL had investigated locals with only 30% of the vote. If 17,096 votes out of 30% were suspect then, at that rate, 56,996 of 100% of the votes could have been tainted, enough by far to put McBride's whole margin into question. But Labor Department arithmetic did not allow for that kind of obvious extrapolation. It was satisfied, after an inspection of only 30% of the votes, that the whole election was "in accordance with the law."

What is involved here is not only strange arithmetic but a fatally flawed basic standard. It may not be possible to complete a thorough investigation of every phase of an election on so vast a scale. If, however, a substantial part of an election reveals serious defects, then the democratic quality of the entire election could be called into question. But the DOL process, with its emphasis on bean counting, does not even permit raising so fundamental a question.

Appealing to Federal Court

Joe Rauh sought recourse in Federal court; but it was an appeal doomed in advance, not because the legal and factual arguments were weak or unpersuasive, but simply because the legal standard for successfully challenging a DOL election decision in federal court is difficult to meet, except in extraordinary circumstances.

In 1975, in **Dunlop v. Bachowski,** the Supreme Court held that federal judges could review DOL decisions in union election cases but only narrowly when it held "...the court's review should be confined to examination of the 'reasons' statement [of the Labor Department], and the determination whether the statement without more, evinces that the [Labor] Secretary's decision is so irrational as to constitute the decision arbitrary and capricious." For an appeal to succeed, therefore, it is not enough to prove that a DOL election finding is wrong, or that its investigation misjudged or ignored certain basic facts. On those grounds, the Sadlowski appeal presented a formidable case. But to prevail, Sadlowski had to convince the court that the DOL finding was not only wrong but "irrational," a standard of proof that can be met only in extreme cases.

In his appeal to the federal court, Joe Rauh could point to inconsistencies in the DOL investigation of Sadlowski's complaint, its probe of only 712 of over 5,000 locals, its refusal to extrapolate the results in those 712 locals to the whole return, its odd arithmetic, the limited nature of the investigation. All in vain. Not enough to meet the Bachowski "irrational" test.

The District Court held that "the entire record in this case satisfies the court that the Secretary's decision was not arbitrary and capricious and was within the bounds of his statutory discretion." Right or wrong as law, the decision did not alter the reality. Sadly, the "discretion" of the Labor Department is a treacherous shifting base for the defense of fair union elections.

Chapter 9: Rescuing Democracy in the International Brotherhood of Electrical Workers

Spurred into action after the miners rebellion and still under the influence of the spirit of the sixties, Dan Boswell, a young electrician, won election in 1977 as an insurgent to the executive board of his Local 164 in New Jersey. Within a few years, he had helped plant, or replant, the seeds of democracy in the International Brotherhood of Electrical Workers.

Chapter 2, above, quotes some of the egregious clauses of the IBEW constitution which, in the days before the LMRDA, subjected members to expulsion for meeting in caucuses or campaigning for office in their local unions. After the LMRDA, the IBEW made a few cosmetic changes in formulation, hoping to pass muster under the new law, and it continued to discipline hundreds of members as though there had been no change.

Three and a half years of LMRDA pass. In the April 1963 issue of its *Electrical Worker*, the IBEW boasted that the U.S. Labor Department had found the union in total compliance, not a single violation of the LMRDA. That same year, *Union Democracy in Action* reported on these patently illegal provisions of the IBEW constitution. Nothing happened for 15 years. The constitution remained intact and enforced until at last, at last, in 1978 came the impulse to change. Early that year, Boswell managed to reach AUD. At the time he was 33, married and had two kids, one 10 and the other 8. In the 1960s, he had been active in the civil rights and antiwar movements. After graduating from high school, he entered the IBEW apprenticeship program, joined the union, and continued his schooling at night. Now Boswell had problems at his IBEW Local 164 in New Jersey. An electrician and local member for 14 years, his troubles began in 1977 after he was elected to the local executive board. In defiance of the local leadership, he opposed ratification of a contract; he criticized the handling of money by incumbents, and charged the officials with favoritism in job referrals. He faced trial on the familiar charges of slander. Boswell's journey to AUD followed a familiar path. Then and in the years that followed, referrals to AUD came from labor educators, union members, lawyers, reporters, government enforcement agencies like the NLRB and Labor Department, and even from high-ranking union officers ("but don't mention my name".)

At the time, his colleague in Local 164, Larry Casey, was taking a college course in labor relations where he got AUD literature from his instructor. With Boswell facing charges, Casey gave him a copy of *Union Democracy Review* discussing the LMRDA Bill of Rights.

Boswell left our office armed with the first installment of our book, "Democratic Rights for Union Members", which explained that the federal court decision in *Salzhandler* barred unions from disciplining members on slander charges. In the IBEW, charges against local officers — executive board members are classified as officers — are tried not before a local trial committee but before an international vice president who serves as judge and jury and imposes sentence. Boswell mounted so effective a defense that he beat the charges. Still the verdict was ominous. J.J. Barry, then vice president and later IBEW president, ruled in effect: not guilty this time, but you'd better not do it again. It was only a brief respite. Boswell simply would not be silenced. Within a few months, he faced a new set of charges and was found guilty, removed from office, fined $1,500, and barred from running for office for five years. He returned to AUD for help.

The charges, the verdict, the penalties, and the union constitutional provisions on which they rested were all obviously illegal. Boswell's rights were clearly protected by LMRDA Title I, the Bill of Rights for Union Members. But there is a catch to it. These putative rights are enforceable only by private suit. If you can't afford a lawyer or can't find one willing to take on a powerful union, or one ready to risk representing you pro bono or on a contingency basis, your rights, valuable in theory, are worthless in practice.

The IBEW possesses talented attorneys and a multi-million dollar defense fund available, if need be, to "defend" itself against its own members. Boswell's resources were what he earned by the hour as an electrician. Nevertheless, he was ready to take on the IBEW. And not only for himself. He agreed that if he could get into court, he would not be satisfied simply with his personal exoneration but would attack the repressive clauses of the union constitution and insist that they be voided.

But first we had to find him a lawyer. Ever since I ran across those astounding provisions of the IBEW constitution, I had been hoping to find some way to challenge them. At last, opportunity knocked. Here was a courageous unionist. But where was the attorney who could confront this tough union? A sympathetic but small and struggling law firm in New Jersey warily agreed to take the case on a contingency basis, but it quickly became evident that the firm simply didn't have the resources to outlast the IBEW. It could easily be bankrupted by the process of depositions, discovery, procedural ploys — the whole whirling dervish rigmarole of protracted litigation that the IBEW with its swollen defense fund could comfortably afford. It was discouraging, but just when it looked bleakest, came a stroke of luck.

Just then, a big, well-endowed law firm, Kramer, Levin, Nesser, Kamin, and Soll, anxious to contribute its tithe to the public interest, was looking for a good charity case to handle pro bono. Robert Mass, a young attorney assigned to finding a case with social significance, sought advice from his friend, George Kennar, a staff attorney at the New York Civil Liberties Union, an AUD supporter, who referred him to our office. By sheer coincidence, just when Mass called, we were ready. "We have just the case," I told him. A legal defense of Boswell would not only afford justice to one unfortunate victim, it could reform the IBEW constitution and bring a measure of democracy for thousands of electricians in one of the country's major unions. We convinced Mass, armed him with documents; and he, in turn, convinced the law firm to take it on. And so Boswell got top notch, well-financed representation. Rob Mass and Susan Gibraltar, both young junior attorneys at the firm were assigned to the case. They filed suit in New Jersey federal district court on August 24,1979 and proceeded to litigate the union lawyers into the ground. The federal district judge in this case was the no-nonsense Frederick B. Lacey. (After leaving the bench some years later, he was appointed the chief monitoring officer in the government's RICO suit against the Teamsters' union.)

As the case wended its weary way — depositions, discovery, procedural arguments — and it became clear that the disciplinary victimization of Boswell was an arrant violation of the LMRDA, the IBEW backtracked and proposed to settle by agreeing to almost all of Boswell's demands: it offered to reinstate Boswell, to compensate him generously for all the trouble, to cover court costs and pay heavy fees to his attorneys. However, Boswell insisted that the union revise its constitution to eliminate those repressive provisions. On that, the IBEW was adamant. If the constitution remained intact, every victimized IBEW member would have to find an attorney and go through the same rigmarole. Most members, discouraged by the costly burdens of litigation, would be wary of criticizing the incumbents and, if disciplined, would be forced passively to accept their fate. If the constitution were democratized, dissent would be encouraged and defensive litigation would be fairly certain of success. If Boswell had agreed to the settlement and taken his money and run, he and his attorneys would have avoided the nerve-wracking uncertainties of continued trial and, with certitude, emerged richer and vindicated. But Boswell would not be bought off; he rejected the proposed settlement, insisting that the union amend its constitution to let democracy breathe in the IBEW.

Aware now that the penalties imposed on Boswell, the individual, were likely to be overturned, the IBEW changed its tune. Insisting that the discipline of Boswell was an individual case, an aberration, not part of a pattern, its attorney argued that this single instance of discipline, even if improper, could not justify a judicial order forcing the union to alter its rules. But AUD was already familiar with life in the IBEW. Over the years, we had received complaints from electricians in one local and then another, and another. Holding firm, Mass demanded access to the union's records. The judge ordered the union to produce its files on discipline; when it failed to comply, he gave Boswell, or his representatives, two weeks to inspect the records at union headquarters. It was a limited right restricted to appeals taken by IBEW members between 1970 and 1980 against penalties imposed under only four constitutional clauses; and the job had to be completed in those ten working days. The records were scattered all over the United States and Canada in 12 separate IBEW district offices. Robert Mass and Susan Gibraltar for the Kamin law firm were able to cover the New York IBEW office. But how to cover all those other places and all that distance in only ten days?

At that moment, AUD had money enough to hire Phyllis Curott, then a young law student, to act as legal coordinator. From the list of AUD supporters, she recruited volunteers in other parts of the country, a mixed bag of young attorneys, some students, all comparatively inexperienced. Of the 12 districts, we covered nine in the United States and one in Canada. But the records in two districts, which could not be covered, remained unopened.

Even that limited search by inexperienced volunteers under time pressure revealed that in those 10 district in that ten-year period, there had been 705 "cases" of appeals under just those four repressive constitutional clauses. That was obviously enough to convince any impartial observer, certainly the judge, that the suspension of Boswell was indeed part of a pervasive pattern.

These were 705 cases, not individuals; in some cases several members were victimized; (For example: In one 1980 case, Local 213 in Vancouver BC, at least six members were fined and suspended.) And these 705 cases involved only appeals from convictions which is why their records ended up in district union offices. But for every appeal there were likely to be several other convictions that were never appealed because the victims would have yielded without appeal, knowing that an appeal could be pointless or even fearing additional retaliation. Records of cases which were never appealed never reached the district offices and so were immune to our investigation. And cases in the two district which could not be covered remained unlisted. Appeals under three other repressive provisions were never tallied.

Taking all these facts into account, we estimated roughly that perhaps 3,000 or more individual electricians had been illegally disciplined in ten years for exercising their lawful democratic rights. There was persuasive evidence of a widespread pattern of repression. But these figures also indicated that the impulse toward democracy, the determination to speak out, was also widespread. Boswell's suit aimed to liberate and legitimize that impulse.

Meanwhile, AUD was busy with its normal affairs which meant trying to raise money to stay alive. In one fund appeal letter in late 1980 we made reference to "Electricians who are standing up for basic civil liberties in their electrical workers union (IBEW)" On the reverse side of the letter, several notables endorsed our appeal, including Joe Rauh who promptly received an indignant letter from Laurence J. Cohen, IBEW chief counsel:

"This reference implies that there is some general movement among members of the IBEW who feel a need to stand up for their basic civil liberties, who are otherwise denied them by the IBEW. I am not aware of any such movement or general trend within the IBEW and feel that the reference in your letter, particularly in view of its context, is quite misleading. Specifically, I am aware of only two pending cases, one involving two individuals, and the other one individual, challenging internal union discipline. And, in both of those cases, you may be interested to know that the discipline which allegedly violated those members' rights of free speech was reversed on appeal within the IBEW."

(Incidentally, the letter also packed a not so subtle threat to Rauh: "I am particularly troubled in view of the fact that you are representing the IBEW, along with other unions, in the pending Right-to-Work case." It was no idle comment. Rauh was, in fact, later dropped as their attorney.)

By this time, we had the results of our court-authorized investigation and forwarded to Rauh the documented record of 705 cases. If it was true that the IBEW's own lawyer knew of only "two pending cases," that fact demonstrates how skillfully the union had kept cases **out of court** whenever the victims seemed likely to get legal backing.

They tried to do the same to Boswell but failed. All charges against Boswell were sustained by international vice president J.J. Barry on February 28, 1979. Six months passed until August 24 when Boswell's complaint was finally filed in federal court. Thereupon the union tried to backtrack. On October 24, the union informed the judge that the patently illegal charges had been dismissed a week before. But Judge Lacey would be diverted by this ploy and the case continued.

Back in court, it became obvious that the IBEW was determined to resist constitutional changes that could unleash a tide of free expression, a stance which threatened tedious time-consuming procedures up and down and into the Supreme Court. But it was not to be; the IBEW, with all its expensive legal talent, managed to trip over itself. In the course of a deposition, Boswell's attorney, Rob Mass, asked Charles Pillard, IBEW international president, what advice he had received from the union's attorneys. Had he been advised that the discipline inflicted on Boswell had been illegal? It was a critical question. Huge sums in punitive damages could be at stake. If the union's action against Boswell was deliberately malicious, that fact would weigh heavily against it.

Pillard refused to answer on the ground of attorney-client privilege. Back for more proceedings and arguments in court. In the end, Judge Lacey rejected the attorney-client claim. Holding that union members had the right to know what advice their lawyer was giving to their elected officers, he ordered Pillard to answer the question. The union stonewalled. It soon became obvious that the issue was so sensitive that the union had no intention of complying. The lawyer asked for a postponement, then an extension, and once again until Judge Lacey become so impatient that he imposed a "final" deadline for the union to conform. When that day arrived and they were not yet ready to reply, Lacey told the attorney to come to the next session with his toothbrush, suggesting a possible jail sentence for contempt.

That did it. The union never did reply to the question. Instead it capitulated. The IBEW was ordered to delete three offending clauses from its constitution and to amend four others to bring them in line with federal law. It reinstated Boswell with full rights, paid him damages, and compensated his attorneys.

It was a total victory except for one detail. Both sides agreed not to reveal the terms of settlement. But everything was on the public record, except the financial figures. AUD, not bound by any settlement, publicized the facts, then reported by the Bureau of National Affairs.

The settlement was finalized on March 12, 1981, but it took much longer — six years! — to dig out the money details. In 1982, IBEW member Jack Mallick asked the union how much the case had cost. Information refused. He died before he got any reply, but Attorney Paul Alan Levy, suing on his behalf and other complainants, finally got the answer. In that single case, for IBEW attorney fees, for Boswell, and for his attorney, the cost ran to about $600,000. One wonders how vast a sum the IBEW has spent over the years to suppress the rights of its own members!

The fruit of victory came swiftly. From that point on, it was open season for publishing independent rank and file newsletters. As the months passed, AUD learned of the formation of independent caucuses, equipped with their publications, in IBEW locals around the country. What had once been a penal offense, had become a normal aspect of IBEW life.

Up to 1996, the IBEW president and other top international officers had been elected at conventions **by openly recorded vote** of delegates from locals. As in most unions, local delegates, leery of offending the international office, usually remain docile and malleable at public convention sessions. Conventions assemble only once every five years, but the international office can reward friends and punish enemies every day. But occasionally things do get out of hand. IBEW vice presidents, on the other hand, were elected by the delegates from their respective regions and **by secret ballot,** which allows for an occasional upset. If they don't know how you vote, they can't retaliate.

Normally no one bothered to run for president. But in 1982, Charles Delgado decided to run for IBEW international president against Charles Pillard, the incumbent. Delgado joined the union in 1955 and had been business manager of the 1,000-member Local 527 in Galveston TX since 1970. He had to possess unusual talents; he had been a critic of the international administration in all those years and survived. His home town credentials were impressive: president of the county AFL-CIO Council and a member of the Democratic Party state executive committee.

In his youth, he admired Saul Alinsky, the militant community organizer. In his declaration of candidacy, Delgado introduced himself as a "progressive candidate" calling for "democracy in our union." A campaign brochure mailed to all locals noted that "he can consistently be found on the side of the consumer, working people, minorities, women's rights, and the poor on all issues." He advocated the right of locals to negotiate their own contracts — with international assistance but not at its dictation. The international leaders, he wrote, interpret the union constitution as though it "was written to serve the international office **against** the members ...I will point out the many abuses of power by our officers using the constitution as their club."

He was encouraged by the initial response from local leaders: no hostility and lots of sympathy; but he had a tough problem. He knew that winning was a long shot, but he hoped, at least, to get his full support recorded; and that was impossible unless the delegates, vulnerable to retaliation, could be guaranteed a secret ballot.

The IBEW constitution required the endorsement of only five locals to begin the process of initiating a referendum on changing the union constitution, a deceptively simple provision as events soon demonstrated. The five required endorsements came quickly. By early April, 170 locals had concurred, an astounding defiance by the locals of the top officialdom. "I have been advised by several locals," wrote Delgado, "that the international office…exerted a tremendous amount of pressure…to suppress our petition drive."

But the referendum was not to be. Locals propose; the international executive council disposes, which is its right under the constitution. It announced "that this referendum would not serve the best interests of the IBEW, and therefore the council has declined to submit the proposed amendment to a referendum vote."

At the convention, eleven locals proposed to replace the open roll call by a secret ballot election. In an open vote, the motion failed. In the openly recorded voting for president, Delgado was defeated; nevertheless, 11% of the delegates publicly declared their support for this insurgent. The last time an opposition candidate had run for president was 1974 when A.J. White eked out 1% of the votes. Delgado lost a reform battle; but he paved the way. Fourteen years later, it was a different story.

Mike Lucas proved to be an even more formidable threat to the established officialdom when, on the eve of the 1996 convention, he announced his candidacy against J.J. Barry, the man who took over as president after Pillard retired. Lucas was well known and respected throughout the union. At 50, he had served for 30 years, as an international representative, then director of organizing, and up to September 1995, as executive assistant to the international president. As organizer, he was a prominent advocate of "salting," a plan to infiltrate nonunion shops with IBEW members.

Like Delgado in 1982, Lucas knew that delegates would be afraid to vote for him in an open ballot. Sentiment for a secret ballot was rising rapidly; eighty locals called for a membership referendum on the issue. The executive council stalled by referring the question to the coming convention, but they realized that a secret ballot posed a real danger to their position.

Apart from Lucas's challenge, there were contested elections for four of the twelve vice presidencies and in six of the nine executive council districts, all by secret ballot. There was no formal opposition slate; but two incumbents, a vice president and an executive council member, openly supported Lucas.

With discontent running high, Lucas had a real chance to pull off a spectacular upset **IF** he could present his views on the convention floor and **IF** he was guaranteed a secret ballot. His supporters planned their strategy accordingly. But the administration concocted a deft plot to bury his chances:

The convention opened at 9:00 AM in Philadelphia on September 16 with delegates from 867 locals representing 718,462 members. A mood-lulling hour and a half was consecrated to the usual boilerplate greetings from notables, a marine marching band, and inspirational entertainment. Then, with the delegates lulled into inattention, the real business of the convention began at about 10:30. Ordinarily, IBEW elections were held late in the sessions, after main business had been completed; and so no one was prepared for the extraordinarily swift movement of events this time.

The report of the rules committee was so routinely adopted that no one noticed the little joker providing vaguely for the election of top officers as a "special order of business"; but the delegates abruptly discovered what they had inadvertently voted for. As soon as the rules were adopted, Chairman Barry announced, without advance warning, that the elections would begin; he reminded the delegates that a secret ballot was not required; he turned the chair over to VP Ed Hill who called on a delegate to nominate J.J. Barry for international president. By now, the Lucas forces realized what was happening — no previous discussion of issues, no secret ballot — Duane Moore, who had been slated to nominate Lucas, announced that because Lucas had no chance to present his views on anything, he was withdrawing his candidacy. "This is a sham, not a democracy," he concluded.

Somewhat flustered, the administration people stalled the proceedings while they conferred and then announced that, whether Lucas liked it or not, his name would be forced onto the ballot. Convention business, by this time, was only a half-hour old, but the election for president was effectively over. In the recorded non-secret balloting, Barry was declared elected with 587,263 weighted delegate votes. Lucas, the unnominated candidate-despite-himself, received 117,381 unsolicited votes, about 16.5% of the total.

The IBEW administration could hardly rest easy with their victory which was not as reassuring as the voting arithmetic might suggest. Delegate votes were weighted according to their local membership. Of the

704,644 cast, a majority was 352,322. Even though Lucas had withdrawn as a candidate and so freed his supporters from any obligation, he received 117,381 votes from independent-minded delegates willing to vote openly for him, even in an obviously hopeless situation. If he had remained in the race, he would surely have received the votes of additional delegates, more prudent, who felt it was pointless to stick out their necks in a lost cause. **Even without a secret ballot, his total in a clear contest could have reached close to 200,000.** With a secret ballot, and all delegates free to vote their convictions and express their desire for change, it would have been a cliffhanger.

In their fear of a secret ballot, the administration's misgivings were well founded; they were in real danger of defeat. That danger became apparent when the disputed issue of secret ballot finally reached the floor. The convention law committee recommended rejection of three local resolutions in favor of the secret ballot. But the delegates voted down the committee by roll call vote of 388,948 to 325,432 — in effect an endorsement of secrecy in voting. Two days later, in accordance with convention rules, the committee brought the proposal back to the floor, this time without recommendation. The delegates held firm. No need for a roll call. A clear majority raised hands for the new system. The battle for a secret ballot which Delgado began in 1982 had finally triumphed over the opposition of the IBEW establishment, but too late to help Lucas in 1992.

Electricians are highly skilled and proud of their trade. In my forty years with AUD, I have been in touch with hundreds of IBEW electricians, independent-minded and jealous of their rights as unionists and as citizens. I note with admiration and not in derogation that this union is rich with jailhouse lawyers. Among them are unionists who know the law and how to use it. Some have become lawyers or paralegals. When Forrest Darby, member in Las Vegas, objects to federal court decisions, he sometimes writes in protest to the judges, letters that are well-reasoned and persuasive, to me if not to the judges; and, unlike the Herzog character in Saul Bellow's novel, Darby mails those letters.

A great hope for a resurgence of union democracy in the construction trades lies with the members of the International Brotherhood of Electrical Workers. It is precisely that potential which makes the top IBEW officialdom so uneasy and so dependent upon narrow bureaucratic devices to solidify their control.

Chapter 10: In the construction trades

All the obstacles to a robust democracy in the one-party union state are compounded in the building and construction trades where the hiring system and the transient nature of work make free expression a risky business.

John Kuebler started working in construction as a truck driver in 1942, hauling concrete to the building sites. A union man, a member of Teamsters Local 282 in Long Island, he told his story in February 1986 at the Citizens Hearings on Union Democracy v. Corruption in the Construction Industry, an event sponsored by the Association for Union Democracy. In 1975, Kuebler insisted on processing an overtime grievance which won $15,000 in back pay for a group of drivers, only to find, he said, that "the arbitration award was overturned." That's when his troubles began. For ten months, October 1976 to August 1977, the company had no work for him; and the union would not help. He joined up with FORE, an opposition reform group, (Fear Of Retaliation Ends, the name was more hope than reality!)

He finally found himself a new union job in 1977, but it didn't last long. "The shop steward told me they were out to get me, they were going after me in my pocket." In November 1977, the steward falsified his work record to indicate that he was not available for work on schedule and he was fired. "The union secretary treasurer said he wouldn't touch this with a ten-foot pole; he wouldn't take it to arbitration, he wouldn't represent me, nothing...People I've known for ten years apologize and say, 'Johnny, you know I can't give you a job' That's it; there's no way I could get a job through Local 282."

His ordeal was part of a pattern. As he explained: "The contracts were not being enforced. The stewards were getting special benefits for not enforcing the contracts. There were nonunion employees on jobs, and the employers were not making payments to the pension and welfare funds for them." About the steward who falsified his work record, he said, "He's still in office, gets a company car, makes $75,000 a year, never works, although he does come in to get his paycheck."

Kuebler found his way to Burton Hall, ace union democracy attorney, who, at his customary rates ranging from zero to contingency fees, filed charges with the NLRB against the union and company. By 1978, an NLRB administrative law judge ruled that the steward had in fact falsified Kuebler's work record. For a long time that administrative victory led nowhere. The NLRB let the company off the hook, but continued the case against Local 282 — and continued and continued and continued. Kuebler was telling this story nine years after his 1977 firing and at that point the case was still ricochetting through the NLRB. By that time, attorney Dan Clifton, for the Hall firm, had taken over the case.

Time marches on. FORE runs opposition slates against local president John Cody in three elections 1975-1981 reaching a high point of 42% in one election but never a majority. In 1984, FORE folded, but its battles were not in vain. The group exposed fraud in the local's pension fund, prompting law enforcement agencies to intervene. Cody went to jail on assorted corruption charges. Later, his successor followed him into prison, and a federal court imposed a trusteeship over the local. During all this time, Kuebler remained blacklisted; the NLRB found the local guilty and ordered back pay to Kuebler and one fellow victim. The two men offered to settle for a token payment of $450 each; but the union refused and continued to resist, appealing through the NLRB and the courts, including a pointless appeal to the U.S. Supreme Court. Having lost all the way on the principles, the union continued to resist through a second round of procedures and appeals on the extent of its financial liability. By 1989 — 12 years after the original firing — the case was still cooking. The union now owed Kuebler $150,000 in back pay, interest, and costs for a case it could have settled for $900.

On June 12,1989, Kuebler died of cancer at the age of 66. It took another round of litigation before his heirs got the money. But Kuebler himself never collected a dime. Was his experience an aberration, a curio? Not at all. It tells us something about life at the NLRB and in the construction trades. If there was anything unusual about this case it is that Kuebler was lucky. Unlike most victimized construction workers, he was able to recruit competent and dedicated workers' rights attorneys.

Union jobs in the construction industry are good jobs with wage rates far above those in manufacturing. The Bureau of Labor Statistics reported the average hourly earnings in all construction, union and nonunion, at $17.54 in March 2000. But it was much higher for union workers in a big city like New York where unions reported that the rate for unionized general building laborers ranged from $19.50/hr for interior demolition workers to $36.40 for mason tenders, including fringes. According to the BLS the annual earnings of all construction workers was $33,346 in 1998.

True, periods of feast are followed by famine, but if a journeyman can work steadily over the years, he can keep his family in good shape. (To that "he," we must now add "she," because women are slowly fighting their way into the trades) Many are not only well-paid but highly skilled, like the electricians and carpenters. Like the operating engineers who run the bulldozers, pile drivers, and backhoes. With good money and valuable skills, comes a sense of pride and an expectation of respect. And so arises the stereotype of the happy hardhat: narrow minded, willing to overlook any injustice, tolerate any corruption, any misdeed so long as they are taken care of. "Who cares if crooks get theirs so long as I get mine." But it is a myth because there is another, more accurate, story.

If you sit in the office at AUD, read the mail, answer the phone, pick up the E-mail, you are soon alerted to the other side. The largest single group of AUD supporter are construction workers. Over the years, AUD has heard from members of virtually every construction union in the United States and Canada. Electrician members of a hundred or more locals of the IBEW. Carpenters in New York, California, Boston, Texas, Michigan, Washington, and more. Laborers all over the country. Roofers in Pennsylvania. Plumbers, Asbestos Workers, Bricklayers, Painters. Everything from individual reports of blacklisting and stolen elections to reports of organized movements for decency and democracy. The battle of operating engineers in Ohio continued for more than 20 years.

The pay is fine, but the work is dangerous. In 1996, 291 construction laborers alone were killed in industrial accidents, the fourth highest of all occupations, exceeded only by sales occupations (where homicide was the leading cause), truck drivers, and farmers. Truck drivers led the pack with 785 killed, but in the **rate** of fatalities per 100,000 workers, construction laborers topped the truck drivers by 35.7 to 26.

Non-fatal work illnesses and injuries show a similar pattern. In 1998, according to the BLS, construction workers suffered 8.8 illnesses and injuries for every 100 workers, while the level in all private industry was 6.7 and in mining, 4.9.

But this is only cold arithmetic. Follow the daily newspapers and read about giant cranes that collapse and crush those operating engineers; scaffold cables that break, killing painters and bricklayers; winds that carry away ironworkers; sand pits give way smothering the diggers; old buildings whose crumbling floors and walls trap demolition workers; huge chemical drums whose residue of fumes suffocate the cleaners. In summer they work under the burning rays of sun, in winter they freeze. Look carefully when they repair the concrete and power and pipe lines on your streets and see how the pneumatic drills and hammers shake their guts apart.

In a world of ill-paid supermarket checkout clerks and fast-food dispensers, workers compete fiercely for high-wage construction jobs. But even for skilled crafts, there is no job security. Work is transient, a job assignment may last for weeks, for months, even — praised be the Lord — for a year or two. But sooner or later — usually sooner — the job is completed, the road built, the building completed, the renovation done, and you must look for another. Construction workers no sooner start working on one job than they worry where the next will come from. Part of the workforce are travelers, the transients who move from city to city to follow the big jobs. But in their pursuit of work, they pay a price: shifting from place to place, they often fail to accumulate pension credits.

Control over the distribution of jobs is a key to the evils in construction. In manufacturing, in public employment, in most other industries, unions win seniority rights to protect workers from discrimination in layoffs, rehiring, and sometimes promotions. Nothing like that in construction. The notion that construction unions have fastened an iron control over work is a fiction. In many construction unions, like the plumbers and painters in New York, union workers hustle for jobs on their own. Some unions, like the IBEW, maintain hiring halls; members may not solicit their own jobs but must take job assignments from the halls. Some union contracts require employers to hire part of their work force out of the halls, say, 25% or 50% but permit them to hire the rest at will. But in most cases, union construction contracts give employers the unilateral, unqualified right to reject any applicant whether dispatched from the hall or not. A model IBEW contract puts it short and simple, "The Employer shall have the right to reject any applicant for employment." One Operating Engineers contract: "The Employer shall retain the absolute and unconditional right to reject any workman referred by the Union." The agreement between Ironworkers Local 580 and the Allied Building Metal Industries, 1983-6, goes further, "The Employer shall have the right to discharge any employees whenever he sees fit except stewards as provided for under this contract."

Employers and union officials are known to maintain formal blacklists, listing the names of unionists who are not to be hired. I met one electrician at an AUD conference who had served briefly as an IBEW local business manager in the mid-west, substituting temporarily for the incumbent, his brother-in-law, who was ill. He told me that he attended one meeting of IBEW local business managers in his region where they exchanged the names of electricians whom they labelled troublemakers. Mike Middleton was 45 in 1983, an electrician for 27 years and a member of IBEW Local 640 in Phoenix AZ when he was tipped off that his name was listed on a "do not rehire" list by the Corbin-Dykes Electric Company. Like many IBEW members, he had studied law on his own; later, he worked for a while at a law firm as a paralegal. Using his connections, he managed to get an actual copy of the blacklist circulated among companies in the area, bearing the names of 261 electricians. He was well acquainted with some of the victims, knowing them as good, hard-working, competent craftsmen.

Blacklists can be just as effective without being recorded on paper, as three union plumbers discovered in 1995 when they tried to get work at the Millstone nuclear power plant in Waterford CT where there was plenty of work. When they tried to register for work at the exclusive hiring hall of Plumbers Local 305, which had the jobs under contract, the local business manager, Terry Quinn, refused to let them sign up. He knew them. The three plumbers, Shane Phalen, Mark Cotton, and Donald Fitzgerald, were members of Plumbers Local 86 in Hartford where they had been campaigning against their own business manager, asking annoying questions about hiring practices. At one point, they opposed him in an election. Earlier, they had complained to the NLRB and won a hiring hall case against the local. Their business manager was Pat Quinn, who also happened to be the brother of Terry Quinn, the BA of Local 305. Terry was ready for them when they turned up on his turf looking for work. Not a chance!

With first class legal representation from AUD attorney, Leon Rosenblatt, they complained successfully to the NLRB. The local was ordered to pay them four months back pay and permit them to register. As usual, the NLRB failed to impose punitive damages and offered no compensation for legal fees. So far, so good, but it was the kind of limited remedy that never acts as a deterrent. Unions and employers can lose this kind of case before the NLRB, chalk up the modest penalty as another necessary cost of doing business, and continue to dispose of the next victims as before.

Not satisfied at the NLRB, the three sued in federal court under the LMRDA where the district judge and the jury were easily convinced that the business manager of Local 305 had violated the law's Bill of Rights which protects union members from retaliation for exercising their free speech rights. It seemed obvious — and of course it was — that they had been denied work because they had criticized their business manager. The jury awarded them $500,000 in punitive damagers and legal fees. Now, there was something for union officials to ponder! That kind of penalty should give them pause before doing it again.

But now we come to the curious part. The AFL-CIO Building Trades Department came to the rescue of Local 305. It filed an amicus brief in the U.S. Appeals Court arguing that, despite the Bill of Rights, the LMRDA permitted the officials of one local to blacklist the members of another local! In an expert display of legal nitpicking, the AFL-CIO came up with the saving distraction. The law, it argued, protects "every member of a labor organization": but, it insisted, the three victims were not members of Local 305 and therefore they had no right to sue under the LMRDA. Preposterous? Nevertheless, the Appeals Court bought the argument and reversed the decision of the district court. And that's how it came about that one construction local can blacklist members of any other local without suffering any penalty under the LMRDA.

In the nonunion — really antiunion — sector of the construction industry, the employer retains total domination of the work force, free to hire, fire, and discipline "his" employees and free to pay wages as low as the market will permit. Unionization brings higher wages, better working conditions, pension and insurance benefits, a measure of dignity at work, job rights that are established in written contracts and enforceable — admittedly with difficulty — in courts and before government agencies. The employer is subject to the union contract; the union officialdom should be subject to control by the union membership. The tragedy of unionized construction is that workers' rights vis a vis the employer and their control over their union officials are undermined by a hiring system which eviscerates those rights.

The prevailing labor system which entails continuing insecurity for the worker, the right of employers to reject any applicant, and the control by union officials over job referrals, is ardently defended by both employers and most union officers. For the employer, it guarantees a work force that is restrained from insisting upon its rights, even from insisting upon rights that are clearly written into union contracts. Some contracts do include provisions for a grievance procedure; but in practice these provisions are often meaningless because it is suicidal for any worker to use them. To file a grievance is usually a no-win event. Win or lose, the grievant loses in the end. Workers know they will soon be looking for work. File a grievance or, even worse, win a grievance, and you find that the door to at least one company is now permanently closed. Repeat the process, and mysteriously all doors are closed. Then if you want to work you must leave town, become a traveller, and look for work where no one knows you.

Union officers accept the system of permanent job insecurity for their members because it permits them to build an impregnable patronage power base in their locals by distributing good jobs to a small coterie of grateful cronies. The job system establishes the framework for a collusive arrangement between malleable business agents and obliging employers. At the convention of the Mechanical Contractors Association on February 9, 1984, D. Quinn Mills, then a Harvard professor and a member of the President's Commission on Employment Policy spoke of the facts of life in construction. In its account of his speech, the *Labor Relations Reporter* (115LRR194) wrote:

"Because unions are willing to work out different deals with contractors, there is less of a direct relationship between contract language and what is actually paid on a job. He [Mills] referred to these deals between contractors and the union as 'business agent concessions'"

Writing about the Operating Engineers in Labor USA, Lester Velie reported "A distinguished arbitrator, Professor Nathan Feinsinger of the University of Wisconsin found to his amazement that the contractors had verbal side agreements with the business agents. The contractors argued that these agreements — which softened the terms of the written area contract — had the force of the contract itself."

That innocuous term, "business agents concessions," is an academician's gloss on what is actually a system of mutually supporting collusion between self-serving construction union officials and unscrupulous employers that goes far beyond minor contractual adjustments and ends in turning the construction industry into a cesspool of corruption. Consenting and cooperating employers are permitted to pay wages under scale, to work employees off the books, to cheat on fringe benefit payments, to run double-breasted nonunion shops, to violate safety standards — in sum, to violate union contracts and fair standards in a myriad of imaginative ways. Most of these devices have been revealed in state and federal court records over and again in criminal proceedings related to carpentry, painting, plumbing, window installation, roofing — virtually every aspect of the industry. Every indictment related to construction cites the same kind of pattern of abuse.

In its final report to New York Governor Mario Cuomo on corruption in NYC construction, the Organized Crime Task Force noted, "[A] common form of bribery is contractor payoffs to union officials to obtain 'waivers' of such collective bargaining provisions as hiring hall and union shop agreements, contributions to employee benefit funds, overtime pay, and mandated ratios of union stewards to workers at the site." And, "Contractors defraud the workers' funds by bribing union officials to permit the double-breasted shops and off-the-books payrolls under which contributions to the employee benefit funds are avoided."

In "Gotham Unbound," NYU Law Professor James B. Jacobs reports the same: "...with the power to choose not to enforce costly collective bargaining provisions (e.g., overtime pay, benefit-fund contributions, on-site union stewards), racketeers solicit bribes from unscrupulous contractors." He tells how Laborers' union officials were paid off "to permit the contractors to operate double-breasted shops (i.e., partially nonunion shops}, avoid employment of union shop stewards, pay workers below scale, and forgo employer contributions to the union benefit and welfare funds."

In return for tolerating these "concessions," crooked business agents get money, but simple bribery (or extortion — call it what you will) is not the most depressing aspect of the system. If it were simply a matter of consenting adults conspiring for mutual enrichment it might be shrugged off as a minor social flaw in a society which is inured to far greater injustices and outrages. The exchange of cash is only one element in a degenerate system which debases the democratic quality of construction unionism. In return for not hearing or seeing, business agents are permitted to place their favored supporters on the best jobs. This small group, perhaps 5% of the membership, works steadily, even in the worst of times, accumulates overtime at premium rates, provides a good standard of living and security for their families. That favored group constitutes the business agents' political machine in the local, the battering ram that keeps them in power.

But let us not exaggerate, even that favored stratum enjoys no more than what every working person deserves: a secure job at a decent wage. But in this dog-eat-dog world, and in this industry which is founded on job insecurity, that privilege is a highly sought prize. In return, these are the members who come to most meetings, who vote as instructed, who on trial committees vote to expel critics of the business agents, who raise their hands for the limousines, salaries, and perks.

All this persists in "normal" sectors of the industry. Where organized crime has infiltrated, especially in the big cities, the system degenerates even further. A tiny band really lives high on no-show jobs, perhaps no more than dozen, even fewer. They serve not merely as voting cattle but as the mob's soldiers to enforce discipline by beatings, even murder. George Morrison of Operating Engineers Local 14 in New York was one of the exceptionally lucky ones. In 1985, he was asked by the State Commission on Investigation how he got hired on a construction job that paid him for 24 hours every day, including overtime rates, while he could relax in Acapulco, with a pay stub of $324,378 for the year. He explained that he just happened to be at the right place at the right time.

A hint of how the system works was offered by Douglas McCarron, international president of the Carpenters' union, in a statement before a

House subcommittee on June 25,1998 describing the situation in his union in New York City: "Despite job referral rules under the Consent Decree [of a Federal court] some business agents routinely violated the rules by awarding jobs to their supporters. Members who supported corrupt business agents were paid off by steward appointments, with some stewards assigned to two job with two salaries. Many stewards often go from job to job while other members wait on the out of work list. Furthermore, members who expressed interest in running for district council or local offices were often threatened with injury or prevented from working." And he added: "Many contractors are double-breasted [operate nonunion on some jobs] and others regularly violate the prevailing wage laws ...no doubt the district council and local unions knew of these problem, but intentionally refused to take corrective action."

On blacklisting: "One reason for this lack of a democratic culture is the sole dependence of members on local business agents for their livelihood. Most construction jobs are short and when a job ended, the member depended on his local's business agents to refer him to another job. If the local refused to refer a member for political reasons, or because of the effects of corruption, he faced significant obstacles in finding work. In addition, a local official could use his power with contractors to 'blackball' the member...This control over work assignments has been used to suppress opposition to incumbents."

McCarron made these rare frank disclosures to the House subcommittee because he was under pressure to justify his program of reorganizing his union under a new system of autocratic centralization. But the evils he described are not confined to New York construction or to the Carpenters' union.

Expert confirmation, involuntary but informed, comes from an usual source, from Laurence J. Cohen, the chief counsel of the IBEW, one of our most important construction unions, who inadvertently revealed the facts of life in union hiring halls. It was the byproduct of an intricate case that came before the U.S. Labor Department:

In 1985, members of IBEW Local 212 in Cincinnati were convinced that their business manager was using their hiring hall illegally to reward his friends and punish his critics. When they sought to prefer charges against him for trial in the local, they discovered that the IBEW international constitution does not permit members to charge and try their own local officers in their own locals. Only the international can process charges against local officers and then only before an international vice president.

And so the IBEW, the Labor Department, and the members of Local 212 all faced a perplexing problem because LMRDA Section 401H requires the Labor Department to take action "upon application of any member of a local labor organization" if "the constitution and bylaws of such labor organization do not provide an adequate procedure for the removal of an elected officer guilty of serious misconduct."

At hearings before the Labor Department, IBEW attorney Laurence Cohen, tried to duck the whole subject and convince the department to dismiss the complaint. He noted that the LMRDA section was applicable only to cases of "serious" misconduct. He contended that hiring hall mismanagement could not be considered a serious offense. In a vain effort to buttress his argument and induce the department to dismiss the complaint, he came up with an extraordinary argument, both in oral argument and in a carefully prepared written brief, where he wrote:

"...NLRB cases involving hiring hall violations are a common occurrence in the construction industry. Administering a hiring hall in an industry marked by transient labor and jobs of short duration is not easy under the best of circumstances...Indeed, the volumes of reported Board cases are replete with decisions finding unions in violation of the National Labor Relations Act because of their hiring hall procedures. But does each one of those warrant the removal of the union officials involved? We respectfully suggest that to ask the question is to answer it. If the answer were in the affirmative, officials of the Department of Labor would be doing little else other than racing from one union office to another in such industries as construction, trucking, etc. in order to remove union officials. even if they had the authority to do so...they would have little time to enforce other provisions of the Act, For the above reasons, the ALJ [administrative law judge] should hold that the allegations of hiring hall misconduct are not allegations of 'serious misconduct'"

The depressing system outlined here is not universal in the construction trades. There are enough local unions, and some regions, where unions are conducted with integrity and dedication to union principles to prove that things can be different. But collusion between greedy employers and unscrupulous union officials is so widespread, especially in the big cities, that it sets the tone and creates the image of an industry mired in corruption.

Every few years, as if commemorating a national tradition, the *New York Times* runs a lengthy exposure of corruption in the construction industry. On June 26, 1972, for example, one part of a typical extensive series quoted the president of a large general contracting company who admitted bribing union business agents, "Although he told a reporter details of his payoffs to inspectors and policemen, he refused to provide specifics on the unions. 'If you look into that you'll get a bullet in your back,' he said without a smile."

A valiant effort to confront construction corruption in New York was launched in 1985 after a familiar wave of muckraking stories in the press; Mayor Edward Koch passed the hot potato to Governor Mario Cuomo who passed it on to the state's Organized Crime Task Force, directing it to open an investigation and bring in recommendations. Another in a long line of scandals and investigations!

AUD ran its own public hearings where construction workers and their attorneys told their stories: laborers, painters, tunnel workers, teamsters. We encouraged construction unionists to come forward in the OCTF proceedings. James McNamara, an AUD Director who had headed Mayor Koch's short-lived committee on construction industry employment relations, served as an OCTF staff consultant. Clyde Summers and Michael Goldberg, both AUD leaders, assisted with advice. I met with the governor's committee and its members several times. Still, as much as we cooperated and as much as we hoped, we remained skeptical, reminding the committee that its assignment was only one in a long line of probes into construction corruption which all ended full of sound and fury signifying nothing. After scandals, interrogations, and even prosecutions, everything always settled back into the same old corrupt routine.

No, this time, the task force leaders insisted, it would be different, because they intended, not only to expose the evil, but to produce a program of action that could help eradicate it. Ronald Goldstock, who was OCTF director, picked a great team to run the Construction Industry Project and backed them up at every point. Thomas D. (Toby) Thacher, a straight arrow, served as project director; he kept a sharp focus on the sordid realities; he understood the need for protecting union democracy as a weapon against crooks. He spoke about these things at AUD's open hearings. "There isn't anybody in this room," he said, "who believes that simply locking up people…is going to change a problem that is systemic. It is the system itself which has got to go…We applaud the efforts of this Association for Union Democracy in making the public aware because only through an informed and aroused public can meaningful change take place."

James B. Jacobs, NYU law professor, served as general consultant and wrote the project reports. "Make no mistake," he wrote, "this Final Report and the criminal investigation associated with it, for better or worse, constitute this generation's major attempt at confronting organized crime racketeering in the New York City construction industry. To allow this effort to fizzle out is to postpone serious reform for at least another generation."

The task force did its best. But without control over the levers of power, they could only advocate. For five years, 1985-89, armed with subpoena powers, court-authorized wiretaps, the right to seek indictments, and the support of law enforcement agencies, the project investigated and held hearings. Its final report, a 285-page book was packed with dynamite. (Regrettably, it failed to detonate!)

The report was more than a repetition of the eternal verities of construction corruption. It recommended sweeping measures of reform. Above all, it underscored the limitations of simply exposing scandals. It called for continuing action on many fronts. To strengthen union democracy, it proposed a two-pronged attack, one, based on government action; and the other, private action encouraged by the government. The state government is urged to establish an Office of Union Members Advocate (OUMA) within the State Consumer Protection Board. The OUMA would "pay particular attention to elections and job referral procedures — two areas often subverted by racketeers to punish those who seek to assert their rights or who dare to challenge corrupt practices." In summary the OUMA would: educate unionists of their legal rights; receive complaints from unionists on abuses in their unions; monitor union elections and job referral systems; gather and circulate related information, issue public reports and recommend legislation. Unions would be required to comply with section 105 of the LMRDA which requires them to inform members of the provisions of federal law on union democracy.

Government action, it emphasized, should be bolstered by civil citizen action supported by private philanthropic foundations to establish a "private sector Center for the Study and Advancement of Union Democracy...for which the Association for Union Democracy could well serve as a nucleus...We recommend that the Governor, the Mayor, and leaders of the law enforcement community provide whatever assistance they can in making such a center a reality." (A little report footnote reads "AUD operates on a meager budget... Nevertheless it plays a vigorous and crucial role..." (Unfortunately that "meager budget" persists, before and equally after the report.)

It was a valiant effort; but in the end, the OCTF report disappeared into the file of incinerated memories. It was innovative, imaginative, unprecedented, with great potential. The trouble was that no one in positions of political power cared; there was no concerned voting constituency or generous campaign contributors crying for action against construction corruption; quite the contrary. Once again, despite the efforts of law enforcement authorities, the basic system that leads to construction corruption remains. In "Gotham Unbound," even though author James Jacobs subtitles his 1999 book "How New York City was Liberated from the Grip of Organized Crime, he writes, "...in many of the city's construction trade unions, such as plumbing, painting, and concrete, mobsters continue to suppress union democracy…Even without the presence of mobsters, widespread and sometimes highly organized corruption exists in the construction industry." Cosa Nostra is still there, even though seriously weakened in places. Organized crime remains side by side with not-so-organized crime. Construction remains cursed by corruption because the call, the urgent plea of the OCTF for a continuing, comprehensive program of private and governmental action, a program that would encourage construction workers to take up arms against the evil, a program that would defend their rights in their unions and on the job, went unheeded. To some, the OCTF report became an embarrassment.

The interim report was published by the Cornell University ILR Press, but when state AFL-CIO labor officials denounced the report as "anti-labor," the ILR press prudently bowed out from publishing the final report, which explains why it bears the imprint of the New York University Press. (James Jacobs, the author, is an NYU law professor.)

Governor Cuomo failed to greet the report with delight or rush it out to the public. Instead, he kept it under wraps for months. Although It was completed late in 1989 and was physically available in book form a few months later in 1990, the governor delayed its release and distribution until January 1991. He was running for reelection and obviously found the report no asset. He kept the book under wraps until the election was over. (P.S. He lost anyhow.) A spokesman for Mayor David Dinkins did not think the recommendations were "realistic or doable." In any event, the report disappeared into oblivion, and surplus copies of the report ended at AUD for distribution to our readers. The message ignored in 1990 remains as urgent as ever.

For years, Stephen Gard, professor of law at Cleveland State University, served as pro bono attorney for insurgents in Operating Engineers Local 18 in Ohio, defending them against blacklisting, violence, unfair elections, and deprivation of civil liberties in the union. In a statement before the Senate Labor Committee on September 29, 1984, he summed up the lessons of their experience in the union hiring halls:

"Exclusive union employment referral systems serve an important societal function — especially in those trades where employment is normally seasonal or otherwise of limited duration… Historically the union hiring hall was a socially beneficial replacement for a system which was disorganized, inefficient, and frequently corrupt. Union employment referral systems, however, also have an inherent potential for abuse, favoritism, and corruption…It is intolerable that no federal statute explicitly addresses itself to this problem of discriminatory administration of union employment referral systems...Simply stated, the union member has been abandoned and is friendless precisely when assistance is needed the most. Indeed, we cannot even rely on the union member who has been victimized by a discriminatory union referral system to speak on his own behalf. Often the union member is unaware of the existence of such discrimination because it is practiced so subtly...Even the union member who knows that it is he who is suffering faces a difficult and lengthy battle to prove the discrimination. It will be a rare and courageous individual who actually challenges the union leadership knowing he is dependent upon their good will for future employment referrals, and may face years of unemployment while his case is pending in administrative agencies or the courts. I would respectfully submit that federal legislation is necessary to correct the intolerable abuses which now exist."

Back in 1938 in "Labor Czar," author Harold Seidman summed it up: "Four vital ingredients — dishonest labor leaders, unscrupulous employers, crooked politicians, and professional criminals — are present in every full grown labor racket."

In the construction industry, after a hundred years of muckraking, scandals, exposures, investigations, touted recommendations, and jailings, that truth continues to be self-evident. There might be nothing surprising here; wars against drugs, against illegal gambling, prostitution and loan-sharking continue interminably without lasting success. Why expect anything different in construction? There is an answer, because a potential force against construction corruption has never been effectively mobilized. A reserve army which awaits the trumpet sound: the thousands, the men — and recently the women — who earn their living in the trades. When the NY OCTF underlined the need for defending their rights in their unions, this is the force they had in mind.

The public suffers from construction payoffs in higher prices and higher taxes. That's only money. But construction workers are there, every day from sunrise to sunset. They lose more than money. The collusive combination under which they work brings unsafe working conditions, theft of pension and benefit funds, violation of their contracts, lack of job seniority, no security, destruction of grievance rights. Above all, they are often forced to kowtow to those unscrupulous business agents and greedy contractor for job referrals and surrender their dignity as free citizens. For all these reasons, the unionized work force in the construction industry is the potential for a peoples movement against corruption. As the principal victims of corruption they have the most urgent motives for resisting it.

The bargaining power of skilled craftsmen organized into strong unions permits construction workers to earn a decent living at decent hourly rates.

And because there is big money, conveniently available for manipulation in this industry, it has attracted an ecumenical assortment of equal opportunity crooks of every description who have debased the industry and its unions. Construction workers are no angels or saints. As individuals, they must adjust to the corrupt system or perish. The rolls are crowded with the names of those who have tried to fight the system, failed, and ended on the blacklist. At AUD we hear from the victims with depressing regularity.

Nevertheless, despite all the risks, there are construction workers, thousands, in every major building trades union in the United States and Canada, who stand up and speak out against favoritism in job referrals, against collusion, for responsible honest handling of union money, in short, for decent and democratic unionism. How do I know? In the course of the last 40 years, I have met with them, heard their stories over the phone, read their letters, studied their newsletters and election campaign literature. The carpenters, electricians, laborers, operating engineers, bricklayers, plumbers, roofers, ironworkers. If this is "anecdotal" evidence, it represents the anecdotes of a lifetime. You can read about it in 42 issues of *Union Democracy in Action* and 150 issues of *Union Democracy Review*. They are the active minority, the gadflies, the instigators, the critics, the independents. Sometimes they are called "dissidents," but the term is a misnomer. A few, but only a few, are eccentrics, like you and me. Mostly they are mainstream America, the kind of people who take their rights as Americans seriously, who don't like to be kicked around, who believe that the Declaration of Independence should apply in their unions as in their country. In sum, the kind of people, who in every other institution, in every other organization, in every walk of life, in the pursuit of every other cause, keep our nation's democracy alive and protect it from decay.

But because they must earn their living in the construction industry, they are always in trouble. They are excoriated by bureaucrats at union meetings, they are denied work, they are put on trial in their unions and convicted on trumped up charges of "slander", framed up, expelled, sometimes beaten. The average member looks on nervously, sees their fate, and gets the message: better toe the line, vote right, keep you nose clean, don't dare to buck the system.

There are hardhats, blue collar construction workers, who do stand up for their rights, for the elements of decency and democracy in their unions. An effective resistance to the corrupt construction kingdom depends upon assuring their survival and defending their rights: their rights in their union and on the job, to free speech, to fair hiring, to honest and democratic union elections, to due process in trials, to protection against intimidation and violence. That defense requires a coordinated effort by legislators, law enforcement authorities, and workers rights advocates. Such was the message of the New York State Organized Crime Task Force, ignored in 1990 but as urgent as ever. Investigations and indictments will come and go, but unless that kind of determined coalition of conscience is activated, one corrupt individual will go, only to be replaced by an identical twin while the corrupt system endures.

Section IV
The Public Impact on the Battle for Union Democracy

Chapter 11: "Outsiders" and the Nature of Union Government

The Steelworkers union was born, with the Congress of Industrial Organizations, in the turbulent thirties, organizing workers employed by the great corporations in mass manufacturing production. Known as one of the "progressive" unions, professing a broad conception of labor's role in society, it cast its 480,725 votes in favor of John Sweeney's coup at the 1975 AFL-CIO convention.

The IBEW, in contradistinction, an old AFL union and still largely a hard-hat construction union, expressing a more limited view of labor's function, voted its 678,232 members in support of the Donahue establishment. Nevertheless, despite the difference of their unions in origins and in attitudes, their leaders reacted to a major challenge to their power with a similar defensive self-righteousness. They both moved to frustrate future revolt by making it more onerous to mount effective opposition.

Sadlowski's strong run for the Steelworkers' presidency in 1977/8 sent a nervous tremor through the union administration. To forestall a repetition of such a traumatic experience, they had sued AUD and its supporting foundations and hoped to silence AUD by goading the IRS against it. When those moves misfired, the official family deployed a more lethal weapon in its war against challengers. In 1978, the union amended its constitution to forbid any candidate for international union office, on pain of possible expulsion, from accepting support in cash or in kind from anyone not a member of the union. This new "outsider" rule was accompanied by burdensome reporting regulations that required candidates to report the names of all members who donated more than a trivial $5.00 to their campaigns.

The rules adopted at the 1978 Steel convention, supplemented later by implementing regulations, are a lawyers dream and a layman's nightmare. Over 50 intricate paragraphs are carefully crafted to hermetically seal every crack and crevice that might permit an insurgent candidate for national office to eke out even a dollars worth of support from friends and sympathizers outside the union. The campaign finance reporting provisions alone tie the victim up in an accounting tangle. Even candidates who receive no "outside" money must complete the nasty paperwork.

Under the new rule, Ed Sadlowski's father, a retired steelworker and former member of the union would be prohibited from donating or lending his son money to campaign. A candidate may not accept donations even from members of the union unless they are in "good standing." The candidate cannot process a check or take cash from a fellow member before discovering whether they may have fallen behind in dues. A Campaign Contributions Administrative Committee is empowered to issue and enforce regulations, to bring charges within the union or to sue in court to punish accused violators. The committee can process complaints "in such manner as it deems appropriate" [A firing squad?] "Decisions of the Committee shall be final and binding and not subject to review by any tribunal within the Union."

The implementing rules make long and dreary reading: every phrase creates another possible violation. In case something might have been missed, an umbrella clause covers any oversight: "These regulations are not intended to be all encompassing but are intended to provide some elaboration of Article V Section 27 [the new constitutional provision.]" The flavor permeating this dizzying concoction can be savored from just one tiny fragment of confusing legalese, "Non-member support may not be transferred to a candidate or supporter irrespective of whether the person on whose behalf it was originally provided ever became an announced candidate".

Only members in good standing can contribute, but the name and local number of any MEMBER who donates a cumulative total of more than $5.00 must be reported to the committee, which will inform all candidates of the names of those who donate more than $25. Still, the enforcement committee retains the right to announce the names of those who have given more than a mere $5.00. [All this is an obvious deterrent to members worried about possible retaliation for supporting insurgents.] It is permissible for candidates to accept only the unpaid volunteer TIME of non-member supporters, but this exception is hedged with eviscerating qualifications. I can do unpaid typing for a candidate, but not on my paper on my typewriter. Here, for patient readers is a fragment of the relevant text, the substance of which is repeated ad nauseam:

"Indirect support. All forms of indirect assistance of a candidate by a non-member other than an individual's own volunteered personal time, are prohibited. Thus a non-member may not provide a candidate, and other member, or any other supporter with such items as printing services, office supplies, office space, meeting space, mailing lists, or other items of value to the campaign unless the non-member charges and is paid the normal commercial price for such goods or services. Nor may a non-member use such items of value to produce or distribute material supporting a candidate, even though the materials are not provided to the candidate or the candidate's supporters." [Paper clips?] A candidate is forbidden to accept even a loan from family or friend. "It is improper for a candidate or other member to borrow money from a non-member for use in support of candidacy, with the following single exception: money may be borrowed from a regular commercial lending institution, on such terms and under such conditions as that institution normally lends money." Steelworkers whose parents are bankers are the lucky ones.

Then there are the intricate reporting hurdles. At rallies, fund raisers, raffles, and other assorted gatherings, the candidate must make sure that no non-member or member not in good standing chips in even a dollar; and the names and local numbers of all members who kick in over $5.00 must be recorded and reported. Try doing that when you pass the hat at a big meeting! All checks and all those fat donations over $5,00 must be listed. And just to make the candidate even more miserable, even unacceptable checks that will not be cashed must be listed and reported! The names, occupations, and employers of all those who donate volunteered unpaid time must be listed and reported. Candidates must provide "a list of the time and place of each campaign rally or other fund-raising event at which cash was collected, together with written proof (including announcements of the events)and a certification by the sponsor of the events that the requirements…were met; the total of cash collected at the event; the costs incurred in conducting the events (itemized); and a list of each cash contribution exceeding $5.00 and the name and local union number of each such contributor." (The reader must forgive these tedious quotes. Otherwise, I could be making it up.)

All that and much more must be reported…on and on. And how reported? For the international election immediately following the concoction of these rules, reports are due monthly on each of these days: January 1, February 1, March 1, April 1.

Then the pace intensifies to April 15 and weekly on all Fridays in May. Then on June 15, July 15, and August 15. (If time for campaigning were not necessary, bookkeepers would make perfect candidates.) Violators are liable under Article XII of the union constitution which allows for expulsion. All this is what Thurgood Marshall, who wrote the opinion, and four other Supreme Court justices later found a reasonable and legal limitation on members rights! When Sadlowski challenged the validity of the new rules in federal court, the case wound its way through the system, ending in the U.S. Supreme Court. Both the Federal District Court and the Appeals Court, finding for Sadlowski, declared the restrictions void. But in a narrow 5-4 decision in 1982, the Supreme Court reversed both lower courts and upheld the repressive provisions. In the vanguard of repression, the Steelworkers union paved the way for officials in other unions who also welcomed the opportunity to erect their own obstacles against effective opposition. The new system quickly permeated the labor movement.

The International Brotherhood of Electrical Workers rushed to follow suit. The Supreme Court's decision came in June 1982. Only three months later at their convention in September, the IBEW officialdom had just warded off the challenge from Charles Delgado. That same convention authorized the IBEW international executive board to adopt rules which, when enacted, exceeded even the reach of the Steelworker rules. The IBEW tried to make it illegal for the members of one IBEW local from donating to candidates in any other IBEW local; but it was forced to back off from that innovation when faced with a challenge in Federal court. In all other respects, however, the IBEW restrictions resemble the Steelworkers'.

Up to then, no one seems to have detected any problem; but soon the cure for a non-existent ailment spread like an epidemic. Ironically, along came the United Mine Workers, then headed by Richard Trumka. The union amended its own constitution, like the Steelworkers', to bar "outsider" contributions to candidates. The irony is that Trumka would never have been elected UMW president if such rules had been in place in 1972, the year that the Miners for Democracy were able to oust the murderous Tony Boyle machine, but only with the assistance of massive "outside" support rallied by attorney Joe Rauh, the same who would later back Sadlowski in the Steelworkers. The miners' victory paved the way for Trumka. However, once lifted into power he, like the others, sought protection against effective challenge.

In New York State, the 50,000-member Public Employees Federation, a union of state and county professional employees, founded in insurgency, followed the leaders with its own brief version of the rule. The Service Employees International Union hopped on the bandwagon in 1984 when its convention routinely amended its constitution to forbid contributions from nonmembers.

In 1996, the court-appointed Teamster election officer, adopting rules modelled upon the Steelworkers', twisted them a few notches tighter: an attorney who, as an employer, could not himself contribute to a candidate, was barred from urging others to contribute.

Like the Teamsters' union, the New York Carpenters' District Council had been dominated by racketeers. In 1999, after top leaders had been convicted of racketeering and the council placed under international union trusteeship, a court-appointed monitor — out of the blue — imposed the now-familiar provision barring contributions by non-members in elections. The restriction was becoming a kind of fad.

The Laborers' International Union of North America [LIUNA], also deeply infiltrated by organized crime, came under federal government monitorship after the Department of Justice threatened a Federal suit against the union. Under the terms of a consent agreement, an outside monitor. authorized to supervise the election of its international officers did a creditable job in running the first honest election in the union's modern history. Unaccountably, however, he too jumped on the bandwagon. For the election in 2001, he came up with the now-standard prohibition on "outsider" contributions to candidates for union office. The ban was so "successful" that no one even tried to run against the ruling regime: all installed without opposition.

The Steelworker election rule which barely made it through the Federal courts and slipped through the Supreme Court by 5 to 4 had now metastasized through the body of the labor movement. Union bureaucrats, government officials, judges, and court appointed monitors, have made these rules the copy-cat crime of union elections. Now that the system has become widespread, its ominous implications are becoming clearer.

Up on cloud nine, the Supreme Court majority decided that exposing the names of union members who donate to insurgent candidates was reasonable and justified because it was a necessary means of enforcing the ban. But they had it topsy-turvy. Precisely because it could be enforced only by such exposure, the rule was a dagger at the heart of union democracy. Is that concern exaggerated? A rule which exposes dissidents to retaliation is now applied by government monitors in the Teamsters, Laborers, and Carpenters, unions which have had a history of penetration by organized crime, more bluntly by extortionists and murderers.

Those misguided monitors in the Teamsters, Laborers, Carpenters, who have promulgated election rules which force supporters of opposition candidates to reveal their names, should read the letter of one high-level Labor Department officer in reply to a union member's request:

"It is not our policy to reveal the source of campaign funding to an opposing candidate for fear of reprisal to those members who choose to support a specific individual."

The experience of the last forty years has demonstrated that the defense of union democracy in the United States depends upon support from the broad democratic community: from the law like the LMRDA, from the courts, from civil libertarians, from people outside unions who share the views of those inside. That need produced the Association for Union Democracy. By isolating insurgents and reformers, the ban on nonmember support cuts away at the very heart of union democracy. To grasp why this is so, we must consider the nature of union government and compare it with public government in the United States.

Union government

A loose federation of autonomous national and international unions in the AFL-CIO makes up the bulk of the American labor movement. (Those with local affiliates in Canada are called "internationals.") The AFL-CIO exercises moral influence over affiliates, but little actual authority; its chief disciplinary weapon is the threat of expulsion of an affiliate, a penalty imposed only rarely and under the most extreme provocations. Full authority in each autonomous affiliate is vested in a general executive board which rules the roost, subject to constitutional limitations which are almost always minimal. In some unions, the international president wields such vast power, even over his own general executive board, that he becomes a de facto one-man despot.

Union constitutions provide for a national convention of delegates elected from each local as the highest governmental authority, theoretically superior even to the president and general executive board which are usually elected by those delegates at the convention. In practice, however, the power of the delegates is normally a constitutional fiction. Hundreds, even thousands, of delegates assemble once every three to five years for a week or less then disperse. In the interim, between conventions or before conventions, and even at conventions, the delegates and their locals are subject to the whims of the powerful general executive board or president. Looking for patronage, or fearing retaliation, or even hoping for simple fair treatment, most delegates learn to remain pliant and compliant. Only under extraordinary conditions, does control of the convention by the top leaders slip out of hand and, even then, only temporarily. If members of Congress and their constituencies were directly vulnerable to the whips of the

President, and if Congress could meet in Washington for only a few days once every five years, what would be the fate of American democracy?

Between government in unions and in the nation, there is a chasm of difference. The Constitution of the United States, unlike the Articles of Confederation which it superseded, establishes a strong national government. At the same time, however, democratic rights are protected by a diffusion of power, by separation of authority among the departments of national government: legislature to enact laws, president-executive to implement them, independent courts to interpret and to apply them. Power is divided between state and nation; the states cannot dissolve the national government but neither can the national dissolve the states. There are freely organized rival political parties on a national, state, and local level; caucuses within those parties; independently organized citizens groups: churches, unions, pressure groups, non-governmental organizations of all kinds.

In contrast, union government is unitary power organized centrally from the top and imposed upon all units below. The general executive board enacts rules as legislature, implements them as executive, and enforces and interprets them as judiciary. It conducts trials as jury and imposes penalties as judge. It decides appeals as Supreme Court. It is the legislative, executive and judiciary powers rolled in one. Other units of union government are subject to its control: it can establish, dissolve, and merge locals and other subordinate units. It can lift their autonomy, remove their officers, and impose trusteeships. No states rights here. No separation of powers.

Unlike the multi-party system familiar in democratic government, unions are what Clyde Summers and William Leiserson characterized as "one-party union states." In unions, as a rule, only one group is permanently and formally organized as a national political force: the administration machine, or caucus, or "official family." In rare cases, organized union-wide political caucuses independent of the ruling administration or in opposition to it have managed to survive but usually only for a few years.

In the one-party union state the internal political power of the ruling administration is intimately intertwined with the official union structure. The union officers, their organizational staff, their professional appointees are the "state" and they are the "party"; the two are inseparable, not in law but in fact. In 1988 in a bizarre ruling, the UAW Public Review Board gave this de facto reality a legal status by granting to a rule adopted by the administration caucus the status of an official decision of the union. The board expressed it bluntly:

"...the UAW is now, and has been for over 20 years, a one-party institution not in all respects unlike that found in many national governments in which a single political party controls the government, and the officials who formally make and administer the laws...are selected wholly by that party. As a consequence, in the UAW the lines of demarcation between party, the Administration Caucus, and the formal governing body, the International Executive Board, have become blurred, for 100% of the personnel are, and traditionally have been, members of the Administration Caucus."

In so doing the PRB transformed what is a defect of union democracy — probably inevitable — into a guiding principle of union law. Ironically, the Review Board, in effect, drew a parallel between the structure of government in the UAW, one of our more democratic unions, with what prevails in a dictatorial state. The PRB unwittingly underlined the depressing fact that democracy is limited and degraded by the one-party government reality in even one of our best unions.

At his union's 1947 convention, Harry Bridges, then president of the International Longshoremen's and Warehousemen's Union, sounded his own variation on the same theme:

"What is totalitarianism? A country that has a totalitarian government operates like our union operates. There are no political parties. People are elected to govern the country based upon their records...That is totalitarianism...if we started to divide up and run a Republican set of officers, a Democratic set, a Communist set and something else, we would have one hell of a time." UAW PRB members would surely be horrified to realize how closely their one-party "institution" resembles Harry Bridges "totalitarianism."

A.J. Hayes, former Machinists president and once chairman of the disappeared AFL-CIO Ethical Practices Committee, told a Congressional committee that there were "16,000 full time national and international officials" at the disposal of unions. That figure is swollen by the thousands of fulltimers on the payroll of subordinate bodies like locals and districts, which normally go along to get along with their national superiors. Add the multitude of staff professionals; the editors, lawyers, PR representatives, educational directors, research workers, advisors, and who knows how many others. No civil service regulations govern their tenure. Under the direction of the top officers, they conduct the affairs of the labor movement. Together they constitute a political army, ready to be mobilized before, during, and after union elections to rally votes for the administration, count ballots, derogate challengers, assure the outcome of referendums, convince members that the latest collective bargaining contract recommended by the officials is the greatest historical achievement since the last greatest one.

Their salaries are generous enough to serve as a readily available political line of credit, a rich fund of instantaneous election campaign cash for the administration. When the Steelworkers' ruling regime faced challenge from Sadlowski in 1977, prompt contributions from 500 generously paid staff representatives quickly filled the official family campaign coffers.

In theory, federal law makes it illegal to employ union resources on behalf of any candidate for union office. But in practice that limitation is meaningless, for the Labor Department has ruled that paid union staff representatives can campaign even on union time when their campaign actions are "incidental" to their official duties, a distinction which covers a multitude of sins. Besides, the top union officers, who are their bosses, are naturally cooperative and understanding when they apply for unpaid or vacation leave to go whole hog for the reelection of those same top officers. Such are the normal, legal, even inevitable, advantage of incumbency even in the best of our unions.

But not every union is of the best. Precisely in those unions where democracy needs protection, other sources of revenue are routinely available to top officials: kickbacks from suppliers, bribes from employers for overlooking contract violations, multiple union salaries, extraction of brokerage fees, commission and finders fees from pension and welfare funds, manipulation of union treasuries. Some of these practices, when exposed, may be subject to criminal prosecution. None is ever effectively limited by mere internal union regulations. Rules restricting union campaign contributions are a burden and limitation mainly on those who are accustomed to obeying rules or who are too inexperienced to evade them. Most of those restrictive rules, however well-meaning, end as a curb on the bureaucratically unskilled insurgents.

An insurgent group, by its very nature excluded from the comfortably ensconced official union apparatus, must survive in a vastly different and harsher world. The opposition has no full time staff; its campaigners work for a living all day and campaign in their limited spare time. They conscript their spouses. No publicists, no professional writers or editors, usually no legal help, no latent campaign treasuries or sources of fast cash.

Any aspiring national opposition is trapped by Catch 22. To become credible, it needs money to make its existence known. But to raise money effectively in the first place, it must demonstrate that it poses a credible challenge. To clear that hurdle is an awesome task. By the time insurgents painfully piece together a campaign fund, time is hurrying out.

When top officers are elected by vote of convention delegates, any insurgency needs big money to solve a double problem. Before the convention, it must get its message to members in locals all over the United States, and perhaps Canada, to urge the election of favorable delegates. At the convention it must appeal for votes from local delegates who are themselves leery of offending the national administration. Generally, convention delegates vote for officers by open recorded ballot. No secret ballot at most union conventions. If, in a rare stroke of defiance, a courageous delegate supports opposition candidates that treacherous act is publicly recorded and risks retaliation.

Where national officers are elected, not by convention delegates, but by direct vote of the membership, money is just as critical, perhaps more so. To begin with, how to get on the ballot?, an enormously difficult venture. To be nominated, hopeful candidates must first win support from delegates or endorsements from locals. The arithmetic makes it burdensome. In the Steelworkers, a candidate for international president in 1999 needed the endorsement of at least 72 locals. In the United Mine Workers, one fifth of the locals. In the Teamsters, the endorsement of 5% of the convention delegates; in the Laborers, 10%. If the nominating obstacle is overcome, along comes the next hurdle: how to police the polls to assure an honest count. All that takes money, big money.

Incumbents in most social institutions enjoy the inevitable advantages of incumbency; but in unions, that advantage is overpowering. The balance of power and resources is so heavily weighted for incumbents that it becomes an overwhelming task merely to initiate a simple protest opposition campaign. By limiting the source of rivals' campaign funds, incumbents have built a protective stockade not only against defeat but even against effective challenge. That assurance against challenge accounts, in part, for the degeneration of so many unions into authoritarianism and corruption.

None of this is to suggest that union government must duplicate the multifarious complex features of democratic public government. Unions, it is persuasively argued, need strong leadership and vigorous central authority to confront the authoritarian power of their corporate adversary. Precisely because that is one inexorable fact we must remember another: the forces that sustain democracy inside unions are far weaker than in society. That coincidence: the need for centralization and the weakness of democracy means that union democracy needs strong public support in the larger society: in law, in the courts, and in sustaining private help from reformers and civil libertarians. Any measure that isolates union members from public support, **like the ban on nonmember contributions**, weakens union democracy. Union rules must meet this test.

It is utopian to believe that insurgents can ever compete on an equal basis with entrenched incumbents who use every advantage in power, prestige, and money to induce members to reelect them, an effort which is only natural and mostly legitimate. What is not legitimate is using that power to silence opposition, to freeze out rivals from reaching the voting membership. If insurgents can never achieve equal opportunity, they do deserve some opportunity to make their voice heard over the deafening din of the administration's fanfare. For that, they need support from friends, relatives, union retirees, members of other unions, and sympathizers who share their aims and values.

The permissible source of support for union candidates is already sharply limited by law. LMRDA section 401g forbids candidates from soliciting or receiving donations in cash or kind from "employers" or unions. Moreover, the term "employer" has been broadly defined by the courts and the Labor Department to include even the most modest of entrepreneurs. An insurance broker who employs a secretary may not contribute to his friends' campaign for union office. The law's restriction applies to **any employer** however distantly removed from the union and collective bargaining processes. A bar owner may not permit union candidates free use of his premises for a meeting, neither may a union local of some other international. A friend who owns a candy store and employs part time sales personnel may not donate money, soda, or duplicating paper. If your father is an insurance agent and employs a secretary, don't accept his money.

In practice, few people who are not "employers" of one kind or another have much money. People with money hire others to do their scut work. So the insurgent has the right under the law to solicit money only from those who usually don't have very much. But the law permits hopeful candidates to eke out campaign funds from like-minded wage-working friends and from cousins, aunts, and uncles living high on social security. Even that kind of chump change, limited as it may be, is now outlawed by those restrictive union rules which isolate insurgents from any possible public financial support. A father who is a member of the Auto Workers and works at Ford may not donate to his son's campaign in the Steelworkers.

Before the new rules became a bureaucrat's dream and a lawyer's delight, no one seems to have noticed any danger in those "outside" contributions. Quite the contrary. Jock Yablonski was able to mount an effective election campaign in the Miners union with public support. After his murder, the Miners for Democracy ended the corrupt regime of Tony Boyle, also with public support. For twenty years, again with public support, Teamsters for a Democratic Union fought for democracy and against racketeers. I.W. Abel had public support when he ousted David McDonald as president of the Steelworkers.

What prompted the change? Only the threat to incumbent officials from a Steelworkers opposition. Rules which are ostensibly framed to protect the **union** from outsiders are actually designed to protect **incumbent officials** from their own members. Under the pretext of enforcing a ban on nonmembers, the rules discourage contributions from **members** by requiring that the names of all **members** who make campaign donations above some trivial amount be recorded and reported. In all unions, members depend on the good will of incumbents to process their grievances. Local officers are reluctant to face the displeasure of their superior national officials. In unions controlled by racketeers or bullyboys, physical threats and blacklisting face known dissidents. In the Teamsters union, election officers appointed by the court, mesmerized by rules which are becoming commonplace, demand that the names of all members of the Teamsters for a Democratic Union be reported because TDU supports candidates for union office. This astounding evolution of the outsider rules seems to cause no stir among civil libertarians.

LMRDA Title I, the Bill of Rights, protects free speech and assembly in unions subject to "reasonable rules as to the responsibility of every member toward the organization." How did the Supreme Court majority find that those "outsider" rules were "reasonable," even though they deeply solidify incumbent power and hack away at the rights of any opposition? The Court majority conceded that the rules "...may limit somewhat the ability of insurgents union members to wage an effective campaign, an interest deserving some protection under the statute."

"May somewhat limit"? The realities of one-sided union power are so stark that they make this comment ludicrous. "An interest deserving some protection"? The whole point of the law, its very heart, is to strengthen union democracy as a means of resisting corruption.

Peering down from the clouds, the Court majority found that "requiring candidates to rely solely on contributions from members will not unduly limit their ability to raise campaign funds" because Steelworkers "earn sufficient income to make campaign contributions." Insurgents, then, must depend exclusively on the voluntary donations of their well-heeled co-workers. The Court' comment might ring true if union officials, in line with that standard, abandoned checkoff, maintenance of membership, and compulsory dues to rely on the voluntary donations of unspecified dues from their affluent members to finance the officials' own salaries. In any event, outsider rules now apply even in unions whose members must live nearer the poverty line.

It is possible under extraordinary circumstances for a rank and file insurgent for top union office to mount an effective campaign and even to win without outside financial support. But democracy will be kept alive not merely by the exceptional activities of unusually ingenious, courageous, or talented advocates. Democracy becomes robust only when full rights are available to the average citizen. No one should have to be a hero or a genius to enjoy full democratic rights. An exceptionally trained athlete can swim across the English channel, but that feat does not make it a normal means of transportation. An African-American may become an eminent Supreme Court justice, but his success does not signify the elimination of race discrimination in America. Tokenism in union elections is no more valid than in employment.

Justice Thurgood Marshall, for the Court majority, noted that In congressional discussions on the LMRDA, "Senator McClellan argued that a bill of rights for union members was necessary because some unions had been 'invaded' or 'infiltrated' by outsiders…"

In his dissent, Justice White replied, "It is true, as Senator McClellan explained that 'impositions and abuses…have been perpetrated upon the working people…by the thugs who have muscled into positions of power in labor unions,' …but the remedy which he proposed and which was adopted was to end 'autocratic rule by placing the ultimate power in the hand of the members' and by giving them sufficient statutory protection to participate in a fair election to unseat an entrenched leadership."

The Steel non-member outsider rules which have percolated through the labor movement were not prompted by any actual conspiracy of anti-union forces to influence union life or by any takeover effort by outsiders. The same kind of sympathizers, even some of the very same people, who supported Sadlowski, the insurgent, in the '70s are now prominent among the intellectuals and professionals sought out by John Sweeney in support of the AFL-CIO. The danger to the union from outsiders was not real but only a pretext.

But if a reasonable assurance is necessary against even remote hypothetical danger, it could be achieved by measures without intruding on the rights of challengers: A cap on the total amount that can be donated by any single contributor; no one can buy a union at bargain basement prices. Disclosure of large contributions. A cap on total expenditures by candidates. Such limitations would be adequate if the motive were really to protect the unions and not its entrenched incumbents.

There remains this fundamental fact: Curbs on financial contributions to candidates for union office will never be burdensome to incumbent national officers. Their built-in campaign resources and ability to find escape hatches make them impervious to any conceivable rule. It is not a matter of whining over this annoying fact of life but of acknowledging it in judging the propriety of any restrictive rule.

Descending from the rarified realm of legal discourse into the sordid world of actual union life, we discover that, yes, there is a real outside danger, before, during, and after elections, posed by racketeers, assorted crooks and operators, and suspect employers whose activities lubricate the machinery of kickbacks, contract sellout, insurance fund manipulation, finders fees, commissions, and other ingenious devices for extracting money from victimized wage earners. These sums, invariably concealed and illegal, generally buttress the position of cooperating incumbents. The practitioners, skilled at evading even criminal statutes and law enforcement authorities, are not likely to be deterred by mere union regulations.

But the union rank and filer, untrained in these arts, is readily trapped and hogtied. The most effective, long term antidote against those outsiders is democracy, especially the right to mount an effective insurgent election campaign. Outsider rules severely limit that right. The irony is that the proliferating 'outsider' rules actually protect union leaders, not from racketeers or employers, but from their own members. Even if that was not precisely their avowed purpose, it is surely their result.

In his dissent, Supreme Court Justice White put it plainly, "If those in office are as unscrupulous as Congress often found them to be, the dimensions of the task facing the insurgent are exceedingly large. Congress intended to help the members solve these very difficulties by guaranteeing them the right to run for office and to have free and open election in the American tradition. It is incredible to me that the union rule at issue in this case can be found to be a reasonable restriction on the right of Edward Sadlowski to speak, assemble, and run for union office in a free and democratic election"

The position of insurgents in unions is analogous to the position of unions in society. The power of capital in the country overwhelmingly outbalances the power of unions. Unions survive and prosper despite this enormous disadvantage because their rights of free speech, press and assembly are protected from the "outside" in a democracy which permits them to mobilize the power of people to counteract the power of wealth. Even with its rights protected by law, the labor movement looks for support from other "outside" sections of society. John Sweeney, AFL-CIO reaches out to intellectuals and stock brokers, to the clergy, to radicals and to business, to professors, students, and low-wage immigrants. All these "non-members" are encouraged to support the official labor movement. In all this, labor leaders seem to detect no danger; their concern for the purity of the labor movement seems to be aroused only when their own position is challenged by insurgents who seek that same kind of support.

The nation faces drug peddling, murder, corruption, spying, terrorism — the whole range of evils that afflict civilized society. But the corrective measures must not be worse than the evils themselves. We could not accept a police state as the answer. The trouble with the court-appointed lawyers and law enforcement authorities who are now running union elections is that they seek to cover every possibility of misconduct by piling one set of complex election rules upon another under the illusion that they can seal every crack by stuffing it with paperwork. It is a fallacy to imagine that the illegal acts of crooks, criminals, and corrupt employers can be exorcised by forcing them to report their misdeeds. The cure prescribed by our doctors poisons the patient.

Chapter 12: The Labor Department labyrinth

Sadlowski's frustration in Steel, the shifting base of Labor Department standards, and the tortuous turn of its reasoning were not a momentary deviation but characteristic of its enforcement performance.

In politically sensitive union election cases, the DOL decision process seems to work backwards: first determine what it is politic to find and then fashion a rationale to reach the required conclusion. It begins with an answer and shapes the question to fit. The LMRDA assigns broad responsibility and exceptional enforcement authority to the Labor Department. The courts have given it ample leeway to exercise ingenuity. Seafarers in the National Maritime Union suffered chronically at the hands of the DOL.

DOL and the National Maritime Union

In 1936/37, in a wave of rank and file revolt, the National Maritime Union, under the leadership of Joseph Curran, wiped out the old corrupted International Seamen's Union and emerged, militant and strong, as the principal union of American seafarers. Years pass. By 1998, the NMU was reduced to a shell of its former power; Louis Parisi, Curran's protege and a successor as president, went to jail for stealing union money. In the intervening years, seafarers who sought to prevent the debasement of their union were victims of the ambiguous role of the U.S. Labor Department.

In 1960, Ralph Ibrahim ran for New York port agent against the Curran administration. Secretary of Labor James P. Mitchell sued to upset the election of NMU national officers charging that the union had violated its own bylaws, had failed to assure secrecy of balloting, and had failed to provide adequate assurances of a fair election. Mitchell had been appointed by Republican President Eisenhower in 1953; but before the suit could be tried, John Kennedy, the new president, appointed Arthur Goldberg to replace Mitchell. Goldberg had always been chief counsel to the labor establishment. He promptly withdrew the suit after the NMU promised to obey the law in the future. No one ever returned to check out that promise.

Prior to the adoption of the LMRDA in 1959, the NMU constitution provided that "Any member who has been in good standing continuously for one year immediately preceding the election...shall be eligible to hold office." By 1966, this simple provision was obsolete. The union constitution had been amended to require candidates to fulfill a combination of sea time and five years continuous good standing.

In 1966, Richard Haake, an NMU member for 23 years, tried to run for national president against Joe Curran, but was eliminated because he couldn't surmount the new road blocks. Two other opposition candidates managed to get on the ballot: James Morrissey, for national secretary treasurer; and Joseph Padilla, for vice president. Morrissey, an NMU member since 1942, had served as a patrolman 1949-53 as part of the Curran team; but he quit the job once he decided that the administration was not interested in aggressive representation for its members.

Morrissey lost, but he did well enough to pose a dangerous future challenge to the Curran administration. In the port of New York where most of the union's seamen strength was located, and the only port where the ballot count was subject to outside scrutiny, he got 47% of the votes. Nationally, he was credited with 5,875 votes to the winner's 11,205. Morrissey, Padilla, and three others who had run for port agent challenged the election in a complaint to the Labor Department, charging that the requirements for office were excessive and that the balloting had been fraudulent. Secretary of Labor Willard Wirtz ignored the charges of fraud, but did agree that the stiff requirements for office violated the law and, on that ground, sued before Federal Judge Constance Baker Motley to void the election.

While the election challenge was pending, Morrissey continued his campaign of criticism, publishing a tabloid newspaper, *Call for NMU Democracy*. The reaction of his enemies was deadly. In August, he opened his post office box and discovered a packet of marijuana which he immediately turned over to the postal authorities where he learned that, earlier, someone had sent an anonymous letter to the post office and to the police, complaining that Morrissey's box was used for a narcotics drop. Obviously a crude attempted frameup. (The NMU constitution calls for the summary expulsion of anyone dealing in narcotics.) A month later, as he was passing out literature at the union hall, he was beaten by thugs wielding a metal pipe who sent him to the hospital with multi-skull fractures. It was a narrow escape from death. The American Civil Liberties Union denounced the attack. Replying to the union's assertion that Morrissey orchestrated the attack upon himself to get publicity, the ACLU said, "It flies in the face of common sense."

While the Labor Department was arguing its case before Judge Motley, Morrissey was dropped from the union rolls and Gaston Firmin-Guyon, insurgent candidate for New York Port Agent, was expelled. The two men had both been witnesses for the DOL in court. Firmin-Guyon, then 39, had been a seaman for 19 years. Franklin Simpson was expelled after simply attending the court sessions as an observer. It required the intervention of both New York senators, Jacob Javits and Robert Kennedy, who asked why the DOL remained passive, before the department acted. On April 23, 1968 (the mills ground slowly), the Department of Justice sued and finally won their reinstatement.

In April 1968, Judge Motley found that only "a fraction of 1% of the members were eligible to be elected to 8 national offices" and that "Of the union's approximately 47,500 members, only about 335...met the prior office holding requirement in 1966." In her decision, she wrote, "It now takes a minimum of ten years to become eligible for national office." She added, "It would be stretching credibility beyond...endurance to suggest that Congress intended the courts to sanction" this kind of restriction on the right to run for office. She ordered the DOL to conduct a new election for all officers, including patrolmen.

A great day for union democracy? Not quite. What the judge made possible, the DOL dribbled away. *Union Democracy in Action* wrote, "Now that the Labor Department is itself responsible for running a new election, it remains to be seen whether it will guarantee the conditions for a democratic and honest election." The forewarning was prophetic. It had taken three years to run through the procedures. At last in 1969, the DOL's New York Region supervised the rerun. What followed was a Labor Department created disaster.

The sorry story opened with the imposition of election rules by the DOL regional director. When NMU officials refused to sit in the same room with oppositionists to discuss election rules, the DOL obligingly met separately and at length with the administration representatives to work out rules to their satisfaction. After meeting cursorily with Morrissey, the director published the rules in a press release, where Morrissey first got the news. He never had a chance even to suggest modifications.

Between 1966 and 1969, the NMU had orchestrated a running denunciation of Morrissey and the other insurgents, in strident speeches, in the issues of the union paper, in statements to the press, attacking them as disrupters, bosses agents, and all-around rotters. One 13-page pamphlet was printed and distributed at union expense vilifying the opposition. The rank and file oppositionists had been afforded no opportunity to reply; now that the election campaign was on, their only practical means of reaching the voters was at union meetings or on the ships when they docked in port.

Then, just when the Labor Department might have exercised its authority to assure the opposition some leeway to reply, to open the door just a crack for a breath of free discussion, it slammed it shut even tighter than before. DOL election rule No. 1 cut down the opposition: "Campaigning by any method, either verbally or in writing, is prohibited in all union halls, buildings, and offices and the Pilot [the union paper] from September 1,1968 until the completion of the balloting." For two years, under Curran, Morrissey had been dropped from the union and barred from the union hall. Under the DOL, he could enter the hall but not campaign.

Opposition candidates were barred by shipowners from boarding the ships, while the administration had easy access under the collective bargaining agreement. Rule No. 2 simply provided that opposition literature could be "placed aboard ship" but "The union...will not be responsible for the safe-keeping of any candidate's literature." *Union Democracy in Action* asked, "Wonder how Hubert Humphrey might feel if he had to depend upon George Wallace to pass out his campaign handbills." Destiny for anti-administration election literature under this rule: deep sea. Morrissey asked that patrolmen on board ship be required to sign receipts upon receiving the literature. Request rejected by the DOL regional director who said such a demand would impugn the honesty of the receiving patrolmen.

The director was obligingly flexible for the administration but rigidly severe for the opposition. He set a deadline for the submission of brief statements by the candidates in the Pilot. After the deadline, some Morrissey candidates asked for permission to modify their statements slightly. Request denied. But then the Curranites, after reading pro-Morrissey statements (only they had advance editorial notices), wanted to change their statements to answer Morrissey. Ever conciliatory to the incumbents, the DOL director switched his policy to permit Curran to make the alterations. In itself, the incident was trivial. But as evidence of mood-obsequious at the DOL, it was deadly, as other incidents soon revealed:

Morrissey printed 50,000 election handbills and cards, exhausting his meager campaign treasury. There were some 95 posts to be filled. To save space and money, Morrissey listed the candidates he supported not by name but only by ballot line number, so that his list of recommendations appeared as a checkerboard filled with numbers. In support of five of the 95 candidates running on the Curran slate for minor posts, Morrissey listed their numbers on his campaign cards. Nothing unusual here. In public elections, any citizen or candidate is free to support any other candidate. But this was a DOL-supervised election, and Curran could count on its truckling cooperation. He challenged Morrissey's right to distribute his literature, and the DOL director promptly agreed. He declared the Morrissey literature "unauthorized" and prohibited its distribution. Voting was about to start. To save time and money, Morrissey and his friends tediously blocked out the offending numbers and attempted to begin distribution. No go! Inspecting the cards like a DNA biologist, the DOL director decided that the offending numbers could still be detected beneath the blackout. He went further by posting notices in Spanish and in English in every union hall excommunicating the Morrissey election literature. It was a disaster, financially and morally, to the Morrissey campaign and a major favor for the Curran camp.

In sharp contrast, was the benign, treatment of an arrant violation by the Curran camp. All candidates had been required to file forms in the union office with "confidential" information about their background. The DOL ruled that none of the candidates were allowed to utilize this "confidential" information. But the Curran camp, ignoring the rule, utilized "confidential" information to blast Morrissey camp. Its literature charged that he was a convicted felon. At 18, he had been convicted of a robbery, a fact he had divulged in filling out his "confidential" form for the union. When Morrissey protested, the DOL director agreed that the use of that information was "a breach of our understanding." But what a difference in treatment! The DOL recorded its position in a private telegram to Morrissey. But it was posted nowhere, not in any language. No anathema against Curran; no Curran literature barred. A body blow to Morrissey; not even a slap on the wrist for Curran.

The LMRDA requires that in international union elections, the results be listed separately by locals; however the NMU is a single unitary union without locals. Every member votes, on a single ballot, for each and every one of the 95 spots to be filled. The port offices, however, are separate administrative units. To make it easier to detect fraud, Morrissey proposed that the DOL, with its authority under the court decree, order that votes from each port be segregated and tallied separately. Request denied.

Morrissey's misgivings were not the product of paranoia. In the 1966 election, later overturned by the Federal court, only non-seamen votes from Panama were listed separately. They were marked with such uniform strokes that Morrissey charged fraud, and they were not included in the final count. In an earlier 1963 referendum, seamen recalled, members in the port of Baltimore were reported to have voted by 1,100 to 1 for a dues increase, a result which would be extraordinary even by totalitarian arithmetic.

The 1969 results in Panama, where non-seafaring voters were Spanish-speaking, were astonishing. Two Morrissey candidates had Spanish surnames: Padilla and Castillo. Two Curran candidates were Miller and Straussman. Incredibly the announced tally in Panama awarded some 40 votes for the Morrissey candidates and over 3,000 for Curran's. (Morrissey himself was credited with 64 votes in Panama; the administration got 3,284.) **Union Democracy in Action** commented, "Either Panama workers have freed themselves amazingly from ethnic loyalties or the announced results are suspect."

Morrissey was declared the loser, credited with 7,317 votes. The administration candidate for national secretary, got 13,507. But Morrissey carried the Port of New York, the heart of the union where ballots were separately counted, by 3,499 to 2,950. Joe Curran, who had denounced the Labor Department in advance, changed his tune after the election. "I will say," he wrote, "...the regional director of the bureau in this area, who was in charge of the Labor Department supervision of the NMU election, did a commendable job when one considers the tough assignment he had." His satisfaction was justified. The Labor Department had been subservient to his administration at every turn; the election was a parody of due process.

The 1983 NMU election

Kirby-Smith McDowell faced the perils of opposing the NMU administration as soon as he tried to run for national president in the 1983 NMU union election. At the time, he was Port Agent in Houston, having held the job since 1962. This 20-year veteran of the Curran regime was moving into opposition. He announced his candidacy in May 1982. Joe Curran had retired; Shannon Wall, the incumbent, had taken over. McDowell charged that the Wall administration was not enforcing the union contract, was passive in the face of job losses, was taking excessive salaries, unnecessarily increasing dues, and undermining union democracy. By October he faced charges of accepting sexual favors for making job referrals and was suspended from office without pay. He denounced the pending internal union trial as a frameup, presenting credible evidence that the officialdom had been trying hard to hang him. In any event, the charges were never tried, because McDowell was saved by a Federal court. Magistrate Gershon, after extensive hearings found, "that the proceedings initiating the trial of charges against McDowell violated the LMRDA and the NMU constitution...that the violation [arose] from a deliberate abrogation of fair procedures...the [NMU] defendant's intentional and far-reaching misconduct requires redress." Federal Judge Charles Haight granted an injunction against the trial and ordered McDowell reinstated with back pay.

The charges against McDowell and the course of the election campaign were proof that the quality of NMU life had not changed, but neither had the quality of Labor Department enforcement.

The organization called the Honest Ballot Association, which tabulated the votes, announced the results on October 18. Of the 15,331 valid votes received, incumbent Wall was credited with 8,958; challenger McDonald, 4,140; For secretary treasurer, incumbent Thomas Martinez's tally was 9,835; Albert Jackson, insurgent, 2,875. Several minor candidates also ran for the top jobs.

Ballots had been cast at 260 different sites all over continental United States, in Panama, and in Puerto Rico. Twenty-seven of these sites were in seamen's union halls; but 233 were at work sites, because half the 30,000 NMU members were not seafarers but worked at shoreside jobs, many at government military installations. Voters picked up ballots at designated spots; they were supposed to mark their choices in secret and then deposit the voted ballots into the nearest U.S. Post Box. From there the ballots went by mail to a post box in New York where they were picked up and delivered to a box at the Amalgamated Bank, and from there to the tallying office of the Honest Ballot Association (HBA).

The process was administered by ballot committee personnel selected by the union. The HBA was supposed to monitor the procedure. But the HBA and the NMU official representatives could be the same person, because the HBA, in many instances, simply designated NMU staffers to serve dually as its representatives.

At least eight separate challenges to the validity of the election made their way up to the Labor Department whose field personnel conducted an investigation over a period of ten months. Even with a massive investment of time and manpower, the investigation covered only 136 of the 260 polling sites. In the end, the Labor Department rejected all complaints and upheld the validity of the election. At this point, however, governed by the 1975 U.S. Supreme Court decision in **Bachowski**, it was no longer enough for the department to dismiss election complaints vaguely as "not suitable for litigation." It was required to submit a "Statement of Reasons" explaining the basis for its decision.

The department completed its investigation on September 30, 1983. In November, 1984, Arthur Fox, the insurgents' attorney, was informed that the complaint had been rejected, but without any explanation. The DOL needed almost five months, until February 20,1985, to compose its

Statement of Reasons. The cause of that inordinate delay is now clear: The DOL field personnel actually in charge of the investigation had recommended that the complaints be upheld and that the DOL act to void the election and demand a rerun. But the Washington DOL office rejected the advice of its own investigators. It needed that five months to figure out how to justify the election whitewash. These facts became public information only later when Senator William V. Roth, chairman of the Senate Subcommittee on Investigations, questioned the department's decision and challenged its Statement as inadequate.

Even while rejecting the complaints, the DOL statements to the complainants revealed that the election process had been a shambles. On the eve of the election, "The union had no membership list." An improvised list was pieced together from one source or another of varying dependability: from the Marine Division Pension and Welfare Fund — but that could cover only half the possible list—; from NMU Port Agents who were supposed to compile the names from employers lists. Polling sites were moved from Army bases but members at those bases were not notified of the changes.

NMU representatives accompanied Honest Ballot Association representatives to voting sites. "The Department's investigation revealed," said the DOL statement, "some instances where union representatives played an active role either in conducting the voting or campaigning on union time or both." At one site, both the NMU shop steward and the official HBA representative who "handed out slate cards for the incumbents at the same time as she conducted the election. At other voting sites, as well, representatives and HBA agents conducting the election handed out slate cards for the incumbents at the same time as the ballots...The campaigning within the polling area and numerous examples of NMU representatives handing out ballots (as well as slate cards) also demonstrates a lack of adequate safeguards to insure a fair election, in violation of Section 401(c) of the Act."

Here was an election in which the elementary requirements of fair play were egregiously ignored, but the DOL found a formula for ignoring the obvious. The violations, it decided, could have affected only 2,459 votes. "However, since the smallest margin of victory for any office was 4,007, the violation could not have had an effect on the outcome of the election." What this distorted rationale ignores are two overwhelming facts: the DOL investigation never reached over half the voting sites; and more important, the violations were a clear indication that the whole election process was tainted.

There was more in the Statement of Reasons to seafarer Anson: At one factory-based site, votes were recorded from members who "did not in fact vote." Didn't matter, because that could only have affected 520 votes. In some instances, voted ballots were handed to HBA committeemen instead of being placed directly into post boxes — and those HBA representatives were actually NMU members selected by the union. Bags of ballots which were supposed to have been sealed were found opened at the bank.

"...HBA Ballot Committeemen and NMU officials at some of the polls collected voted ballots from voters, either directly or by the use of ballot boxes. The ballots boxes used ran the gamut from flimsy cardboard boxes to metal and wooden boxes with locks and/or seals.[Who had the keys!] Ballots were collected often at the instruction of polling place officials who insisted upon collecting the voted ballots from the voters. In any case, every post-voting procedure which did not require the voters to take his or her ballot outside of the polling place and deposit it in a post office mail box (except in Panama) violated the union's own constitution and its election rules." (from statement to Concepcion)

In Panama, physical control over ballots was minimal because it was not permissible to use U.S. prepaid postage envelopes. Voters dropped their ballots into locked ballots boxes [keys?] and ballot committeemen brought "all voted ballots to the NMU Panama office where they were sealed and mailed in a large envelope to the Amalgamated Bank Of New York." The DOL recorded all this as ordinary procedure, but in an election riddled with hanky-panky a normally skeptical participant would wonder what happened to those ballots in the union office before they were "sealed" and mailed.

Other critical issues were simply evaded by the department. In 1963, the requirements for running for office were so restrictive that Judge Motley voided the election. This time, the complainants pointed out, the requirements in 1983 were even more stringent than in 1963.

The insurgents complained that 17% of the addresses supplied for their mailings were defective. They complained that for most of the election period they had been barred from passing out election cards and literature at military bases while the incumbents had free passage. They complained that they had been denied any possibility of observing the printing of ballots. All ignored.

In 1985, two years after the election, William V. Roth, chairman of the Senate Permanent Subcommittee on Investigations, directed his staff to review the record in the 1983 election. What they found contradicted the DOL at every major point and vindicated the charges of the NMU insurgents. Roth forwarded the findings of his staff in a long letter to the Secretary of Labor. His letter made public precisely what Arthur Fox, insurgents' attorney, had learned in private. "Staff members of both OLMS [the DOL's election agency] and the Office of the Solicitor [of the DOL]," Roth wrote, "recommended that the Department institute legal proceedings to overturn, and eventually rerun, the election. Subcommittee interviews with personnel from these offices reinforced the belief that significant and numerous violations of Title IV of the LMRDA had occurred during the NMU elections and that these violations could have affected the outcome. Therefore it is somewhat difficult to reconcile these recommendations with the final decision of the Acting Assistant Secretary...not to institute proceedings to overturn the elections results."

Roth went on to express his concern, among other things, that "The Department of Labor has not accurately expressed the reasons for its decision in its "Statement of Reasons" as required by *Dunlop v. Bachowski*...one must wonder whether a challenge to the Statements under the 'arbitrary and capricious' standard of *Bachowski* could be sustained when the 'statements' do not reflect all of the Department's 'reasons'." His staff also confirmed a serious charge levelled by insurgents: the same violations that occurred in 1983 "have been encountered in NMU elections prior to 1983."

"Although the above concerns are specifically related to the NMU election investigation, I believe it is reasonable to ask whether the Department of Labor is generally enforcing the provisions of Title IV in a vigorous manner."

Senator Roth added, "I am also concerned that the 'Statement of Reasons' drafted in the NMU case do not contain any mention of the above considerations even though these reportedly played a significant part in the final decision [to reject the election complaint]."

Was "the impossible dream" worthwhile?

Eli Wier, a minor candidate for NMU president, poured out his story in a letter to Arthur E. McInerney, an attorney who had represented Jim Morrissey in the NMU many years before. McInerney replied, "You and others like you are modern-day men of LaMancha — dreaming the impossible dream. Perhaps some day your dream will come true and justice will prevail."

Will "justice" ever prevail in the labor movement? The question is loaded with larger philosophical implications. Will justice ever prevail in society? Under absolute monarchy, justice seemed embodied in the Republic. Then, in Democracy. Then in Social Democracy. And then? Under slavery, justice was embodied in liberation. Free at last! but it was not enough. Then in civil rights. Then in a myriad of new social goals.

Justice is an elusive ideal, eternally approached but drifting tantalizingly out of reach. The battle for justice persists in the labor movement because, as in all society, it is eternal.

If the insurgent seafarers lost their battle for democracy, so did the union lose its battle for survival. In 1983, 15,331 valid votes were cast. In 1998, there were only 1,617 valid votes; and of these, only 768 came from seamen. The union was on the road to extinction when it finally dissolved into the Seafarers International Union which superseded the NMU as the dominant union of unlicensed sailors.

The DOL and the painters

My own misgivings over the erratic quality of DOL LMRDA policies came quite early in its career as an enforcement agency and my own as a union democracy advocate.

In May 1962 — Arthur Goldberg was Secretary of Labor — *Union Democracy in Action* noted briefly that Frank Schonfeld, in a complaint to the Labor Department, had challenged the validity of the 1961 elections in Painters District Council 9. "It remains to be seen how this case will be listed in Mr. Goldberg's next set of election statistics," I wrote in UDA.

Two months later, to my surprise, I received an unsolicited letter from John Holcombe, then commissioner in charge of DOL enforcement under the LMRDA. He acknowledged Schonfeld's complaint but found my report "incomplete" because, he wrote, "The results of [the DOL] investigation clearly indicated that there had been no violation of the Act. The Washington office...concurred with the conclusion of the New York area office."

I was perplexed because 1. I hadn't requested any information from the DOL, and 2. No one had ever informed Schonfeld of the decision, verbally or in writing, and 3.Holcombe's letter to me violated the DOL's own policy as elaborated in its 1961 report: "At any time it becomes evident that inadequate evidence is available to establish that there has been a willful violation, the investigation is terminated. No routine notice of the results of such investigation is given," Why, then, did the DOL depart from its own policy to give the election a publicly written clean bill of health? The answer seemed obvious to me: it was eager to perform a PR service for the union.

Three years pass. *Union Democracy in Action*, able to monitor DOL enforcement activities because the department's annual LMRDA reports were still available, continues to raise sensitive issues. Goldberg is replaced as Secretary of Labor by Professor Willard Wirtz. In the hope that the new secretary might inject vigor into LMRDA enforcement, I wrote to Wirtz on

September 2,1965, about those four years of repression and suspect elections in the Painters union: "Under your predecessor, to put it bluntly and with perfect accuracy, the DOL simply and deliberately acted to whitewash the accused officials rather than protect the rights of union members."

Two weeks later — which for a government bureaucracy means instantaneous — James Reynolds, the new assistant secretary for LMRDA affairs, replied that Wirtz was "greatly concerned," and they were dispatching someone from the Branch of Special Investigations to meet with me in New York. I met with Peter Cattaneo, who must have been important; two years later he became assistant director of the LMRDA division. Things were moving. Action at last? Ah, vain illusion!

When I met with Cattaneo and Edwin Dooley, New York Area Director, it soon became clear that this was a public relations gesture to reassure me that all was well. On the whole, Cattaneo politely insisted, I must be mistaken because the department was doing all it could and should. Demurring, I repeated that the department had done nothing to protect painters from election fraud and intimidation. We left on cordial terms. Cattaneo invited me to come up and see Dooley whenever I felt the department could help. "As a matter of fact," I replied, "I'll accept your offer, because something is coming up." "Be glad to see you," said Dooley. I had in mind the recent election in Painters Local 1011.

In June 1965, Schonfeld had run as an insurgent for two positions in Painters Local 10ll. Of the 500 votes cast, he was declared defeated by only 35 for local chairman and by only 11 for council delegate. When he complained to the Labor Department, he seemed to have an airtight case even for the most dedicated bean counter. He proved that his campaign literature had been mailed by the union to an outdated obsolete membership list while the incumbents had the use of an accurate up-to-date mailing list compiled by the insurance fund. More than 70 envelopes were returned to Schonfeld marked addressee unknown. He was sure that many others, sent to an old address then forwarded, had arrived after the election was over. Surely elections decided by 11 and 35 votes could have been affected by those 70 misdirected envelopes.

Immediately after the election, I decided to cash in my invitation and prepare the DOL office for what was coming. At the DOL, I met with my old friend Dooley and a Mr. Nash, his assistant. Mr. Nash must have been a rapid-fire analyst with a hair-trigger mind, because I had hardly completed outlining the facts when he interjected that the case was baseless and that the department couldn't accept the complaint. I couldn't believe it; the election outcome had obviously been "affected." Mr Dooley was more circumspect;

offering no encouragement, he said maybe a complaint could be considered. "But why do **you** come to us?" he asked, "Why don't the painters come themselves"

"But you issued me this invitation," I reminded him, "I thought it would help to talk it over in advance." They weren't interested. Dooley said he would be pleased if I didn't rush into print and turn the case into a publicity show. And so I held off writing about it until later when the case got into court.

It was no surprise, therefore, when the department rejected Schonfeld's complaint, but its written comment was startling: "The investigation disclosed that a violation of Section 401 of the Act occurred. However...there is not probable cause to believe that the violation found in this case may have affected the election outcome. Accordingly...the case has been closed. Nevertheless the violation has ben brought to the attention of your union officers so that appropriate steps can be taken to ensure compliance with the Act in future elections." (Remember that we were still in those days before *Bachowski*, when the Labor Department could reject election complaints without explanation.)

The decision seemed bizarre to Schonfeld; and when he sued the Secretary of Labor, Federal District Judge Edward C. McLean agreed. Defending the bureaucratic stockade, the DOL argued that its decisions in election cases could not be appealed because they were immune from judicial review. In rejecting that position, the judge wrote: "There is nothing in the Act [LMRDA] to indicate that the Secretary has 'absolute discretion' or that decision is 'totally committed' to his judgment. Assuming plaintiff's allegations to be true, it is hard to see how the Secretary could have concluded that probable violation of the Act which prevented plaintiff from communicating with over 75 voters, could not have affected the outcome of elections which he lost by 35 and 11 votes respectively. On the face of it, the Secretary's decision seems arbitrary."

And so back to the Labor Department, where Schonfeld's complaint moldered while the department mulled over the judge's finding. Time passes. In 1966 another election takes place in the same Local 1011 where William Papson, a Schonfeld supporter runs as an insurgent for trustee. And this time, precisely the same violations as in the previous election, except that Papson lost by only 28 votes. But the Labor Department, was better prepared for him. The fumble it made in Schonfeld's case was to admit that violations had occurred. In Papson's case, it recovered simply by not referring to any possible violation. This time, it wrote: "...an investigation was conducted by this office," it wrote, "...it has been determined that this case is not suitable for litigation under Section 402 of the Act; therefore this case has been closed." The department had learned how to maneuver. It was not yet required to explain and it did not.

The standards: How does the DOL make up its mind?

To repeat: before the DOL will uphold an election complaint it must find not only that the law was violated but that any violations may have affected the election outcome. Sounds reasonable; but for a complainant, that criterion poses a dilemma. How to prove that you might have won an election if it had been fair when in actuality it was crooked? Not so easy.

Armed with investigators with subpoena powers, how does the Labor Department decide whether violations could have affected the outcome? In the quest for illumination, I wrote to the DOL and got this answer on December 17, 1976: "...The Secretary's finding of probable cause is dependent not only upon the particular violation alleged, but also upon the facts and circumstances which have been developed by the investigation in each case. Since each complaint filed under section 402 is investigated and reviewed individually, the Department has not issued any guidelines, standards, or directives." Plenty of elbow room here. Without definite standards, the DOL can make any decision short of demonstrated irrationality.

Without clearly defined standards, what does guide the department in LMRDA cases? For that, we must study its record, which has become difficult even for authorized government personnel and virtually impossible for ordinary citizens. Between 1959 when the law was first adopted and 1978, the Labor Department issued detailed annual reports on its LMRDA enforcement record, often running to 100 pages, including detailed facts and statistics on election and trusteeship cases. Its final report in 1978 described 137 court cases in which the department itself was engaged, including 112 election cases. Nineteen pages listed criminal cases under the LMRDA and 56 civil cases initiated by private litigators. You might not accept the DOL analyses, but facts were there for making up your own mind. But abruptly, in 1978, those reports were discontinued; public accountability effectively ended.

In 1999, upon request of John Boehner, chairman of the House Subcommittee on Employer-Employee Relations, conducting hearings on union democracy, the General Accounting Office reviewed the Labor Department's role as an LMRDA enforcement agency. It required 14 months of work by 11 staff members to produce its report, and even then, the result was skimpy. For a private individual, it is now impossible to penetrate the workings of LMRDA enforcement.

My own conclusions are based upon 40 years of monitoring the DOL, studying the reports of academic analysts and hearing stories told by unionists who have gone through the mill. One DOL investigator once told an AUD class that the primary guide of the agency in any situation was the well-known principle: "Cover your ass." That explanation, however accurate, is too roughly formulated to be scientifically illuminating.

The DOL is most comfortable with simple technical violations of the statute that do not require it to discover other reprehensible misdeeds. The law clearly mandates the election of local union officers 1. by secret ballot, and 2 for a maximum term of three years. If either of these obvious requirements is not fulfilled, the DOL may find violations, may uphold an election complaint and, if necessary, may sue the union for compliance. Maybe, but not necessarily, because the DOL always retains its own right of prosecutorial discretion.

However, when complexities arise, it's bad news for the complainant. You never know how the DOL will jump. You may have been denied the right to post observers at a dozen sites where you are sure more votes were stolen. Here's what the DOL told Sadlowski in its statement of reasons: "The denial of the right to an observer is plainly a violation of the Act. But there must also be some evidence that the violation may have affected the outcome of the election. This possible effect cannot be shown if the investigation disclosed that the election was otherwise properly conducted." But how can you prove improper conduct if no one was allowed to watch?

Trusteeships

One of the glaring abuses exposed at the McClellan Committee in the late fifties was the imposition of repressive trusteeships over locals union by their internationals. LMRDA Title III was intended to correct those abuses, an aspect of the law considered so vital that it was one of the few major sections that permitted alternative roads to enforcement. Complainants can seek recourse against improper trusteeships either by appealing to the Labor Department or by filing their own private suit in Federal court. Because it does afford these alternatives, Title III provides a means of testing the effectiveness of the Labor Department as an enforcement agency. The department's record under Title III can be compared with the record of enforcement by private suit.

The trouble here as with most aspects of the law is that, with time, devious union officials have learned how to circumvent its provisions. (To get around the restrictions of Title III, they can simply dissolve locals or merge them out of existence) Title III presumes that a trusteeship is valid for the first 18 months, usually time enough for a despotic national union officialdom to cement its control over a recalcitrant local by dispensing favors to submissive friends and threatening retaliation against stubborn critics. If the actual purpose of a trusteeship is to repress a rising dissident movement, the international can easily conceal its real aim. It need only learn how best to fill out the DOL reporting forms. The DOL never goes beyond these reports to test their accuracy. In the 40 years since the LMRDA was enacted in 1959, the DOL has never reported a challenge to the validity of a trusteeship during that first 18 months. In this respect, the case of Painters District Council 9 in New York City, reveals a DOL futile to the point of absurdity.

In the Miners union

A decisive test of the effectiveness of DOL in trusteeship cases came early in its career with a challenge to long-enduring trusteeships in the Miners union.

Back in 1944, 21 of the UMW's 31 districts were under trusteeship. By 1959 when the LMRDA was adopted, some had been in effect for more than 18 years. In 1961, complaints were filed with the DOL but for three years it passively contemplated. Finally in late 1964, the department filed suit to void trusteeships in seven districts: 4, 6, 7, 17, 23, 30, and 31. Immediate delay! Under three different secretaries of labor, the department allowed its suit to sleep on the dockets for more than six years, finally bringing it to trial in 1971 only after Jock Yablonski had been murdered and hundreds of UMW members had complained to their congressmen about DOL somnolence. In February 1970, 19 of the 23 districts of the United Mine Workers were still under trusteeship, forming a solid base for the self-perpetuating bureaucracy that ran the union.

Meanwhile, private suit was filed by the Miners for Democracy against trusteeships in seven other districts: 2,12,14,19,20,28, and 29. So that in this instance two series of trusteeship cases proceeded simultaneously, one by the DOL and the other by miners. The difference in outcome was startling. The DOL had fiddled for 11 years without resolution. The private suits were filed by the Miners for Democracy in March 1971. By May 10,1972—after only 14 months—they had won their case against two of the trusteeships, one of which had been in effect for 20 years. The DOL cases were still pending in court. By making an end run around the DOL, the insurgent miners accomplished in 14 months what the DOL belatedly achieved after about 12 years. Based on his experience, Chip Yablonski told AUD, "The lesson is: If you've got a trusteeship, for God's sake, don't go to the Secretary of Labor to get it lifted. Title III permits union members to go directly to court to remove unlawfully imposed trusteeships, and there surely are plenty of them out there."

Defining away LMRDA rights: an officer is not an officer

In 1967 I was in touch with the leaders of Machinists Local Lodge 837 at the McDonald Douglas plant in St. Louis. The 22,000-member local was one of 14 locals affiliated to District Lodge 9, with a total district membership of 46,000. Bruce McArthy, Lodge 837 president, announced that he intended to run for directing business agent of the district at the head of a full insurgent slate of 22 in opposition to candidates supported by the international administration. It was the first such challenge in the district's history. McArthy, with powerful backing from his huge local, was front runner virtually assured of election.

But it was not to be. The union barred his slate from the ballot on a contrived technicality: the local had transmitted formal notice of the nominations on stationery that lacked an impressed seal. Without opposition, the international's own candidates sailed in, free and clear, "elected" without opposition. When McArthy complained to the Labor Department, it threw out his complaint on the ground that the post of directing business agent was not a union "officer" and hence the election was not subject to DOL review. (LMRDA Title IV regulates the election only of union "officers", but it defines that term broadly to include "any person authorized to perform...executive functions of a labor organization, and any member of its executive board or similar governing body.")

It is common knowledge that the directing business agent, sometimes called business manager, is actually the local CEO, the official with greatest power. And so it was in IAM District Lodge 9. In an editorial on August 18,1966 entitled "A Labor Department Fiction" the St. *Louis Post Dispatch* put it plainly:

"The Department of Labor's ruling in the Connor-McArthy case [C. was the incumbent] strikes us as unrealistic and so narrow and unreasonable that it reverses the intent of the law and sets a precedent of great potential harm to the labor movement... Everyone connected with the labor movement in St. Louis knows that Mr. Connor is the machinists boss ...That could not be good enough for Mr. Beaird [the DOL solicitor] of course, but the District 9 constitution should have been...it gives Mr. Connor 'full power to remove any member from his job' and to call shop meetings 'for any reason he deems necessary.' The District's nominal president can do neither and draws not a dime in salary. Is Mr. Connor boss or isn't he?" [Connor was paid $20,000 a year, good money in those days.]

It was soon the end for McArthy. When the local tried to retain a lawyer to represent its interests, the international imposed a trusteeship, obviously to crush opposition. But the Labor Department, a la Painters DC 9, upheld the trusteeship because the union filled out the proper form stating that its aim was to restore democratic practices! One thing led to another and McArthy was expelled.

Twenty-five years later the same issue was raised in IAM District Lodge 70 in Wichita KS. In 1992 Keith Thomas, the young leader of an insurgent caucus, Unionists for Democratic Change, ran for directing business agent of IAM District Lodge 70, which represented 11,000 Boeing workers in the Wichita KS area. In the three-way race, he was credited with 1,032 votes to the winner's 1,312. When he challenged the validity of the election, the DOL dismissed his complaint out of hand on the ground that the directing business rep was not an "officer" with executive responsibilities but only an "employee" performing "ministerial" functions.

On the face of it, a ludicrous ruling. Consider the DOL's own regulation 452.19 which acknowledges the reality: "...a directing business representative or a business manager usually exercises such a degree of executive authority as to be considered an officer." This time, AUD's access to information under the FOIA provided insight into the DOL process of reaching absurd conclusions.

IAM officials told DOL investigators that the DBR "conducts the day to day operations of the union" because he is the only paid union official; none of the "officers" are paid full time by the union. The DBR can "call the executive board into session" and these sessions deal "only" with "contract administration and the members' livelihood." Only! How did the DOL decide that all these vital functions were only "ministerial." Simple. When DOL investigators asked Alex Bay, assistant to the international president, if the DBR was an officer, he denied it. When he was reminded that **the district bylaws actually referred to the directing business representative as an officer**, Bay explained away that inconvenient fact: the word "officer" he said was simply "misused." While the interview with Bay was in progress, an IAM international vice president walked in. He too assured the investigator that the DBR was no officer, and the DOL readily accepted these self-serving assurances even though they contradicted common knowledge.

Violence and reprisals: How Section 610 got lost

Two provisions of the LMRDA, taken together, would provide strong protection for union members against retaliation — if they were enforced. Section 601 gives the secretary of labor the "power when he believes it necessary in order to determine whether any person has violated or is about to violate any provision of this Act (except Title I...) to make an investigation and in connection therewith" he can inspect records, question witnesses, and order the production of records.

Section 610 provides for criminal penalties: "It shall be unlawful for any person through the use of force or violence, or threat of the use of force of violence, to restrain, coerce, or intimidate, or attempt to restrain, coerce. or intimidate any member of a labor organization for the purpose of interfering with or preventing the exercise of any right to which he is entitled under the provisions of this Act." Violators are subject to fines up to $1,000 and jail terms up to one year. There may be fossil evidence that this section was once vigorously enforced. I have never unearthed any. When Jock Yablonski was assaulted and called for a investigation (later murdered) in 1969, when two reform painter leaders in California (murdered in 1966) called for an investigation of corruption, when seaman Morrissey was almost killed in New York in 1966 the Labor Department took no action.

Reprisals

In early 1963, I tried to discover how the DOL protected unionists from intimidation or violence in the course of an election. A chain of extended correspondence followed, back and forth, signifying nothing. In the end, it became obvious — not clear but obvious, the DOL made nothing clear — that it would do nothing. If violence occurred during an election, I was informed, the victim could file a post-election complaint. If the offense could have affected the outcome, [virtually impossible to prove], the recourse was a possible new election. If the violence could not have affected the outcome, the complaint falls into a black hole. But what about the victim's rights under Section 610? That, DOL Commissioner John Holcombe informed me, "would be separately handled." Vague! When I asked how many complaints of retaliation the department had received. The answer: we do not keep such statistics. Then, in another, related, contest Mr. Holcombe replied that the DOL did not keep "nice, but not necessary, statistical data."

In the years that followed, unionists told me of many threats of violence, but I never learned of any action against the perpetrators under Section 610. And so on January 5,1999, in preparation for these lines, I wrote to the DOL under the Freedom of Information Act requesting information on enforcement action under that section. In reply, the DOL informed me that it referred such cases to the Department of Justice and that it did not, itself, maintain statistical records on how many complaints it passed along. Next came anther stream of correspondence between me and the Justice

Department, which wrote that several of its "components" should be individually contacted. The Civil Rights Division replied that it had no records and referred me to the Criminal Division and the Executive Office of the Attorney General. They referred the question to the FBI which turned back the request because they had no information on Sec 610 investigations.

A month later, on May 24, 1999, the DOJ Executive Office "complied," so to speak, with my request. Success at last? Not so fast. A DOJ envelope transmitted a sheaf of indecipherable computer code printouts. I wrote to the DOJ: "The data supplied is in so cryptic a format that no normal citizen if anyone, could find it intelligible." Apparently my latest complaint found its way back to the starting point at the Labor Department which replied on October 4, "...under the FOIA, agencies are only required to provide existing records in response to requests. The FOIA does not require an agency to create records...agencies do not have to organize or reorganize file systems to respond to a particular FOIA request." In other words, they will produce cryptic indecipherable "records" but not necessarily translations into comprehensible information.

And so, what enforcement action has been taken under Section 610? I doubt if any living person is capable of providing an accurate answer. But however you try to break the computer code, one fact seemed evident: not much activity. In any event, a 1971 Yale Law Journal study found, "While there have been some prosecutions under sec 610, they have been rare enough to persuade union members interviewed that the statute does not deter campaign violence."

The "politics" of DOL enforcement

Morris Weisz, a former assistant director of the BLMR, the agency then responsible for LMRDA enforcement, wrote me to express misgivings over my treatment of the DOL in *Union Democracy in Action.* While he sympathized with my efforts, he insisted that I was frequently unjust because I failed to acknowledge the legal limitations on DOL authority and criticized it for not doing what it was unable to do. I first met Morris in the early thirties when we were both members of the socialist-oriented Student Forum in New York City College, and I remembered him as a fair-minded, objective person of 100% integrity; and so I did pay attention. I do understand that the DOL, as an administrative agency, feels compelled to tread delicately through the bureaucratic political mine field. But UDA's role (and later AUD's) as an independent citizen agency is to put moral pressure on government agencies to do their job and so, in a way, helps them to fulfill their responsibilities. We are not unfair; we are simply different. The LMRDA certainly does need strengthening. Meanwhile, however, the problem is not simply that the DOL is limited by law but rather that it prudently avoids vigorous exercise of what authority it does possess and never presses urgently for additional authority.

The feeble quality of DOL intervention flows inexorably from its fundamental flaw as an LMRDA enforcement agency. In pursuing its main work — mediation, health and safety, statistics, monitoring wages and hours, labor-management relations — the Labor Department requires the amicable cooperation of union officers. But union democracy disputes pit insurgents and rank and file workers against the leaders above. If the department were to defend with zeal the legal rights of insurgents, it would inevitably arouse the hostility of those very union officials whose goodwill it so eagerly desires. These contradictory responsibilities — to cultivate union leaders and to protect unionists against those leaders — places the DOL in an irreconcilable conflict of interest position.

The leaders, armed with union treasuries and sustained by prestige, pack impressive political clout, a fact which enables the labor movement to serve as a necessary countervailing political force to big business and reinforces democracy in the nation. But that same clout also serves to entrench their position inside their unions against critics. Insurgent rank and filers, in opposition to their leaders, are politically inconsequential and dispensable.

And so we are asking the Labor Department to do the impossible, to cultivate excellent relations with labor leaders and at the same time vigorously defend the rights of union members who criticize or even seek to overthrow these same leaders. Something has to give. Who must be sacrificed, leaders or insurgents? In this sorry world, the answer springs instantly to mind: Justice yields to power.

The Labor Department was established as a government body which would advance the interests of labor. In selecting a Secretary of Labor, most administrations, Republican and Democratic, cultivate the approval of top union leaders, or at least try to avoid irritating them. All this is to be expected, even desirable. The Department of Commerce exists to advance the interests of business. Why not the Labor Department, of organized labor? The tilt of the Labor Department toward union leaders was taken into account when the National Labor Relations Act was adopted, establishing norms for collective bargaining between unions and employers. Enforcement was assigned, not to the Labor Department, but to a new, independent agency, the National Labor Relations Board.

In time, however, I learned that referring to the Labor Department as "it" fails fully to recognize that the DOL, like other government agencies in a political democracy, not only has contradictory assignments, it has a split personality. On top, making strategic policy decisions are political appointees whose loyalty is to the administration in Washington. Beneath, are the career officers responsible for the day to day workings of the agency. The career personnel, including the investigators, merely propose; but the political appointees dispose. All decisions are handed down in Washington; it is from this lofty perch that statements of reasons dismissing union election complaints are composed.

We have met DOL career staff reps who are impatient, as we are, with the slow and erratic pace of LMRDA enforcement and frustrated when their reports and recommendations are reversed.

Upon invitation from time to time, the DOL has assigned personnel to explain its work at AUD conferences. They were invariably friendly but, in their public addresses, never strayed from the official line. Privately, however, some DOL personnel at all levels subscribe to our Review, circulate copies to their colleagues, and donate modestly to our efforts. In 1991, when two members of the executive board of Texas Chapter 247, National Treasury Employees Union, were expelled from the union for criticizing their chapter president, AUD submitted a brief on their behalf to the Labor Department and eventually won their reinstatement. Written by Lauren Esposito, then an AUD legal intern and now (2001) an NLRB field attorney, the brief was circulated by DOL personnel to its regional offices as a guide to its LMRDA-type enforcement responsibilities for federal employees.

The opposing forces that tug at the DOL were defined in a book-length report in 1979 by Doris McLaughlin and Anita Schoomaker of Michigan State University who were commissioned by the DOL to examine the effectiveness of LMRDA enforcement. After the DOL itself would not print the report, it was published by the university. Most of its findings, more than 20 years ago, square with our own experiences.

The authors wrote: "Who are the real makers of DOL policy? ...We asked that question of a half dozen long-time DOL officials, past and present, and a dozen additional close observers, primarily labor lawyers, who have been concerned with the enforcement of the LMRDA...[They say] that the everyday decisions are left to the career civil servants. Key decisions, on the other hand, are made by the Solicitor and the Assistant Secretary for Labor-Management Relations. In an unusually sensitive situation...the Secretary of Labor himself might become involved — but only then. Ordinarily...the Assistant Secretary, with the advice of the Solicitor, is the really key figure."

To what extent are these decisions political? The question is not whether decisions are based on narrow partisan (i.e. Democratic v. Republican) ground but whether they are influenced by the "nonpartisan" social and political pressures on the DOL to conciliate the very union officials they would be forced to antagonize by scrupulous LMRDA enforcement. On this score, the McLaughlin study reports, "Four DOL spokesmen in the national office agreed that the two tasks were incompatible, being both the intermediary between management and labor and the union policeman is unfeasible...20% of those we interviewed did believe that the DOL has two incompatible functions...and because of the political pressures that inevitably flow from trying to fulfill both, over two-thirds of these respondents thought that the Act should be administered elsewhere, or at least additional safeguards should be imposed...Four national office DOL officials said that they wished that Congress had created an entirely new government agency, autonomous of any existing one, whose only charge would have been to administer the LMRDA...The new agency...could have pursued enforcement of the Act single-mindedly, devoting its entire attention to protecting members' rights."

An earlier study completed at Yale Law School in 1971 under the supervision of Professor Clyde W. Summers dealt with similar issues and reached similar conclusions: "There is a common perception among both attorneys for Title IV complainants and union counsel that 'political influence' is brought to bear on this decision [whether to sue in election cases]. Complainants and their attorneys tended to view this influence as being exerted in specific instances to forestall litigation — by the national union to protect an incumbent local officer, or by the AFL-CIO to defend a national official. It is, however, virtually impossible to evaluate or document such asserted political bias." And in a footnote, it added, "The charge of political influence at the Washington level could be evaluated more systematically if the reports and recommendations of field personnel could be compared with the decisions coming out of the Department's litigation conference. This avenue of inquiry could not be pursued, however, because the Department's files of internal correspondence are not open for inspection."

Since then, however, we do have new evidence. The DOL itself has never reported on how often recommendations from the field are vetoed by the politically minded operatives in Washington. But the report of the Government Accounting Office in the year 2000 confirms with statistics what we have always suspected. In the two years, 1998 and 1999, the GAO reports, the DOL found election violations in 162 cases, a figure that the GAO thinks may be an underestimation because of faulty records. In 67 cases where the field personnel proposed legal action against the offenders, Washington rejected the recommendations, closed 44 cases without taking any action, and reached some kind of agreement with the union officials in 23 other cases.

Like McLaughlin, the Yale study reported, "Union attorneys suggested a systematic bias in favor of incumbents resulting from the fact that the Department and specifically the Assistant Secretary for Labor-Management Relations, depends upon good relations with labor leaders in order to deal with them in labor-management disputes."

The DOL remains the weak link in LMRDA enforcement, In 1984 at an AUD conference, Joe Rauh proposed eight amendments to strengthen LMRDA. His first was "Shift enforcement of the law away from the Labor Department whose job is to comfort and coddle unions and can't be an enforcement agency over them." Nothing in AUD's experience in the years that followed justifies a modification of that view.

Section V
Years of Promise

Chapter 13: The Teamster Revolution

In the years following 1959, the wave of insurgency and reform stimulated by the adoption of the LMRDA reached a high point with the victory of the Miners for Democracy in 1972. By then, however, the United Mine Workers had dwindled in membership and lost its dominating position as labor's mover and shaker. The great event which reverberated through labor movement and helped change the guard at the AFL-CIO came in 1991 with the Teamsters revolution.

During the Miner's battle, the U.S. Labor Department had lumbered along ineffectually, but it was finally prodded out of its lethargy by the murder of Jock Yablonski. However, in the events leading up to the reform victory in the Teamsters' union, the DOL played a negligible role. The defeat of the racketeer-dominated Teamsters officialdom was effected by a combination of two forces: the rise of an extraordinary rank and file democratic reform caucus, the Teamsters for a Democratic Union, and the intervention of the Department of Justice under RICO, the Racketeer Influenced and Corrupt Organizations Act.

The RICO statute, adopted in 1970 as part of the Organized Crime Control Act, had created new, effective legal weapons against the mob. There had been massive exposures of organized crime since the Kefauver hearings of 1951. But, in time, it became clear that organized crime could not be effectively combatted by dealing with racketeers as individual offenders. (Between 1976 and 1986, for example, over 200 Teamster had been prosecuted. One, sent to jail, was replaced by another.) RICO was intended to give law enforcement authorities the power to break up the racket organizations that were debasing so many aspects of public life:

ordinary business, weapons production, securities industries, services to local government.

RICO made it a federal offense to conduct an "enterprise" in a pattern of racketeering. James Jacobs characterized it as "the most important substantive and procedural law tool in the history of organized crime control" permitting the government to charge defendants "with all sorts of different crimes allegedly committed at different times and places" and allowing the government "to join all the members of a criminal enterprise in a single trial."

RICO criminal provisions provide for stiff sentences, up to 20 years for each violation. From the standpoint of labor reform, the civil remedies are decisively important, permitting government to reorganize, even dissolve, offending "enterprises." According to Jacobs, "...since 1981, 19 bosses, 13 underbosses, and 43 capos (crew chiefs) had been convicted...Between 1983 and 1986, there had been 2,500 indictments of Cosa Nostra members and associates...There were major prosecutions in every city where organized crime families have been identified."

In 1982, for the first time, the Justice Department wielded RICO against organized crime in the labor movement when it filed civil suit against Teamster Local 560 in New Jersey. Racketeering in this local seemed intractable, with a record of extortion, beatings, and two murders. For over 20 years it had been run by Anthony Provenzano, a capo in the Genovese crime family, a member of the Teamster's international executive board, and a suspect in the murder of James Hoffa, senior. When Provenzano went to jail his brothers and then his daughter took over. The union-racket combination in Local 560 was one of the worst. But on the other side, the law enforcement team was the best. The assistant federal attorney in charge of the suit, Robert Stewart, determined to see it through, remained with it, postponing retirement, for the 13 years it took to finish the job. District Federal Judge, Harold Ackerman, who presided over the case, was familiar with unions, and surely sympathetic to the labor movement; as a young attorney, he had represented the New Jersey CIO. Clyde Summers, an AUD director and top expert on union democracy law, was a key prosecution witness.

Judge Ackerman ruled in favor of Justice and later appointed Edwin Stier, a former federal prosecutor, as trustee with full power to run Local 560. Stier was a shrewd and able trustee. Supported at every critical juncture by Judge Ackerman and federal attorney Stewart, and armed with all the resources available through the FBI, he was able to root out the old Provenzano gang, develop an alternative leadership, and restore the local to autonomy. But it took 18 years, between the first filing of the suit in 1982 and the restoration of self-rule in 1999. Even then, Judge Ackerman retained jurisdiction, just in case.

For Justice, Local 560 was a trial run. In 1986, after the case wound its way through the courts, and the Federal Court of Appeals upheld Ackerman's decision to impose a trusteeship over Local 560, the way was open to use the RICO statute against the racketeers who controlled the International Brotherhood of Teamsters. In its suit, filed on June 8,1988, the Justice Department proposed to remove the entire international leadership and establish a full Federal trusteeship over the international, modelled upon Local 560's, to run the union.

To avoid a total takeover by the government and their own removal from office, the Teamster officialdom dropped their opposition to government intervention and reached a compromise, one accepted by the D of J to avoid legal proceedings that could have dragged out for years. The agreement was signed and sealed in a consent decree approved by Federal Judge David Edelstein.

The terms of the consent decree left the incumbent officials in office, but subject to extensive controls. Three court appointees, supplied with the necessary staff and budget, were armed with powers to root out corruption and strengthen union democracy. An investigations officer would bring charges against those accused of cooperating with organized crime or defrauding the union on their own. An independent administrator, and later a three-person Independent Review Board, would try the charges. An election officer would supervise the nomination and election of international officers. The old system of electing international officers by delegates at conventions was superseded by direct vote of the entire membership.

In accepting these terms, it is obvious, the established officialdom was overconfident. As far as anyone could remember, they had always manipulated the membership, intimidated critics, and maintained a political machine fueled by a force more effective than nuclear power: money. Nothing had succeeded before, not even jail sentences against errant officials inept enough to get caught. How could anything succeed this time? (Later, it turned out, they were even suicidally overconfident when election time rolled around. In a squabble among themselves they ran two opposing candidates for president against Ron Carey, the reform challenger.)

Their self-confidence seemed amply justified; it was not the product of wishful thinking but based on solid reality. In the years after 1957, every effort to clean up the union had failed. In 1957 when James Hoffa, the elder, was first elected president, a committee of 13 rank and file Teamsters sued in federal court to prevent his assuming the post; and for a time the union was subjected to a weak, and eventually powerless, court-imposed monitorship. But at that point, there was no organized opposition; the rank and file group was precariously composed of squabbling individuals, some of whom were later obviously bought off by Hoffa. The dissident group, which succeeded only in delaying Hoffa's assumption of total power, soon disintegrated.

Despite exposures at the McClellan hearings, the 1950's federal monitorship, and the expulsion from the AFL-CIO, racketeers held the union in a grip tighter than ever. As Steve Brill put it in "The Teamsters", "Teamster insurance funds became a source of venture capital for organized crime." Murders continued as routine. Tony Provenzano was a member of the international executive board when two critics were murdered in his Local 560; he died in prison while serving a life term for one of those murders. Jimmy Hoffa, after leaving prison and planning a comeback as IBT president, was assassinated. Teamster presidents followed one another into federal prison on corruption charges: In the late fifties, President Dave Beck; followed by Hoffa, then by Roy Williams. President Jackie Presser, under indictment and likely to carry on the tradition, beat the rap by dying in office. Scores of Teamster officials at various levels were convicted of racketeering, but the corrupt combine continued unshaken. As convicted union representatives were sent away, they were succeeded by an endless stream of duplicate replacements. When Hoffa went to jail, the official family appointed a pliant Frank Fitzsimmons in his place. The mob seemed comfortably ensconced and powerful. Its influence in the labor movement and in national politics remained high. It seemed unlikely, even with the RICO prosecution, that the hold of the corrupt combine over the Teamster could be broken.

But this time, unlike 1957, with its abortive monitorship and easily fragmented dissident group, a new force staked its claim, the missing link in the battle to change this union. Beginning in the early 1970's, a strong rank and file movement for democracy and against corruption had emerged: Teamsters for a Democratic Union. The record of its origins and its persistence make an inspiring chapter in contemporary labor history.

The miners' movement for union democracy led by Jock Yablonksi in 1969, and later the victory of the Miners for Democracy, had demonstrated that no entrenched corrupt union officialdom was invulnerable. In the person of Ralph Nader, we find an early link between the miners' and the teamsters' crusades. "...the influence of social activist Ralph Nader, who had taken a strong interest in the corruption of the Boyle administration and in the issue of health and safety in the coal industry, [was one of the] crucial factors in Yablonski's decision to run for the UMW presidency," wrote Paul F. Clark in "The Miners' Fight for Democracy."

In 1971, consistent with his work on auto and road safety, Ralph Nader enrolled several hundred truck drivers into a new public interest association, the Professional Drivers Council, or PROD. Arthur Fox, a young attorney on Nader's staff, who became PROD executive director, brought truck drivers to testify at Senate hearings on the use of amphetamines by drivers. Fox argued that drivers were often forced to use drugs, not for kicks but to fight off fatigue, because neither the law nor union contracts protected them against excessively long working hours.

When PROD called upon the union to support its legislative safety program, IBT President Frank Fitzsimmons denounced Nader for making "slanderous accusations" and "sensational ill-founded charges" against teamsters. PROD was forced to transform itself into an insurgent union caucus; it was impossible to campaign effectively for the enforcement of safety measures when the union failed to defend drivers who protested hazardous conditions. PROD recruited members, published a tabloid newspaper, *Dispatch*, and continued to campaign for drivers' safety. In 1976, PROD published a major research report, "Teamster Democracy and Financial Responsibility" listing in detail the overgenerous salaries enjoyed by Teamster officials and simultaneously recording the erosion of members rights. The report, financed by a grant from the Field Foundation to the Association for Union Democracy, was widely distributed in the union on the eve of its 1976 convention in Las Vegas. PROD never succeeded in enrolling a massive membership; but, according to Brill, "PROD's impact was greater than its numbers suggested. By 1977, it was impossible to find a local union where PROD activities weren't talked about frequently by the rank and file…"

Meanwhile, independently of PROD, a new and broader insurgency was forming inside the Teamsters union, one which took final form in 1976 as the Teamsters for a Democratic Union. PROD drew its strength from older, over the road drivers; TDU was organized by younger Teamsters. In 1975, on the eve of negotiations for a new national freight agreement, representatives of several scattered rank and file groups met to plan a campaign for strong provisions in any new contract. They set themselves up as Teamsters for a Decent Contract, electing Ken Paff to run the new organization. Encouraged by the response to their appeals during the 1976 national strike, the participating groups agreed, that year, to make their organization permanent and to broaden its scope. The group took the name of Teamsters for a Democratic Union to express its new aims, no longer limited to proposals for decent contract terms, but for a wide-ranging program of democracy and reform.

Some of TDU's founders, like Ken Paff, who continued as its national organizer and de facto head, were young socialists, well-educated idealists who knew how to articulate the aims of their fellow unionists; not pie in the sky but wages, working conditions, democratic rights, dignity on the job, the spirit of American freedom. Within a year or two, TDU expanded far beyond its original base, enrolling several thousand union members in a genuine grassroots new movement. In 1979, TDU and PROD merged under the TDU name. Ken Paff continued as chief organizer. Arthur Fox, who resumed full time work as a lawyer for Public Citizen, became one of its volunteer attorneys.

There followed years of intensive activity; annual national conferences attended by 500 Teamsters, a small full time staff, a monthly tabloid, *Convoy-Dispatch*, the formation of local chapters, some with their own newsletters, special bulletins for each section of the industry at contract time, publication of a comprehensive "Teamster Rank and File Legal Rights Handbook" prepared by Ellis Boal of Detroit, who developed into a skilled union democracy attorney. There were booklets on how to organize chapters and how to edit newsletters. There were court suits to protect members rights and defend pension funds. It was an extraordinary record of achievement. TDU arose and grew as a genuine rank and file movement without the support of a single labor leader, not in the IBT and not anywhere else. It could count on moral support from Victor Reuther, but he had long been retired, was without power or access to money. Moreover, because he was an outspoken critic of established labor leadership, he became persona non grata in his own United Auto Workers union.

On the other side, the corrupted Teamster old guard basked in the moral and political support of the AFL-CIO, of a big piece of the U.S. Congress, and of aspiring eminent political figures.

As soon as the news broke, that the Justice Department was preparing its suit, and even before it was filed, Teamster officials could count on widespread ecumenically diverse moral support. On December 10,1987, 264 members of Congress signed a letter to the attorney general warning against any intrusion into union affairs. Prominent labor leaders sponsored the formation of "Americans Against Government Control of Unions" to oppose the suit. Among them was Richard Trumka, Miners president and later the new AFL-CIO secretary treasurer. (It was his good fortune to lose that battle; had his viewpoint prevailed, he could never have dared bid for power in the AFL-CIO against Tom Donahue)

In September, the Teamsters old guard summoned 4,000 local officials to a rally against the pending RICO suit. Among the dignitaries who expressed support were several international union officials and four aspirants for nomination as candidates for president of the United States: Jesse Jackson, Alexander Haig, and Jack Kemp attended. Paul Simon sent a message.

And finally, just when it seemed possible, for the first time, to shake up the racket dominated Teamster officialdom, the AFL-CIO rode to the rescue. In a powerful public relations coup, the Teamsters union, as corrupt as ever, won readmittance to the AFL-CIO, welcomed enthusiastically by AFL-CIO President Lane Kirkland.

In a press interview on August 23,1990, Kirkland criticized the government's move against the Teamsters, "I still do not like it, and I continue to oppose, the principle and the proposition…I think that the government shouldn't have gotten into it in the first place other than through the enforcement of the existing laws."

Nevertheless, TDU was growing steadily; it amassed a list of some 10,000 sympathizing supporters; its rights were protected by federal law; here and there its supporters were elected to local offices. But it was slow going. The prospect of dethroning the racket kingdom still seemed like a utopian dream. Back at the 1981 Teamster convention, where delegates elected national officers, Pete Camarata, a TDU delegate from Detroit, ran as a token candidate for president with trivial support. When Diane Kilmury, TDUer from British Columbia, proposed an Ethical Practices Committee to root out corruption, she was hooted down in an orgy of vituperation. This giant seemed too big; this David, too small. Commenting on PROD and TDU in 1981, Paul Clark wrote, "Their significance, to date, has been so minor that they have been largely ignored by the membership they sought to rouse."

But the balance of power shifted massively when the federal government intervened.

While the government's threatened RICO suit against the Teamsters faced a hostile reaction from the labor establishment, it also touched off an internal debate in our union democracy family. There were union reformers, radical union activists, and labor intellectuals who expressed misgivings over any drastic government intervention into the life of unions, even into the Teamsters. Not apologists for corrupted union officials, they were partisans of reform and outspoken allies of the Teamsters for a Democratic Union against the mob. Their skepticism over the RICO suit was summed up simply: "You can't trust the government." In defense of that position, they pointed to President Reagan's destruction of the air traffic controllers union, injunctions against unions, and disenchantment with the National Labor Relations Board.

The Association for Union Democracy, on the other hand, was forthright and insistent in calling upon government authorities to intervene in support of embattled reformers in the Teamsters union. Even before the 1988 RICO suit, in *Union Democracy Review*, AUD argued that it was the obligation of law enforcement authorities to help defend union workers against racketeers, that unionists had the same right to protection against criminals in their unions as any residents to protection in their neighborhoods, that no unaided and unarmed citizen, should be required to resist a murderous organized crime combine without government backing. Clyde Summers, for AUD, compared the RICO action against the mob with the post-war denazification campaign against the fascists to restore German democracy.

Distrust of government cannot by itself serve as a policy or program. Everyone distrusts government or some major aspect of it! Conservative Republicans don't like "big government;" the FBI doesn't trust the CIA and vice versa; the President distrusts Congress and vice versa. Labor distrusts the courts and the NLRB, but makes use of them nevertheless. The key to union reform policy is to utilize the power of government, which unionists may not trust, against mobsters whom they surely distrust — and fear — even more.

When the LMRDA was enacted in 1959, labor leaders, almost unanimously denounced the measure as an impermissible intrusion on the right of unions to run their own affairs. More than forty years of experience have exploded that objection. It is obvious now that, in regulating certain aspects of union government, the law strengthened the right of workers to run their own unions. The RICO suit, subjected to the same kind of objections by the same kind of union officials, extended the principle embodied in the LMRDA: it strengthened the right of workers to run unions free of racket domination. As Federal Judge Loretta Preska, who took over after the death of Judge Edelstein, succinctly summarized the aims of the Teamsters suit, "The goals of the Consent Decree are to rid the IBT of the hideous influence of organized crime and establish a culture of democracy within the union." (The "culture" still remains elusive even after the departure of organized crime.)

Despite protests from members of Congress, despite the mantle of respectability provided for the IBT by the AFL-CIO, despite the moral boost to Teamster officials by eminent politicians of both parties, despite the supportive rally of a consortium of labor leaders, the Department of Justice stood firm and filed its RICO suit before Federal Judge David Edelstein. From then on, under the terms of the consent decree, the Teamsters union was submitted to firm court-imposed monitorship.

In the next three years and four months, charges were filed against 214 Teamsters, many of them officials at some level, including 66 who were charged with organized crime connections. By the time of the election, late in 1990, the air was clear for a free and open campaign. Prodded by the judge, the election officer meticulously conducted the international elections. The pages of the union's magazine, mailed to all members, were opened to the candidates, who campaigned vigorously. There had been nothing like it in all the union's history. Ron Carey, backed by TDU in a three-way race, won the presidency with over 48% of the 400,000 total votes and carried his entire slate with him. It was a total defeat for the old guard. The three-way combination of forces that had led to reform victory in the miners union brought victory over a racket-infiltrated apparatus in the Teamsters union: an organized union reform movement, supported by a civil libertarian network of prolabor supporters, and backed by the power of federal government.

After the Teamsters experience, the debate over drastic government intercession against corruption was definitively resolved. Reformers, supported by government action in court, achieved what they could not win by their own efforts alone: direct elections so that members could break through old guard control of the union apparatus, and an honest count so that ballots would be tallied as they were actually cast. But something else was decisive, less tangible but no less urgent. It was essential to lift the climate of fear and convince members that a power was now on the scene superior to the mob so that unionists would feel free, or at least more free, openly to nominate and campaign for candidates to office against the machine. That became clear when the court-appointed monitors, backed by the presiding judge, brought charges against scores of officials accused of corruption or organized crime connections and drove them out of office and even out of the union.

Sweeney and his friends had contributed nothing to Teamster reform, but the way was now open for their rise to power in the AFL-CIO. Encouraged by the changing moral atmosphere and assured of support from Carey and his New Teamsters, they were emboldened to challenge Lane Kirkland and won control of the AFL-CIO.

In the years that followed, Federal monitorships, of one degree or another, were imposed on three internationals: Laborers, Hotel Workers, Teamsters, and on several local and district unions, all accused of mob infiltration. Not all the monitorships were success stories. At least one was a total failure, but in no case were the unionists worse off after than before. Even where there was been no spectacular change, unionists who had been intimidated into silence by mobsters, found courage to speak out. Federal monitors alone cannot make a free gift of a decent and democratic union to its members, but they can provide the tools of democracy. To the extent that reformers organize and use those tools, unions can be transformed. Such is the Teamsters lesson.

Summary of post-LMRDA period

In the years that followed the adoption of the LMRDA there have been significant reform and insurgent movements among: Machinists, Paperworkers, NMU seamen, Marine Engineers, Painters, Masters Mates and Pilots, Teachers, Musicians, Steelworkers, Miners, Operating Engineers, Auto Workers, Postal Workers, Electricians, Hospital Workers, Public Employees, Plumbers and Pipefitters, Carpenters, Electricians, Transit and Transport Workers, Packinghouse workers, Railroad workers, Laborers, Teamsters,

It would require the talents of an experienced labor historian to do justice to rise of movements independent of the incumbent power structure in all unions, those who were spurred on by the Labor-Management Reporting and Disclosure Act in 1959 and then those who were inspired by the victory of the Miners for Democracy in the United Mine Workers union in 1972, and finally by the rise of TDU. This account is not intended as such a history, but mainly as a partial record of what came to the attention of the Association for Union Democracy and its precursor, *Union Democracy in Action.*

A reinvigoration of union democracy was effected, not simply by rank and file movements, but also from within the union leadership cadre itself. In the mid-level leadership there were Ed Sadlowski in the Steelworkers, Jerry Tucker in the Auto Workers, Charles Delgado and Mike Lucas in the IBEW. At the top, there was Jock Yablonski in the Miners union. At the very summit, in his own way, John Sweeney, the latecomer.

Each insurgency was impelled by unique interests and pursued its own course. Some disappeared, some have persisted, some were successful. They were mainly isolated from one another. Taken together, however, their cumulative force triggered an explosion of democratic activity inside the labor movement, legitimized the right to dissent, and thereby helped open a new stage in the life of our labor movement.

Postscript: The cutoff date for most of this account is the 1995 AFL-CIO convention when John Sweeney took over the AFL-CIO presidency. However, in 1996 after Ron Carey's reelection, Teamster reform suffered a severe setback when he was removed from office by the court-appointed Independent Review Board and expelled from the union.

Carey had been propelled into the Teamster presidency by the reform revolution of 1991; but Teamster locals were then, and remain, dominated by those who had cohabited with organized crime figures for decades. From the moment Carey took office, they initiated an unremitting campaign for his defeat and ran James Hoffa Jr. against him in 1996. Nevertheless, Carey was reelected that year by a more comfortable margin than in 1991, but still a narrow majority. But during the 1996 campaign, desperate to match the $4,000,000 campaign funds of his enemies, Carey had retained a sleazy PR team. They devised a crude money laundering scheme which derailed funds from the union treasury into the 1996 Carey campaign. After the operation was exposed, the 1996 election was voided by the court-appointed election monitor.

Carey, who denied authorizing the scheme or knowing about it, was barred from the rerun ballot by federal monitoring authorities. In 1998, Hoffa coasted into office, sustained by the mystique of his father's name, backed by an overwhelming majority of the old local officials, and opposed by a rival candidate without name recognition.

In 2001, Carey was prosecuted in federal court on the same charges on which both the Teamster election officer and the union's Independent Review Board forced him out of office and ordered him expelled from the union. But, on October 12, 2001, a federal jury promptly found the evidence against him not credible and reached its verdict: Not Guilty.

Nineteen ninety-eight was the year of the Teamster counter-revolution. But nothing in these depressing events erases the profound impact of the 1991 Teamster reform victory on the AFL-CIO. The battle for reform continues in the Teamsters union under far more favorable conditions today than when it first began. The shift of power inside the AFL-CIO has not been reversed.

Chapter 14: The power of union democracy

In 1995, John Sweeney proposed to inject new vigor into the labor movement and restore its influence by a two-fold program: a stepped-up drive to organize the unorganized and an intensified political action program. In his mind, the two objectives were interlinked: Only by enrolling masses of new members would the labor movement be taken seriously enough by politicians to affect government policy. Labor could not go far unless it could lift its membership far above that 13% of the nation's entire workforce and only 9% in private industry. Sweeney was — and is — convinced that the key to advancing the cause of social justice is through strengthening labor's political power in the nation. Organizing, he argues, will strengthen that power.

"Organize the unorganized" has been labor's perennial theme, usually the subject of resounding convention resolutions. But Sweeney went beyond words, adding money and manpower wherever he could, using the moral authority of his new office to spur leaders of international unions to do the same. He toured the national proclaiming that "American needs a raise." His exhortations succeeded — mildly — in changing the mood in the labor movement. Some unions displayed new activity and sensitivity to organizing in their jurisdictions. With effort there have been some organizing successes, notably in low-wage service industries. "A culture of organizing has developed," he asserted, somewhat optimistically.

And yet with all the concentration on organizing, the graph of success is a roller coaster. In 1999, union membership rose by 240,000, but a year later it dropped by 200,000. At the rate at which new organization now takes place, it would take generations even to reach the previous high, assuming even the current rate could be sustained. In *WorkingUSA* (Spring

2002), Michael Eisenscher notes, "To raise union density one point requires that the labor movement organize about 1.2 million...According to Andy Stern, president of the Service Employees International Union, it costs about $1,000 for each newly organized member. At that rate...to increase union density one point would cost the labor movement $1.2 billion."

As it became clear that the drive to organize was bringing only modest — and so, disappointing — results, a soul-searching discussion opened among labor activists and pro-union intellectuals in universities, an assessment of experiences, a criticism of shortcomings, a multitude of suggestions for ideological, technical, methodological, and organizational changes to make organizing more effective, some of them excellent ideas. But the grim reality remains that even with the most ingenious approach, organizing is bound to be an onerous uphill task in the conditions of American life today. The main difficulties lie not in failures of dedication or strategy but in those harsh realities. The fault is not in unions but in their stars, in cut-throat global competition, in the intensity of employer resistance, in hostile government policy, in the conservative drift in American politics, in the nervous fear even of workers who would like to be organized that now is not the time to jeopardize their jobs. So that unions must try harder to make even modest gains or hold their own today in preparation for a possible massive breakthrough under more favorable conditions tomorrow.

Meanwhile, Sweeny summoned all unions to the political battle; and, in reply, the labor movement has poured more money and manpower into the effort. Sweeney promotes a smooth campaign of advertising, television, public relations. Here too, as in organizing, there have been modest but not massive successes. The balance of power in the nation continues to tilt back and forth between the two main trends in American political life. The division of influence remains evenly balanced, seldom so close as in election year 2000.

Labor political action has been effective whenever unions work hard to get out the vote of those who are already convinced. That is, it activates those who already agree with its political aims. And that, in the context of America politics, is sometimes enough to tilt the delicate balance from one side to the other. But it is not enough to effect the big political change which labor needs. It brings to the polls those who are already its political followers. It has not succeeded in winning over that great section of American workers who still vote repeatedly for labor's adversaries.

It is reported that roughly 60% of union workers generally vote Democratic. But that statistic, by itself, is deceptively consoling for labor leaders. In the year 2000, blacks constituted 15.3% of the total union membership. Their vote choice is not necessarily determined by any special union loyalty; they, like other blacks, voted Democratic by at least 90%. The reality is that the vote of the non-black union workers splits fairly evenly between the two main camps of American politics, just like the general population of voters.

The urgent need is to break out of the political stalemate, change the mood in the country, and create a new balance of power favorable to proposals for social justice and, by that token, hospitable to the rise of the labor movement. The nagging question is: How can the labor movement win the heart of America if it is not able to convince a major section of its own membership? So far, Sweeney has succeeded in prodding sections of the unions' staff cadres; he has rallied support from religious leaders, especially for organizing the underprivileged; he has won back sympathy from intellectuals. Judged by labor's public image of yesterday, it is remarkable progress. Compared to the needs of today, it is grossly inadequate. With all its concentration on political action, the AFL-CIO has succeeded only in avoiding a total political route and in sustaining a continuing precarious balance. To fight its way back, labor needs, not a minor momentary political shift but a major breakthrough.

Here, then, is the vexing dilemma, a classical Catch 22: To increase their political power unions must organize. But in order to organize on the scale to which it aspires, the labor movement needs political power, power to change the climate of opinion in the nation. For that, there is no open sesame, no get-rich organizational or ideological scheme. It does pose the subject of democracy, democracy in unions, union democracy — not as a magic bullet, but in preparation for the long haul.

By bringing a measure of democracy into the workplace, the labor movement strengthens democracy in society. In that ongoing conflict in America, the eternal contest between democracy and aristocracy, between people and privilege, the labor movement has been a powerful force for democracy precisely because unions represent the organized power of people against the concentrated power of wealth. The labor movement and individual unions, are sometimes right, sometimes wrong on the political and social issues that face the nation; but on the whole the labor movement has been one of the principal countervailing forces to offset the big corporative powers and, by that fact, a principal pillar of American democracy. In effect, these ideas are now embodied in the nation's law. By adopting the Wagner Act in 1935, Congress acknowledged the special role of unions, embodied the principle of collective bargaining in federal law, and required employers to recognize unions chosen by their employees.

The labor movement, so crucial to our democracy, is far weaker today than it has been for decades. That stubborn fact partially explains the social stalemate in America which wraps the great issues in fluff, robs our politics of content, and turns election campaigns into television sound bites, image projections, and popularity contests. Labor's weakness today is distressing compared to its power of yesterday. Weakened, yes; but still a giant. Its 16,000,000 members remain a powerful potential social force in the life of the nation.

Strain as it may, the labor movement can never come even close to the material resources available to its principal adversary, the big corporations. The assets of a single one of these multi-billion companies exceeds the wealth available to the entire labor movement. They outspend labor and never notice a burden. But with all their influence and all their money and all their access to the media and to politicians, rich corporations can never match the most valuable asset of all: the power of people. Over sixteen million people are still enrolled in unions. While the leaders devote themselves vigorously, with money and manpower, to the roller coaster of new organizing, the hard practical reality is that, in the political arena, they depend upon that 16,000,000 already organized. Despite the rhetoric, the resources, and the PR, unions have not succeeded in mobilizing this, their own army, as a unified moral force in the nation.

Those 16,000,000 men and women with their families constitute a force of perhaps 50,000,000 people. Even at its ebb tide, here is labor's unmatched resource, a cross section of mainstream America, all races, all crafts, all religions, all national origins, in small towns and big cities. Right now, a cadre of perhaps 100,000 officers, organizers, and staffers are imbued with a sense of loyalty and active enthusiasm for this movement of theirs. Imagine now if labor could inspire its multi-million member army with that same conviction that this is indeed their movement, that it stands up for their rights outside and inside their unions, that they need not cringe before employer bosses or union business agents to work in dignity, that union hiring halls are fair, that members are welcome to run for union office, that they know their rights in society and in their unions. In sum, that their labor movement truly stands for decency and democracy, not only in the nation and at the workplace, but also in their own union halls.

If these 16,000,000 unionists believed all that, in their hearts, they would transmit that message person to person throughout the nation...at their social gatherings, at their churches, in shops at lunchtime, wherever people gather to talk. That lesson is, or would be, that here is no special interest but a peoples movement for social justice. That would be the beginning of a new moral majority in the nation because there is no power greater than the message delivered from neighbor to neighbor, greater than anything money can buy. That's what a flowering of union democracy could do for the labor movement — allow it to emerge as truly a peoples movement and a great force for social justice.

Of course, of course! There are limits. By itself, the most beautiful democracy is not enough. Rights must not only be available, they must be exercised, and wisely. Global capitalism, concentration of wealth at the top, competition from sweatshops at home and abroad, taxation, the contraction of mass production manufacturing, race and sex, the environment, free and fair trade, social security, part time labor and the rise of spurious consultancies — these and so many other great issues confront the nation. And no one in public life, in politics, in academia, in labor, in the professions has come up with answers that inspire an enthusiastic consensus. It would be absurd to suggest that the spirit of democracy by itself, magically, will somehow supply the answer to these questions.

The existence of democracy does not eliminate the need for intelligent leadership nor does it automatically supply constructive policies; but it does serve as a means of finding that leadership, arriving at those policies, and rallying public support for them. Meanwhile, the discussion, the debate, the political and social battles continue while we search for answers. It is not absurd, in fact it is essence of realism, to suggest that an infusion of the spirit of democracy in its own internal life will make the labor movement a more powerful force and give it more moral authority in the defense of social justice as the battle over social policy continues.

Transform the mass of dues-payers and draftees into an enthusiastic army of labor...Walter Reuther had that in mind when he told UAW conventions that the union had to do more than organize the unorganized. We must, he said, unionize the organized. Sweeney and co-thinkers seek that aim by rhetoric, by lectures and classes, by teach-ins, by advertising, by devising clever slogans, by union-sponsored credit cards, by every gadget and gimmick of public relations. They look everywhere except to what is most effective: the free independent democratic activity of union members inside their own unions. What makes democracy powerful in our country is the untrammeled right of citizens to organize in free association, to protest, to demand, to run for office. You can teach that effectively in classes only when it exists in reality.

The lesson to the labor movement is: Open up! Let members run for office without niggling restrictions or intimidation. Let them speak their mind without fear of retaliation, without blacklisting. Fair trials before truly impartial tribunals. Open union papers to dissenting views. Expand the right to elect stewards and business agents and to vote on contracts. The idea, simple but powerful is union democracy. Is it a realistic idea? For union leaders, everything else that must be done to restore labor power requires long hard work. The strengthening of union democracy requires only the will.

The divided soul of American labor leadership

The labor movement usually can be counted on to stand up for democracy **on the outside, in the nation.** But **on the inside** large sections of the labor leadership are uncomfortable with democracy in their own unions, even hostile to it. That hostility to internal union democracy, in large measure, accounts for the inability of the labor union leadership, of its bureaucracy, to inspire its own membership, to "unionize the organized." Here we reach the great paradox of the American labor movement: democratic for the outside; restrictive and bureaucratic for the inside.

Here then is the divided soul of labor leadership. In most of the great issues that face the nation, in the key political conflicts that separate the parties, the labor movement places its power on the side of liberalism, enlightenment, civil liberties, equalitarianism. It stands on the side of people against the privileges of wealth, for workers rights against corporate power. But on all the issues that involve the rights of workers inside their unions, that same labor movement, as represented by most of its top officials, stubbornly defends limitations, restrictions, repression.

In court cases, high and low, state and Federal, enlightened union leaders stand on the side of decency and social justice whenever the interests of workers — and of the nation — are threatened by the greed of profiteers. But Dr. Jekyll becomes Mr. Hyde. In more than 50 years since the adoption of the LMRDA, in every case that has come before the courts involving the rights of workers in their unions, those same union leaders resist democracy in the interests of their own authoritarianism. They are on the right side on issues that affect public life but almost always on the wrong side of internal union life. (And I write "almost," just to be on the safe side.) A host of entrenched officials, not secure enough behind the stockade of mere centralized incumbent power, buttress their position by an assortment of supplementary devices, some legal, some illegal.

Where union officials control job referrals, as in the construction trades, they use that power to freeze critics out of work and to build a political machine of favored kneejerk supporters.

Control over the unions trial and disciplinary machinery permits them to fine, suspend, or expel rivals. Control over the election machinery permits the manipulation of dues referendums, contract ratification, and the selection of officers,

In some of the most egregious cases, critics are threatened or beaten.

Intricate meeting attendance rules are enforced, disqualifying over 90% of the membership from running for office. According to a study in 1994 by AUD legal interns of ten international union constitutions and nine other unions involved in lawsuits, unions with a total membership of 4,447,000 enforced such rules. That year, when the U.S. Labor Department requested briefs on the subject, 15 unions and the AFL-CIO favored unchanged enforcement of those rules; not one union called for any change. Only AUD and one small law firm called for their abandonment.

Despite section 105 of the LMRDA which requires unions to inform their members of the provisions of the act which protects democratic rights, only one union, the Masters, Mates, and Pilots was in voluntary compliance forty years after the 1959 law was adopted.

Most major unions disqualify aspiring candidates from running for union office unless they have remained in continuous good standing usually for the two years immediately before nominations. Union members who have held membership for 20 years or even more are disqualified if union records show that they have inadvertently fallen behind just a few days in a single month.

Local unions which displease their international officers, can be placed in trusteeship and their autonomy lifted, or they can be dissolved or merged out of existence.

Collective bargaining contracts can be imposed on union members by their internationals without membership ratification, a familiar event in the construction trades.

Practices like these led to the adoption of the LMRDA in 1959. Some of these malpractices continue even though they violate the law. Others persist because of loopholes in the law.

And so the labor movement sends out contradictory signals to its own members. In confronting its corporate adversary in politics, in organizing, in striking, in demonstrations, its message is: speak out, stand up, rights of Americans, demand justice, assert your rights, human rights before greedy profiteers, fair play for all, justice, democracy, integrity, decency, But in everything related to the union's inner life, the message conveyed, sometimes brutally, sometimes subtly, is: sit down, shut up, and pay your dues. Don't rock the boat. Critics, election opponents, those who demand fair hiring, information about staff salaries, contracts, union constitutions, mark themselves as troublemakers. Jump these hurdles if you want to run for union office. Maybe you'll get an honest count. Maybe not.

The drive of the labor officialdom for stability as a bureaucracy conflicts with the needs of the labor movement as a movement for democracy and social justice. As a bureaucracy, it seeks restrictions and its own security; but the labor movement needs openness and the spirit of freedom.

What is union democracy?

What is this union democracy we keep talking about? In posing this question we risk soaring into a dizzyingly thin stratosphere where commentators delight in rendering all things profound, what someone (was it Jesse Jackson?) characterized as paralysis through analysis.

Those who are uneasy with the advocacy of 'union democracy' because it is too "simplistic" remind us of the debates so familiar in those far off days when if you called for democracy against dictatorship you were confronted with...analysis. How simplistic! Is democracy superior to equality? to security? Can a starving person eat it? Do you mean bourgeois democracy or proletarian democracy? Peoples? social? industrial? economic democracy?

To bring the subject down from the Olympian heights, we must talk about democracy-democracy, that is, the kind of rights written into the U. S, Constitution and into federal law in the LMRDA: the right to free speech, free assembly, to select or remove representatives in free and fair elections, due process in trials before impartial tribunals, the right to criticize officials without intimidation or repressive retaliation.

Some are put off by the sometimes disorderly behavior of a robust democracy and feel more secure when it is restrained and restricted by a strong authoritarian hand. They might reflect on the words of Alexis de Tocqueville, the French aristocrat who surveyed American democracy in the early 1830's:

"If a certain moment in the existence of a nation is selected, it is easy to prove that political associations perturb the state and paralyze productive industry; but take the whole life of a people, and it may perhaps be easy to demonstrate that freedom of association in political matters is favorable to the prosperity and even to the tranquility of the community."

The **idea** of union democracy has been legitimized inside the labor movement. That change in mood is one of the great moral victories of the last decade. The principle was clearly written into federal law in 1959 and sank firm roots in the life of unions after more than 40 years of insurgent and reform activity. By now, most labor leaders accept the idea or are at least reconciled to it. The heads of those big unions who organized inside the AFL-CIO to elect John Sweeny as an insurgent gave an impulse, involuntarily or not, to union democracy. If it was legitimate for them to organize against Kirkland, it is legitimate for their critics to organize against themselves. Those who give lip service to the principle of union democracy but violate it in practice pay homage to its virtue.

However, while the principle of union democracy, as an idea, has made great headway in unions in the last generation, the **practice** of union democracy as an active reality still falls far short of that ideal. Its full potential, for the labor movement, and for the nation, is yet to be unleashed. The defense of union democracy is not a narrow "labor" issue, because it fills needs that go beyond unions.

The three faces of union democracy

1. Every decent labor leader on every level of authority respects the power of democracy in mobilizing workers under the banner of unionism. When the union appeals for workers to join; when it organizes strikes, and boycotts, and demonstrations; when it rallies voters to the polls at election time, it calls upon workers to stand up, to speak out, to act together, to demand respect. Most labor leaders welcome this aspect of union democracy with an enthusiasm they share with activists, radicals, and reformers of every stripe.

2. However, a second aspect of union democracy is not so universally popular: union democracy as a weapon for union members to control their own officialdom, to criticize, even to replace them. Here, the ardor of even progressive leaders often cools. The AFL-CIO publishes loads of informative literature and runs excellent courses in its institute on how to advance the rights of workers in society and defend them against abusive employers, but not much about the legal rights of workers in their unions and nothing about defending themselves against abusive union officials.

3. There is a third aspect of union democracy, neglected but just as vital: union democracy as a means of releasing the power of workers in the cause of democracy and social justice in the nation. At Sweeney's initiative, the AFL-CIO council endorsed those gallant words, "to bring economic justice to the workplace and social justice to our nation." To achieve so sweeping a change in American life requires more than "organizing" as commonly understood. It requires the intervention of a new moral force capable of moving the conscience of the nation.

In their understandable preoccupation with recruiting new members, our labor leaders underestimate the power of the old. The force that can move the nation is already available. But only as a potential: those 16,000,000 union members. The monumental task is to release that power. The instrument is democracy, union democracy.

Notes:

General: Through the Association for Union Democracy and, earlier, as publisher of *Union Democracy in Action*, I was directly involved in or wrote about most of the events discussed here relating to the Machinists, Painters, Teamsters, Paper unions, NMU, MMP, MEBA, and IBEW electricians; and, as these events unfolded, they were reported in *Union Democracy in Action* and in *Union Democracy Review.* The related documents are on deposit at the Walter Reuther Archives of Wayne State University. Otherwise, there is no attempt here to provide an extensive bibliography, only a few publications that are of particular interest or relevance are listed.

Chapter 1

Quotes are from Sweeney campaign literature on file at Walter Reuther archives. "Decline of the Labor Movement and What Can Be Done About It," by Solomon Barkin. Pub by The Center for the Study of Democratic Institutions 1961.

Chapter 2

All the documents on the Lodge 113 case are on deposit in the Benson collection at the Walter Reuther Archives, including those assembled as exhibits in the case of Irwin Rappaport and Marion Ciepley v. IAM filed in U.S. District Court, Northern District of Illinois. Eastern Div. Case No. 60 C Civil Action, 1959.

In 1962, as one of its series on comparative union governments, the Center for the Study of Democratic Institutions published "Democracy in the International Association of Machinists" by Mark Perlman. In a review in *Union Democracy in Action No. 12* (5/64), reprinted in *Dissent* magazine,

I noted that it was so full of inaccuracies and distortions, especially in its dealing with Lodge 113 that it amounted to a whitewash of the IAM regime. Paul Jacobs, one of the Center's staff editors was asked to comment on my review and Perlman's book. In part, he wrote on June 11,1965, "I agree almost completely with Benson's analysis of the book...Had it been my responsibility, I would not have published the book, but, in fact, it was not my choice to make...All we did was commission the work to be done and in Perlman's case I think we got stuck with a lemon and a damn sour one at that."

Raskin on "shining hour": "Unions in Transition: entering the 2nd century," p15. Seymour Martin Lipsct, ed. ICS Press 1986. **Kennedy's speech at ABW convention,** 9/8-12/58. Daily proceedings. The three years and thousands of pages of testimony at the McClellan hearings are partially summarized in "The Imperfect Union" by John Hutchinson. Pub. by E.P. Dutton, 1970.

Chapter 3

"A Miner's Life,: autobiography by John Brophy p 218. Pub. by Univ. of Wisconsin Press 1964. — IAM 1954 constitution Art. XXIV Sec. 1. **On MMP**: *Progressive*, "Captains in Revolt," September 1960. **ILGWU constitution**, 1959 Art 8 Sec 16. **On the Forward:** Union Democracy in Action No 2 p. 2. **On the Potters:** p.193 Sourcebook of Labor. Ed. Neil W. Chamberlain. McGraw-Hill 1958 **IBEW Smith case**: UDR No 3 p 6O. **On LMRDA**: "Individual Rights Within the Union, "by Martin H. Malin. BNA Books. 1988; "The Internal Governance and Organizational Effectiveness of Labor Unions" ed. by Samuel Estreicher et al. Pub. by Kluwer. 2001;— "Union Democracy and Landrum-Griffin" by Clyde Summers, Joseph Rauh, Herman Benson. Pub. by Association for Union Democracy, 1986. — (Some Congressmen, hostile to union power, seized upon the LMRDA proceedings to amend the Taft-Hartley law and make it more onerous for unions.)

Chapter 4

Most of the documentation on this period is on file with the Walter Reuther Archives; *Liberation*, April 1960; — "The Government of the Steel Workers' Union," by Lloyd Ulman. pub. by Wiley, 1962;— "The Enemy Within," by Robert F. Kennedy. Popular Library 1960;— "Right to Challenge," by John Herling. Harper and Row. 1972;— UDA 1960-1972.

Chapter 5

On Brooks: "The Internal Governance and Organizational Effectiveness of Labor Unions: essays in honor of George Brooks ed. by Samuel Estreicher. Pub. Kluwer. 2001; **Maritime:** "The Maritime Story." by Joseph P. Goldberg. Harvard. 1958; — "Captains in Revolt" in *Progressive*, September 1960. **On Pulp, Sulphite:** "The Paper Revolt" by Harry Edward Graham. Univ. of Iowa Press. 1970

Chapter 6

On Haskell, unpublished autobiography Vol 1 p. 95 at Reuther Archives. **Contemporary story:** *Union Democracy in Action 1959-1972.*

Chapter 7

On CLC: UDR No.26, Dec. 1981. **On Rauh**: "Union Democracy and Landrum Griffin," p11; **On PEF:** UDR #63 p 8 **On icy indifference:** UDR 37 p.1,

Chapter 8

On Yablonski: *Union Democracy in Action No.37* Feb 1970; **Books:** Death and the Mines," by Brit Hume. Grossman. 1971; — "Fire in the Hole." by Curtis Seltzer. Univ. of Kentucky. 1985; — "The Year of the Rank and File," 1973 Officers Report to the UMWA 46th Constitutional Convention.

Chapter 9

These events were reported in detail in UDR between No. 5, Fall 1973 and No. 39, March 1984.

Chapter 10

On Boswell: Detailed reports in UDR No.18-22, May 1980-April 1981. **Legal Ref: Civ.** 79—2571 DJ Lacey NJ; **On Delgado:** UDR No. 28-32, April-Dec.1982. **On Lucas:** UDR Nos 106-109, April-Nov.1996. **On the Kramer firm**: Partner George Soll was secretary of the American Civil Liberties Union. In later years, Federal District Judge Marvin Frankel, who had presided over the trusteeship case in Painters District Council 9, joined the Kramer firm after leaving the bench.

Chapter 11

Text of Steel rules in UDR No. 17; **DOL Letter**: Larry Yud to George Waialeale 11/98; **Public Review decision:** UDR 65; **Harry Bridges**

quoted: "Labor and Communism," by Bert Cochran p.339. Princeton. 1977. **Hayes on staff**: "Unions in Transition" ed. by Seymour Martin Lipset ICS Press, 1986. p332 n.31; **Outside support in Steel:** "Right to Challenge," by John Herling. Harper and Row 1972 p250

Chapter 12

On Local 282: "The Teamsters: Perception and Reality." by Stier, Anderson, and Malone. 2002 and UDR No. 71, Aug. 1989; **On work-injuries:** "Profiles of Fatal Work Injuries in 1996, BLS report on Compensation and Working Conditions, Spring 1998";— **On Plumbers in CT**: UDR No. 95, Aug 1993;— **On Mills**: 115LRR194;— "Labor USA" by Lester Velie, Harper. 1958;— **Final OCTF Report** "Corruption and Racketeering in the NYC Construction Industry" NYU Press.1990;— **"Gotham Unbound"** by James B. Jacobs. NYU Press, 1999; — **Morrison, the engineer**, UDR No. 48, Sept. 1985;— **McCarron** at House Subcommittee on Employer-Employee Relations, June 25. 1998 and UDR No.120, Sept. 1998; — **Laurence Cohen**; UDR No.79, Dec. 1990; — **Thacher at AUD hearing**: UDR No 52, May 1986; **"Labor Czar"** by Harold Seidman. Liveright. 1938;

Chapter 13

On the NMU: Detailed reports in UDA No. 21 and after; — BLMS reports, 1961 p. vi, 1962 p. iii; — 1983 vote tally, Pilot 11/83; — Fox letter, 11/14/84. **On the painters**: UDA Nos. 6, 11, 30 and others; *Schonfeld v. Wirtz* SD NY 66-558; **Annual reports of DOL,** 1961 through 1978 entitled "Compliance, Enforcement, and Reporting under the Labor-Management Reporting and Disclosure Act": **On GAO report:** "Department of Labor: administering the Labor-Management Reporting and Disclosure Act." June 2000 GAO/HEHS-00-116; and UDR No. 133, Dec. 2000 **Miners trusteeships:** "John L. Lewis" by Melvyn Dubofsky and Warren Van Tine Quadrangle 1977. p 450; — "Year of the Rank and File, 1973: report to 46th UMW convention," p.86; UDA No. 37, Feb. 1970; UDR No 8, Spring 1975; **On DOL and business managers**: UDA No.26, June 1967 and UDR No.93, Feb 1993. **On Section 610**, UDA No 11. **Books:**"The Landrum-Griffin Act and Union Democracy," by Doris B. McLaughlin and Anita W. Schoomaker, Univ. of Michigan. 1979 pp. 171-4; — "Union Elections and the LMRDA: thirteen years of use and abuse," in Yale Law Journal, Volume 81 January 1972 pp. 407-574: **Rauh on DOL**, p14 "Union Democracy and Landrum Griffin" pub. by AUD. 1986.

Chapter 14

Background: Stier and Sheridan and Brill; "The Teamsters: Perception and Reality," report by Stier, Anderson, Malone. 2002; — "The Fall and Rise Of Jimmy Hoffa" by Walter Sheridan. Saturday Review Press. 1972; — "The Teamsters," by Steven Brill. Simon and Schuster. 1978; — "The Miners' Fight for Democracy" by Paul F. Clark. Cornell ILR Press. 1981. **On PROD:** UDR No.3, Spring 1973. **On TDU:** "Rank and File Rebellion," by Dan LaBotz. Verso 1990;— "Teamster Rank and File," by Samuel Friedman. Columbia Univ. 1982. **On the 1991 IBT election:** "Collision" by Ken Crowe. Scribners 1993. **On RICO:** "Busting the Mob" by James Jacobs. NYU Press. 1994. **On Local 560:** "The Liberation of IBT Local 560," by James Jacobs and David Santore. In Criminal Law Bulletin March/April 2001.

Chapter 15

On membership: BLS report January 2001; **On organizing "culture":** Sweeney interview in "The Future of the Labor Movement," by Hoyt N. Wheeler, p212; **Discussions on organizing:** UDR No.140, Feb.2002, "Why is it so hard to get organized.?" **On how unionists vote:** Exit poll in New York Times, November 12,2000, reported 1. That 59% of unionized workers voted for Gore. and 2. That 90% of all blacks voted for Gore. DOL report on union membership in 2000 reported total union membership at 16,300,000 of which 2,489,000 were black. Release 01-21, 1/18/00. Calculations: Black membership is 15.3% of total. Ninety percent of 15.3% is 14%. Of the 59% of all unionists who voted for Gore 14% of that 59% or 8.2% voted as blacks. Deduct 8.2% from that 59% and you are left with 50.7% of the non-black union membership that voted for Gore. This may not be scientifically precise, but it does point to the essential truth. The non-black **union** voters split evenly between the two parties.

About the Author

Herman Benson began his labor-related career in 1930 when he joined the Young Peoples Socialist League at 15. As a toolmaker and machinist, he joined the United Auto Workers, the Rubber Workers, the United Electrical Workers, and the International Union of Electrical Workers.

Between 1960 and 1972, he published **Union Democracy in Action** to rally support for reformers who fought for democracy and decency in unions. Meanwhile, 1967 to 1973, he worked for Frank Schonfeld, who, as an insurgent and then secretary treasurer of Painters District Council 9 in New York, battled the mob. After two Painter reform leaders were murdered in California, Benson helped found the Association for Union Democracy. He edits its publication, **Union Democracy Review.**

Printed in the United States
22895LVS00003B/224

9 781414 057767